TRAIN GONE

A CODA EX-JW MEMOIR

By Rebekah Mallory

An Unkind Press, LLC Publication

This is a work of creative nonfiction, memoir. All events
described in this book happened to the best of the author's
memory including dialogue and location. Only a few small
liberties were taken regarding certain occasions and their
timelines; some events depicted herein are composites of
different experiences. Names and identifying details of the
people described in this book have been altered (and at times
embellished) to protect their privacy. Any offenses are
unintentional.

Cover Design by BookBrand
Formatting by Jo Harrison
First printing edition 2020

Rebekah Mallory

www.rebekahmallory.com

UNKIND PRESS

ISBN Print: 978-1-7358221-0-5
ISBN ebook: 978-1-7358221-1-2

"Rebekah writes a story familiar in many ways to any of us who grew up in a harsh belief system. If you've ever struggled to find your own peace and gain a sense of self—if you've hoped that freedom and joy were possible on the other side of what seems like an impossible journey—I'm sure you will gain a lot from this memoir."

Jacob Nordby, author
Blessed Are the Weird: A Manifesto for Creatives & The Creative Cure

"Mallory's *Train Gone* is a must-read for anyone in search of themselves and the truth that comes only from one's own heart."

Lauren Sapala, author
Between the Shadow and Lo & The INFJ Revolution

"I sent my Soul through the Invisible,
some letter of that After-life to spell:
And by and by my Soul returned to me and answered:
I Myself am Heaven and Hell."

~Omar Khayyam

"Praise makes me humble, but when I am abused, I know
that I have touched the stars."

~Oscar Wilde

"I've seen a lot of strange stuff, but I've never seen anything
to make me believe there's one all-powerful force controlling
everything. There's no mystical energy field that controls my
destiny."

~Han Solo

Table of Contents

Introduction

BOOK INTRODUCTIONS BORE ME. As do acknowledgements, forewords, prologues, and prefaces. My brain gets impatient. And here I am forcing an introduction on you. I promise it'll be quick and painless.

This book took me *years* to complete. It still doesn't feel complete. How could so many pieces of one's life be complete? I can say the writing process was not *nearly* as painless as the introduction will be for you. You lucky bastard.

Reliving the particulars of my sordid life in such detail, to paint just the right picture, felt like tearing skin layer by calloused layer. Kinda like much needed therapy does.

This book isn't meant to bash anyone's individual faith. You can praise a head of lettuce for all I care. Your relationship with your chosen entity is between the two of you. If you think you might take it personally when I reveal ugly truths about how I was raised, and the havoc one denomination's version of God has wreaked on my life, then this book might not be for you.

While writing, I wasn't looking for absolution or using it to clear my conscience. The things I've done—no matter how shameful—are a direct result of the calculated mind control I experienced, and the very tight, theocratic, misogynistic chains I was trying to break free from. I found it increasingly difficult to make good choices—critical thinking was a foreign concept to me. I grew up in a culture of every decision being made for me, and when I left, experienced decision overload; I had no idea what I was doing once I was left to my own devices.

I've done many immoral things, while tangled up in my own insolent rebellion, simultaneously baffled by my severely damaged moral compass. That being said, this book contains sexually explicit content; consider yourself forewarned.

If you think you might be comforted knowing you're not the only one who's been betrayed, exploited, abandoned, or afraid of *anyone* who's forced you into blind submission—I hope you find solace within these pages.

If you also have Deaf parents—or parents requiring you to grow up in a hurry and protect them in some way, while being subjected to nonsensical, religious dogma, or *any* other systemic, oppressive body—then turn the page, my friend. This one's for you.

I only ask one favor: give each character a chance, including mine. It's much easier to vilify than it is to deify. Every person described within these pages is real (names have been changed), and real people fuck up. I couldn't have gotten here—to this place of self-acceptance—without everyone in this book. *Especially* one very special four-year-old.

I'm proud to be who I am, and it took me years to be able to say that. Although I may not be proud of every choice I made, I'd like to think those choices led me here to writing this book. Even if that means I'm seen as *mentally diseased* for creating and publishing "apostate literature." Fuck it, I healed and that is why I wrote this. To heal. I hope my story helps you heal whatever you may need to heal.

Cheers to the heroes and the villains.

Opportunity Knocks

I SAT WITH MY legs crossed, ankle viciously twitching in his direction. *I shouldn't even be here*, I thought.

"You're nervous," he said. "It's normal. Walking into this office means confronting the shame you may feel about crossing that threshold."

He's already analyzing me, and I haven't even opened my mouth.

The stigma attaching itself to the letters "PhD" next to his name on the door wasn't what bothered me. It was the fact I'd repeatedly been told, "All the advice you'll ever need is in the Bible."

Sitting on the couch, with clipboard and pen in hand, I stopped shaking my ankle and made eye contact with the man. Across from me in his leather office chair, he released a tiny sigh and smiled. He had kind eyes and grey, thinning hair.

"It might help you to think of me like you would an uncle... Uncle Joel. Have you ever been to a therapy session before, Rebekah?" he asked gently.

Uncle Joel. Okay, I guess. I sighed and looked down at the clipboard. "No."

"First thing I need to ask, as you're filling out that form is, have you ever tried to hurt yourself or anyone else? Ever try to take your own life?"

"Do all sessions start out like this?" I asked, nervously scribbling my birthdate.

"Yes, it's protocol, and the only reason our session would no longer be confidential."

"I've never tried to hurt anyone else." That was the God's honest truth.

"And yourself?"

The pen stopped. I looked up from the clipboard.

"If it was in the past, it stays here. If you're actively planning to take your own life or have tried recently, it has to be reported."

"Oh." I thought for a minute. I guess thinking of taking my own life at fourteen isn't the same as making plans to do it today, which I wasn't. "When I was fourteen, I thought about it."

"Did you have a plan?"

"No. Not really. I was just...in pain. Behind our house, I stood on the railroad ties at the tracks. I stared at the rushing water underneath for a while and..." I shrugged, "...thought about jumping."

"What stopped you?"

I shrugged again. "I guess I wasn't hurting enough to actually go through with it?"

"Okay. Nothing recently though?"

"No." I felt queasy. *I really shouldn't be here.* "I wasn't supposed to need this," I muttered under my breath, signing the form.

"What's that?" he asked.

I sighed. "I wasn't supposed to need...*therapy.*"

A bird flitted by his office window and landed on a tree branch. I watched it tweet and twitter playfully.

"Supposed to? Need it? Who told you that?"

"Well... My parents. My brothers...just about everyone in the Truth."

"The Truth?" He crossed his leg and leaned back.

"Yeah. I was raised a Jehovah's Witness, JW, a J-Dub. We were told all we'd ever need was everything they gave us."

"What did they give you?"

Wow. How do I even answer that? What had they given me? Self-doubt, ostracization, panic attacks, indecisiveness, this newfound orphan-hood— "I don't know how to answer that," I said quickly, interrupting my own spiraling thoughts before they had time to suck me in.

"Okay, before we get too deep here, tell me a bit about you. Where do you live? What do you do?"

"Um, well, I live in Silver Spring, alone, in a basement apartment. I'm a sign language interpreter. I have one cat and two dachshunds. Um..." I squirmed a bit and contemplated leaving.

He must've noticed because he asked, "Would you be more comfortable starting at the beginning?"

"The beginning? The beginning of my life?"

"Sure, earliest memory. If that's what you think would help. This is your time, Rebekah. Your session." He grabbed a steno pad and ball point pen from his desk, adjusted his glasses, and looked at me. "Ready when you are."

The beginning. That felt like a lifetime ago...

******

MY MOM LAY ME down on the cold bathroom floor, in the new house that we'd built, changing my cloth diaper. It was the first time I'd experienced—and was fascinated by—pain. *My* pain.

Mom was shifting things, moving the cloth, folding this over that and I felt something stick me. *Hard.* I screamed. Mom barely heard me.

Maybe I'd moved, maybe she'd moved. I don't know. All I knew was that something sharp poked me, and I wanted to see it. I needed to see it. I just had to inspect the source of my pain. I looked down and saw a bright yellow piece of plastic, covering a thick needle.

******

"A safety pin?" Joel asked.

"Yeah. The old school kind."

5

"Why did she barely hear you?"

"Oh, she's Deaf. So is my dad."

"Ah, okay. And your fascination with pain?"

"Well, I guess that's why I'm here with you; I need to inspect the source of my pain."

He jotted something in his notepad. "Tell me a bit about your parents."

******

MOM GOT SPINAL MENINGITIS when she was three months old and subsequently lost her hearing. Dad was born Deaf like his older brother and sister. Three out of eight kids in his family were Deaf and Dad was the baby.

Mom and Dad met at American School for the Deaf (ASD) in Hartford, Connecticut. As students of ASD, they'd been exposed to a twisted kind of programming, forced to fit into a mainstream hearing world.

Mom is Hard of Hearing (HH), which means she has *some* residual hearing. Any audiogram would show her decibel loss wasn't nearly as profound as Dad's. Their education consisted of speech, pronunciation, lip reading, and the importance of fitting into a mainstream hearing world.

The school fervently discouraged the use of American Sign Language (ASL), for a time, during the post-WWII era. So, they missed out on what most people see as a normal education, which likely affected their critical thinking, egos, and self-confidence, I'm sure.

******

"Wow," Joel said.

"Yeah, I mean, can you imagine being dropped off at a residential school at the age of three? Their parents didn't sign, they had no clue what to do with either of them, so they just sent them to ASD."

I CRINGED AT THE thought of Grandma Nina dropping Mom off at ASD at just three years old. Thinking about what that must have been like for both of my parents, made it easier for me to understand why they fell prey to asinine, doomsday gospel.

On a typical day at ASD, teachers routinely held little pieces of paper near the mouths of Deaf students while they practiced reciting letters like P and B to ensure the puff of air forcing the paper to waver occurred. If the paper didn't move, or if words were mispronounced, they were punished. Dad told me he was slapped in the mouth often. If he and other kids were caught signing, their knuckles were whacked with a ring of keys.

Twisted programming.

The institutionalized techniques, coupled with piss-poor communication efforts of their respective families, didn't allow Mom and Dad the opportunity to rightfully find and use their own voices. If they attempted to use their own voices (literally and figuratively), they were quickly hushed, and left with jagged pieces of dignity.

Dignity they relinquished once and for all, during a coming-to-Jesus moment, in a swimming pool at a summer convention of Jehovah's Witnesses.

******

"So, because of this *twisted programming* you believe your parents easily fell for another type of mind control?"

I nodded as he scribbled something in his steno pad.

"How did they become Jehovah's Witnesses?"

******

DURING A HEATED ARGUMENT—in Mom and Dad's Section 8 apartment in Danbury, Connecticut—hands were flapping, guttural grunts were exchanged, floors were stomped in frustration, and light switches were vehemently flipped on and off. Their shouts, passionate hand waving, and light switch flipping suddenly came to a halt when they felt an incessant rattle at the front door.

Red-faced, Dad flung the door open. And there stood a short, plump woman clutching the recent *Watchtower* and *Awake!* magazines.

This woman, realizing she had interrupted a battle from the shadows below, whipped out her Bible, and gave them marital advice. The tiny butterball communicated with my folks the way almost every hearing person does while interacting with a real live Deaf person—by yelling and over-enunciating everything.

She shouted Bible verses at the doorstep as if they would pounce from the leather-bound book and penetrate their Deaf ears miraculously.

This divinely inspired, second-rate, drive-thru therapy led to brief visits with the butterball. And while planting seeds of the Truth, this woman quickly turned short visits into home Bible studies—complete with shouting and exaggerated lip movements.

The mind control oozing from the pages of JW faith-based literature the little woman left with them, seemed harmless enough. Mom and Dad had already experienced oppression and feelings of worthlessness at ASD and in their childhood homes; a little spiritual persuasion couldn't make things any worse than they were at the time. Living forever on Jehovah's paradise earth with restored hearing, perfect egos, and perfect health tickled the damaged hair follicles in their ears.

Mom and Dad started to attend the Kingdom Hall of Jehovah's Witnesses in Danbury, Connecticut three times a week to sit through meetings they barely understood—which was no different than attending ASD. There was no qualified interpreter for the Deaf and hardly any brother or sister in their new faith learned ASL past fingerspelling their name.

For years, my parents struggled to understand it all. *Years.* Publications given to them, talks from the platform, songs sung in praise, and unheard prayers literally fell on Deaf ears.

******

"Tell me about the rest of your family."

"There's a lot to tell, where do I even start?" *I've never been to therapy. What exactly does he want?*

"Well, how about brothers? Sisters? Grandparents?"

******

SISTERS MIGHT'VE BEEN NICE, but sadly, no. No sisters. All brothers.

Brother number one, Johnny, had been on the scene since 1965; he was Mom's firstborn from a previous high school romance gone awry. Mark was born in 1970. Luke, in 1971. And I, in 1977. The three of us—Mark, Luke, and me, the only fruit of Dad's loins—Johnny, and later Jesse (our adopted brother) equaled five Children of Deaf Adults (CODA).

When I was two, Mom and Dad moved us from Connecticut to Northfield, New Hampshire (NH). We built our mint green, black-shuttered, three-bedroom raised ranch. It set on a small hill, on a dead-end road, zoned for residential and commercial spaces.

After settling in NH, they excelled at keeping our non-JW, worldly, extended family, and respective in-laws at bay. We visited Connecticut for long weekends but never holidays, which infuriated my mom's mother, Grandma Nina; she loathed anything associated with Jehovah's Witnesses.

Grandma Nina was *not* a cheek-pinching grandma, feeding you treat after home baked treat. Oh, no. Grandma Nina was a take-no-shit badass with mafia blood running through her veins. No doubt from the days our family smuggled olive oil during WWII. Which explained her no bullshit character and why she always had plenty of olive oil on hand for pans of lasagna.

I craved long weekends in Connecticut with extended family. It was the only time things ever felt semi-normal. Packing up our bags, loading up the ol' Caprice Classic, and Dad signing a quick prayer to Jehovah before the four-hour drive to Grandma's one-bedroom apartment always got me excited.

Once in Connecticut at Gaylord Towers, Grandma's senior apartment building, we buzzed #801.

For our parents, the intercom was nothing but a metal box with pin-sized holes protruding from the wall with names and buttons beside it. Every time we visited, they'd wait for one finger to press #801, eight little, CODA eyebrows to signal, and four routine CODA head nods, before yanking the lobby door wide open.

From the intercom, Grandma answered with a raspy, perturbed, "Yeah?"

"We're here!" my brothers and I would shout.

Mom and Dad stood ready, eyes bugged, hands gripping the lobby door.

Eight CODA ears heard a loud buzz, unlocking the lobby door. Eight thick, CODA eyebrows danced, four CODA heads nodded, and the imaginary gunshot I heard in my own head, released us all from our Post Positions.

And they're off!

Dad yanked the lobby door wide open, and said, "Hurry up! Hurry up!"

He pushed us through as if the door would close on us like a guillotine blade. Once we all rushed into the tiny, orange elevator, we took a deep breath in—pressed against each other, motionless. Until we reached the eighth floor.

The elevator dinged, the door opened, we exhaled. And there stood Grandma in her doorway. Annoyed. Arms akimbo. Kitchen towel draped over one shoulder.

"Hi Mummy," Mom voiced, leaning in to kiss her.

"Hullo, Mom!" Dad shouted.

"Shh! I can hear you!" she said. Grandma was never as happy to see Dad as he pretended to be to see her. Their relationship was forever changed once he made the executive decision that our family would identify as J-Dubs. "You're late, you should have called. The lasagna's cold." She said every word slowly and clearly, glaring at them both.

"Sorry," my parents voiced in unison.

In Grandma Nina's one-bedroom, industrial-tiled apartment— heavily decorated with old bric-a-brac, collectibles, and family photos—we were practically on top of each other. My parents slept on the sofa's hide-a-bed, while the boys took turns sharing a fold-up cot kept in the closet. Being the youngest, I didn't get to flip for the cot. I slept on Grandma's floor, next to her bed.

Grandma's room felt haunted. There was an air of desperate loneliness that morphed into cloudy, milky, white spirits, circling around her neatly made twin bed, crying all night. Her room was chill, dark, and sad. No doubt it was filled with a million secrets she'd never tell. It was eerie, despite one window looking out over the street.

Her polished vanity table showcased a pair of Mom's first Mary Janes, bronzed. Next to the table, a doily-covered dresser held up more useless bric-a-brac. I slept on a nest of sheets between her bed and dresser. Most nights, I lay shivering and awake, staring under her bed, worrying she'd forget I was there, and step on me when she got up to use the bathroom.

I was always the last to get up, cursing a horrid night's sleep. At the table, with my customary bowl of corn flakes and skim milk, Mom and Grandma whispered loudly over coffee. They had the same conversation every visit: skim milk—friend or foe?

Dad sat in Grandma's recliner reading the newspaper, most likely thanking Jehovah for his profound decibel loss. And the boys roughhoused in a basketball court across from Gaylord Towers. I stayed in, watching *I Love Lucy* reruns.

My saving grace from boring, dietary trend discussions, was my mom's sister, Kathy. She came over, often rescuing me from dull skim-milk-food-talk, Grandma's lonely lair, and the brotherly beatings that usually took place whenever the boys inevitably grew bored.

Aunt Kathy and her husband, Ron, took me to the mall, the movies, Bristol Pizza, and the roller-skating rink. Some days I went back to their house and spent the night in their guest room.

******

"Did your family go to another Kingdom Hall while on these trips?"

"No, we usually just stayed a couple of nights. If we went to a meeting, it probably would've pissed Grandma off." *I could see her scowling in my head.*

"Did not going to a meeting affect you in any way?"

"Oh, for sure. The nights I stayed at Kathy and Ron's I could barely just *enjoy* being with them."

"Really? Why?" Joel adjusted his glasses.

******

I WAS SCARED WHAT God thought of me being with worldly family members. I mean, would I know what to do when faced with temptation? If I'm not with other God-fearing Christians, am I just further dooming myself? All I could hear was, 1 Corinthians 15:33: "Bad associations spoil useful habits," over and over.

At Kathy and Ron's, they'd have get-togethers in their basement bar—which had its own bathroom, a stocked bar, barstools, a door leading out to the backyard, cushy sofas, expensive stereo equipment, fish tanks, and one questionable, life-sized, cardboard stand up of Humphrey Bogart.

I never liked the way his eyes followed me around the room. *Just look at him, with that fancy hat and cigar. Tsk, tsk, bad association.*

I tried to ignore Bogie by zeroing in on Uncle Ron, behind the bar, mixing a Shirley Temple for me. I felt so chic, sitting at the bar, with their friends, drinking my special concoction. I didn't understand anything they laughed about, but I laughed anyway. Yet, I couldn't help wondering: was the laughter blasphemous enough for Jehovah to sweep them away like he did in Noah's day? "...and they took no note until the flood came and swept them all away," Matthew 24:39.

I decided to go to bed. Kathy tucked me in, closed the door, and disappeared down the hall to re-join the party. My curiosity got the better of me, and I snuck through the guest room, cracking the door, to have my ears tickled. Revelry commenced.

They're bad association, but I want to know why.

This was fascinatingly different than evenings spent at Grandma's, and most definitely more action-packed than nights in NH where we would most likely be home preparing for the next meeting, or at the Kingdom Hall. I didn't miss the meetings one bit during our long weekend visits. Even so, I felt guilty I wasn't at a meeting or at the very least with Mom and Dad, safe in my J-Dub bubble.

Curious still, I opened the door and snuck out of the guest room, tiptoeing down the hall. I stood in front of a full-length mirror at the top of the stairs, lost in my tiny reflection.

Uninvited cigarette smoke floated up five measly steps, encircling me. I panicked as an aggressive death cloud of stench drowned me in predestined lung cancer. Cigarette smoke, worldly whoopla, and a night away from my uber Christian household weren't things I knew how to handle.

I stared into the mirror, holding my face in both hands. Standing there, in my worldly Flintstones nightgown, I ran my fingers over my cheekbones and thought my face looked very lean—leaner than yesterday. My heart thumped wildly.

This is what I deserve for being with worldly family members. Their skim milk, cigarette smoke, and Shirley Temples are going to give me the AIDS.

******

"Wait, Rebekah, AIDS? You thought you might contract AIDS as punishment for spending time with extended family?"

"Yeah. I know…stupid." I scoffed at myself.

He jotted something down in his notepad. "No. It just underscores the grip this religion has on you. Continue."

******

AIDS, THE STEAMING HOT topic it was in the early 80s, scared the crap out of me. My brother, Luke, and Grandma talked at length one night about AIDS, how it was "airborne, spread by an African monkey, and gay men who'd wind up with bony faces and skin lesions once they got sick."

Remembering their conversation got me spooked.

These people—my aunt and uncle's friends, as nice as they could be—were still bad association. Jehovah would punish me for being with them, and they were definitely doomed for death when Armageddon came.

Bad associations spoil useful habits.

I just knew one of those cigarettes was in the mouth of a worldly AIDS victim. They weren't living in line with Jehovah's commands, and they did *something* to get the AIDS.

The cigarette smoke, wafting up the stairs, surrounding me, had me convinced they were blowing their dirty AIDS right in my gaunt, little God-fearing face. Lost in my own gaze, I imagined that my face was getting bonier by the second. I didn't recognize myself.

Oh, no. I haven't got much time, I thought. *Armageddon must be close. Jehovah might kill me just for associating with them!*

"What are you doing up?" Kathy asked, coming around the corner.

I gasped, tiny paws still gripping my cheekbones. "Umm, going to the bathroom." I lied.

"Get back into bed. We have some fun things planned for tomorrow." She smiled, ushering me down the hallway.

"Okay."

I wandered down the hall back to the guest room. I tried to sleep but it was near impossible as thoughts of infectious disease, death, and Armageddon spun relentlessly.

Tonight's the night. I'm gonna die. My parents will be so upset I didn't make it through Armageddon so they could finally hear my voice. Please, Jehovah, don't kill me. I'll be good. In Jesus Christ's name, amen.

When morning came, I was still alive. My prayer must have worked. Before leaving for breakfast, Kathy started cleaning out one of her pock-ah-books to give me.

"Here, you can have this packet-book," Kathy said in her Connecticut accent, removing her cool, grown-up things. "Oh, here's a qw-ah-ter. You can keep that." She handed me twenty-five cents.

Kathy was my idol. I wanted to *be* her. I hoped to grow into the same gorgeous, mysterious, Italian look she and my mother both had.

When it came time to leave, I hated every minute of it.

"It's my last 'U' day here," I said as Kathy drove me back to Grandma's.

"'U' day?" she asked, cocking her head inquisitively, turning a corner.

"Yeah, we always go the Kingdom Hall on days that have a 'U' in them; Tuesday, Thursday, Sunday, and even sometimes on Saturday." I inspected the packet-book she gave me. "And when we go back home, we'll be at the Kingdom Hall on another 'U' day, not here with you. I like being here for 'U' days."

"Oh? You don't like going, huh?"

I shrugged. "Meetings are three times a week, and long. Tuesday is the book study at our house for an hour. We set up chairs in the basement, the boys get the wood stove going, and we have Bible book studies there. Only the people in our congregation who live close to us come, like maybe twenty; our house isn't big enough for everyone. The Thursday meeting is two hours and at the Kingdom Hall, it doesn't end until 9:00 at night. But sometimes—if we're good—Daddy takes us to Weeks' Restaurant for ice cream after the meeting. Sunday is the big meeting—the talk and *Watchtower* study is for two hours. I draw a line down a piece of paper and write Jehovah on one side and Satan on the other and make tally marks on both sides to show I'm paying attention," I said.

"Oh. What happens on Saturday?"

"Sometimes we go out and talk to people about the Bible."

"Is that when you go around neighborhoods, knocking on people's doors?"

"Yeah, I have a panda bear book bag I use for my Bible and magazines. Maybe I'll use this one next time." I smiled at her while holding up the packet-book she gave me.

"Oh. I'm glad you like it." She smiled.

Being in Connecticut was always more enjoyable than being at the Kingdom Hall or at school. But at least once we were home, I had our backyard, and the B&M Railroad trains.

******

"The B&M Railroad?"

"The best part of my childhood was a little wooded area off our backyard where I'd wait for the line of old Pullman trains. Every day, since I was about four years old, I'd follow the brook that ran alongside our house, leading me into the forest. That was when my love of solitude was born."

"Oh, really? Talk about that." Joel crossed his leg.

"As long as I can remember, I've felt different. I constantly thought—and still think—there's something about me that no one else could possibly understand. Like maybe, there's even something wrong with me, which is why I'm here, I guess," I said, chuckling nervously. "I feel like I've had some inside secret, into some dark and magical world, that no one else is, or was, ever invited to—except for me. I dunno, like, because I'm special in some undefined way. Does that make sense?"

He nodded and kept writing.

"Anyway, as a kid, I wanted to feel that way all the time. Alone. Special. So, I'd escape to the woods behind our house and isolate myself. I felt whole there...more like *me*, I guess. I envisioned disappearing somewhere into the great unknown of New England, on the line of Pullman trains that cut through the wooded area of our backyard. I fuckin' worshipped that train—sorry, do you mind if I swear?"

"Go right ahead."

"Anyway, I was obsessed with clocking its exact time every day. I guess I thought, maybe the Pullman conductor would take me away from all the demons."

"The demons?" He raised one eyebrow.

I sighed. The more I said, the crazier it all sounded.

"Yes, demons. My brother Luke had me convinced our basement was infested with them. One day, Luke lured me into our dank, moldy basement. He opened the door, and as I stepped onto the industrial, burnt orange carpet glued to the cement floor, he slowly brought me to our father's prized possession—the cast iron wood stove.

"He leaned over me and whispered, 'We have demons. Satan's demons. There are shoe prints all over Dad's stove, and the clean laundry that was folded on the couch is now all over the place. Just a mess.' I just stood there, holding my bear, scared shitless. I told him it was probably our Maine coon, Bubba, but he vehemently disagreed. He said we had demons. And I sure wish I had known then that the basement dwelling demons Luke introduced me to would pale in comparison to those I'd meet later."

Joel set his elbow on the armrest of his chair, chin on the palm of his hand. "Same time next week?" he said, smiling.

"Definitely."

Regardless of what anyone in the Truth thinks.

Miseducated

SAME TIME, SAME COUCH the following week, and I was a bit more relaxed about telling a complete stranger the sordid details of my life. The more I said out loud, the more absurd some of it sounded, and the less awkward I felt.

"What was school like for you?"

"School was...a special kind of hell. I think because my mom and dad had such an awkward time themselves, it influenced *my* experience."

"How so?" Joel grabbed his pen and steno pad, crossing his leg. I was slowly unclenching—giving in to the idea of therapy. To my own astonishment, I was okay with him scribbling down pieces of my life.

******

AN ORDINARY DAY IN our house was most definitely not what most folks might consider normal.

Whenever Dad called for Mom, his voice reverberated throughout the entire house. "Yyyuuhh!" he'd bellow. And to get Dad's attention Mom would stomp her foot, shaking both the kitchen and living room floors.

Along with grunts and floor stomping, there was a lot of screaming, pounding, and light-switch flickering. In most houses this isn't welcome. In our house, it wasn't indicative of anger; it was a way to attract attention using visual and sensory cues, initiating eye contact, inciting conversation.

Light switches were strategically placed by every door, at both ends of the hallway, and at the top and bottom of the stairs; all for the ease of attention grabbing. It really was quite normal for us, as were the plethora of mispronunciations.

My dad has always called me Bucky; always. To him, the air conditioner was an *ay-kah-geesha*. When he wanted us to calm down, he'd say, *clam dawn*. If he was angry, he'd tell us to "Go rye affa bed, no wash pop-a-bie show!" (This meant go to bed without supper and no Muppet Show). But ask the man to say Alexander Graham Bell and he can say it beautifully.

******

"Alexander Graham Bell? You mean, the telephone guy?" Joel said.

"Yup. A little fact about Alex—the telephone guy—the man is an asshole. He was in favor of sterilizing all Deaf people so they couldn't reproduce. He *himself* had a Deaf mother and wife. If my parents had been sterilized, I wouldn't be here right now."

"I did not know that."

"It's true. Anyway, my mom called me Mecky. If she was angry—Make-ay. When Mom called us to supper for beef stew, she said, *miff-shwoo*. If she was in a good mood, she'd giggle, saying it over and over, trying to get it right. Catch her in a bad mood, and talk back to her, she'd shriek, 'Go 'head! Talk mehind me my mack! I Deaf, not shtupid! I not hear you, but I know you do!' She was right; we usually were 'talking mehind her mack.'"

My poor mother.

"What does this have to do with school?"

"Sorry, I know, I'm all over the place, but I swear I have a point. My parents had a narrow education, with a heavy focus on lip reading and correct pronunciation. And it obviously didn't work for them. So, when it came time for my brothers and I in school, it was almost too easy. Boring, even."

"Oh?"

"Surprisingly, we didn't have any speech impediments or narrow vocabularies because of our parents' lack of adequate schooling or their many verbal slips. We all learned to read before going to elementary school and we each skipped the line to kindergarten. My brothers and I had mortgage letters, Bible verses, and bank statements to interpret. Mom and Dad relied on us; not because they're stupid, but because they were raised in a questionable residential school program, deprived of language access, and forced to morph into a hearing-centered world. And I think this shaped how I viewed school in general. School was a peculiar institution my parents didn't fit into and neither did I."

"Do you think their experience influenced yours somehow, dooming you to the same fate?"

"You could say that, yeah. My mom and dad weren't members of the PTA; you wouldn't find them wasting time in Satan's wicked system, sitting in the bleachers for any athletic competitions or theater productions. Not only did my parents carry around a communication barrier for the school to grapple with, but remember, they were raising us as J-Dubs. That was worse than being a CODA. It definitely affected our scholastic and social experience," I said, taking off my shoes, making myself comfortable on the couch.

"Tell me more about that."

******

WHEN SCHEDULED TO MEET teachers that I was assigned to at the start of every year, the main objective was to explain our beliefs and provide a list of Jehovah's Witness approved activities. This is seen as an opportunity for JWs to *give a good witness* to worldly people. The goal was to give the *Jehovah's Witnesses and School* brochure to the teacher, stirring conversation.

This brochure and countless others are printed at the JW Headquarters, Bethel, in Brooklyn, New York. Though Bethel in Brooklyn has since been sold, consolidated, and certain facilities have been relocated, this publication still exists and is designed to inform teachers and faculty what to expect while having a J-Dub in their classroom. And maybe they'd see something in the brochure, then change their hedonistic, worldly ways.

"No pledge flag. Bucky stand respect flag fine. No say pledge, no hand on heart," Dad voiced to the teacher.

"Yeah and no holiday party, no holiday schoolwork. No school dance, no sport, no after school thing," Mom chimed in. "She do normal schoolwork fine. Play with other kids outside fine. No holiday or patriot thing, you know?"

The word *no* was routinely uttered, full force ahead, every year. JWs submit to a do or die organization. *Do* what the *Society*, Governing Body (GB), says *or die* at Armageddon. Simple as that—

******

"Sorry, the *Society*? Governing Body?"

"They're one in the same. It's the ruling council for the entire worldwide organization. They write the literature, they make the rules, they control it all. I can never remember how many of them there are, eight? Eleven? I think the number fluctuates."

"Continue."

******

LIFE OUTSIDE THE KINGDOM HALL was unnecessary, and faithful witnesses were expected to *always keep on the watch*.

My teachers stood at attention and nodded to my parent's demands every year. No doubt they felt sorry for me, and probably weren't in the mood to carry on a conversation with fanatic religious nuts, coming complete with their own conversational roadblocks.

I regularly missed Halloween costume parties, candy giveaways, coloring Thanksgiving Day turkeys and pilgrims,

Christmas parties, cookies, gift exchanges, and Valentine's Day parties. I remember thinking, *I want someone to like me enough to gift me Valentine Sweetheart conversation candies, but the Watchtower Society told us that Jehovah says no.*

If holiday activities took place at the end of the school day, I was dismissed early, and went home to watch *The Price is Right* and *$10,000 Pyramid*. If parties took place in the middle of the day, I'd leave the room to sit in the library with a book or uncompleted schoolwork. It didn't really bother me, given my already established love for solitude.

I was also excused from attending holiday concerts for chorus. If the concert had holiday cheer, *and* a mix of other songs on the program, I could attend. I'd sing the non-holiday songs, then simply stand, looking down quietly on the chorus bleachers while my classmates sang "Grandma Got Run Over by a Reindeer." I didn't understand then why a harmless song, or a festive sweater and antlers, hurt Jehovah so much.

By third grade, my classmates knew better than to give me Valentine's treats, share Halloween candy, or give me a Christmas gift. If they did, I was instructed to smile, say thank you and use it as an opportunity to *give a witness.*

I felt bad when I couldn't return in kind and worse for telling my classmates, "I don't want you to die at Armageddon, so please take this *School and JWs* brochure and get baptized." It was easier to keep quiet whenever possible to avoid these uncomfortable exchanges.

The kids in our neighborhood knew our house was not one you bothered to trick or treat. If anyone came to the door in Halloween gear, we politely answered and said, "Sorry, we don't have any candy." As they left, I'd run over to the window and watch them—parading happily in their Ames costumes.

They strutted away laughing. Every year, I wondered if they were laughing at me and hoped they didn't mention it at the bus stop the next day.

******

"Did you make many friends at school?" Joel asked.

"A few, but not really. J-Dubs gladly ostracize themselves, and unabashedly cringe at the general populace to please the ol' Governing Body. This *training*, this...*inculcation*—and the fact I was already accustomed to, and liked, isolating myself—made me feel older and more mature than most of my classmates. I had more conversations in my head than I did with anyone at school.

"I mean, I was the kid who knew the truth about Santa's existence, and while my classmates were practicing cursive letters to Santa, I knew those letters were for naught. And even if Santa *did* exist, he was most definitely going to die at Armageddon. The way I saw it, he'd burn to a crisp at Armageddon for claiming to have godlike powers. I was also the kid busy protecting my parents from the bad, hearing people who were trying to take advantage of or make fun of them."

"That's a pretty hefty responsibility for any elementary aged child," he said scribbling on his notepad.

"One day, Mom and I were in line at the bank. Being at the bank meant money. I was just dying to get my grubby little hands on the red-headed Cabbage Patch Kid at Ames. My mom was making small talk with me in her Miss Piggy voice—"

"Miss Piggy?" He looked up from his steno pad.

"Yeah, her HH voice always sounded like Miss Piggy to me. She doesn't know she sounds like a Muppet, but she does. It's insanely adorable. Anyway, I hear this tall, fat bastard with a beard behind us, making fun of her. She can't hear him teasing, but I can. He must have thought I was Deaf too, until I turned around and glared at him. I told the asshole to stop. I wanted to kick him right in the gut."

"You protected them a lot, then?"

"I guess. I felt guilty anytime I was embarrassed by them, though..."

******

MOM AND DAD'S DEAFNESS—coupled with submission to a publishing company, disguised as a godly organization—was nothing more than a sharp-pointed stick, heavily wrapped in *Watchtower* and *Awake!* magazines. The stick jabbed anyone that came too close, jabbed at any clique that *might* have welcomed me. This happened every time they came to school for any reason.

My dad walked around each school like he owned the place, talking to everyone. Out loud. With his voice. He didn't sound like Miss Piggy. He sounded more like a mix of the Swedish Chef, Statler, and Waldorf—nonsensical and sometimes grumpy. I thought I'd die the day he wandered into my third-grade classroom.

"Bucky, you fuhget you lusshh money," he voiced and signed simultaneously. He walked up to my desk, handing me lunch money. "See later," he said, pinching my cheek as he left.

Then some of my classmates started in.

"What's wrong with your dad? He retarded or something?" one classmate asked while waving his hands idiotically.

I sighed and rolled my eyes. "No, he's Deaf."

"Death?" another classmate asked.

"No. Deaf!"

"Oh, he can't hear?"

"No, he can't." I had to wonder if *they* were retarded, or something.

"What kind of music does he like, *Bucky*?" Some of my classmates heckled in small groups. *Friggin' children.*

That same year I was given the role of Paul Bunyan's mother in our class play. *Paul Bunyan is okay,* I thought. *I don't think Jehovah has it out for him. He's made-up, anyway.*

I had a sore throat but insisted on going to school because of my very important role of sitting in a rocking chair, knitting, while reminiscing over my boy Paul Bunyan and Babe the Blue Ox; I needed to rehearse. Dad brought me to school and walked me into the cafeteria where the rehearsal was already taking place.

"He okay now. He have horssshh in throat," Dad said to my teacher while running his forefinger up and down his throat, demonstrating the sign for sore throat.

Some classmates laughed at him as he smiled and walked out of the cafeteria, waving, oblivious that my classmates were mocking him.

"You have a *horse* in your throat?" my classmates said.

I rolled my eyes. "My throat is hoarse."

"That's not what your dad said! Why did he call you a 'he'?" They kept chuckling.

I knew they wouldn't understand if I said what I was really thinking...

My dad called me a 'he' instead of a 'she' because English pronouns mean almost nothing in ASL. In ASL, English pronouns (he, she, they, and it) are replaced by a finger pointed toward the person or object you're addressing. In Deaf Culture it isn't rude to point.

You might know a fraction of this if you paid one tiny speck of attention during our English lessons. What's more—I was chosen to play Paul Bunyan's mother. You obviously haven't matured enough to be cast for such an adult role. Friggin' amateurs.

For most of my school career, some students assigned me cute nicknames like, "Jumpin' Joho," "Jehover" or instead of saying, "She's a Jehovah's Witness," they'd simply call me "a Jehovah," which drove me crazy. Being called "a Jehovah" was the worst.

No, I'm not the one plotting cosmic revenge to cleanse my name from the devastation cast upon mankind. I'm just Bek. My Deaf parents drag me to the Kingdom Hall three times a week and force me to disturb people on Saturday mornings.

I suspect my classmates knew I disliked attending the Kingdom Hall and being labeled "a Jehovah," because I didn't openly preach to them during the school day like some J-Dub kids did.

I'd briefly entertain their questions about my supposed faith whenever a hand-written invitation to a popular girl's house, for a birthday party or sleepover, made its way to my desk. My little burst of inner jubilation was immediately cut short when I remembered to say, "No, thank you."

Even though I was openly disinterested in my own religion, it didn't stop them from teasing me and shouting things like, "I hate Jehovah's Witnesses!" as soon as I walked into class, which usually drove me to the bathroom in tears.

******

"Sounds rough." Joel took his glasses off and began wiping his lenses.

"It was. I felt like I had no one in school, really. And the few friends I *did* have were either other J-Dubs—trained to police each other and me—or worldly kids I couldn't really hang out with. I guess it makes sense that I took to solitude."

"Were you angry with your parents?"

"Yes and no. I mean, I know they didn't have an easy time raising me or my brothers. I'm sure their decision to become J-Dubs was literally a godsend for them, since they'd maybe had an overcast existence up until the day opportunity knocked in the form of a little, Christian butterball. It most likely helped them handle four, rambunctious, hearing kids."

"Interesting. I'd like to hear more about rambunctious CODAs." Joel smiled and closed his notepad.

"Oh, you will. Same time next week?"
He nodded.

Brotherly Love

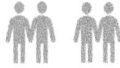

I DON'T KNOW WHY it took me as long as it did to notice, but my therapist looked an awful lot like Larry David, which made the whole experience easier. Maybe he'd make some crack about Festivus, or man-hands.

I wonder if he's got any Superman action figures lurking around...

"How well did you get along with your brothers?" the Larry David look-alike asked that following Thursday.

"Heh. We may not have enough time to cover them this week."

"Well, let's give it a go." He grabbed his notepad.

"My brother, Johnny, told me on many occasions that I was born on a Thursday. He remembered because everyone was excited to finally have a baby girl in the house. He said he, Mark, and Luke used to sing this song to me all the time, and I'd giggle."

"What was the song?"

"Something... 'I'm gonna love you...' doesn't sound familiar to me at all, but it was obviously special enough for him to remember. Johnny was baptized at age fifteen; Dad promised him a dirt bike if he took the plunge. He was dunked, got his dirt bike, and then a little over a year later he was disfellowshipped—"

"Disfellowshipped?"

"Yep. The ol' GB pride themselves on keeping Jehovah's earthly organization squeaky clean. Immorality, wrongdoing, or even *doubt* among the rank-and-file warrants a judicial committee hearing. And if the baptized person isn't repentant, a disfellowshipping—to rid the congregation of unrepentant filth—follows. With a quick announcement from the platform during a Thursday night meeting, the shunning begins, and your entire J-Dub network completely cuts you off. Johnny was disfellowshipped for dating a worldly girl at school and getting her pregnant."

"How old was he?"

"He was seventeen when he left home, I think. I was so young, I'm not sure. One day, he was just...gone."

"Go on."

"Soon after Johnny left, a new brother moved in and took his place. It was as if Dad traded one boy that wasn't biologically his for another without even blinking."

"Interesting. How did this happen?"

******

A SISTER IN OUR congregation needed a ride to Boston. Dad, a fearless city driver, offered to take her.

In one of Boston's overcrowded apartment buildings, he met her nephew, Jesse. With almost no warning, Dad brought him home, and he immediately became my new sixteen-year-old, Black-brutha-from-anutha-mutha—a man of smooth dance moves and the originator of duck lips.

I was so young when Johnny left and Jesse came, that I simply accepted he was my new brother. I didn't question why his skin color was different than ours. The only thing plaguing me was Johnny's exodus.

For Jesse, there was no official adoption process when he moved into our spirit-infested basement. He automatically became the oldest, knocking Johnny right out of the line-up.

I think in most religious settings, congregation members consider each other brothers and sisters in the faith. J-Dubs take this arrangement to a whole new level. Children of any age are often looked after by spiritual brothers and sisters, and it rarely matters who the host family is. As long as they're

Witnesses—vowing to raise that child in the Truth, fearing the one true God, Jehovah—no one bats an eye.

Boston, and its surrounding cities, weren't hospitable to Jesse; he came with baggage. That baggage was one reason my dad took to him so quickly and brought him home.

Jesse still saw his family in NH and Boston regularly. And soon I realized, Dad didn't take Jesse away from his family; Jesse joined ours, brought us into his, and two families became one.

Jesse spent time with me, included me. We took drives in Dad's red Toyota Corolla, blasting Whitney Houston's, "The Greatest Love of All." He showed me the same kindness Dad had shown him. He carted me around NH, visiting his family, and occasionally to Boston to see his mom and grandma, where we watched BET and VH1 endlessly.

One Thursday night at the Franklin Kingdom Hall, just before the last song and closing prayer, my cool, brutha-from-anutha-mutha, Jesse, and almost all the brothers he was friends with were disfellowshipped from the congregation.

A list of about five people, that the Christian congregation of Jehovah's Witnesses could no longer mingle with, was read from the platform. They were to be dismissed and forgotten. And just like that, brother number two was gone, and I had no idea where he went.

He may have been gone and easily forgotten by most uptight passers-by at the Kingdom Hall, but for me it was devastating. I did not forget him, our drives with Michael Jackson, Whitney, and New Edition. I didn't forget him teaching me how to do the cabbage patch in the basement while the demons were sleeping. Or the one time he permed my hair, pulling every strand on my head until I screamed. Jesse'd just keep yanking and say, "We're almost done. Beauty is pain."

Well, that pain paled in comparison to losing another brother simply because the old men at the *Watchtower* printing press told us we had to cut him out of our lives. Over the years, Jesse bounced in and out of the Kingdom Hall like the sparkly balls I coveted in the fifty-cent bin at the A&P.

My brother Mark was Mom and Dad's carefully planned firstborn, and third in the line-up of five. He and I never had a deep-seated relationship as brother and sister. With seven years between us, the only thing we shared were awkward glances around the house.

In a feeble attempt to win him over, sometimes I'd peek into his room while he was lying on his bed. His face was usually buried in a big, blue, hard covered *Watchtower* publication—*Aid to Bible Understanding*.

I stood in the doorway and asked, "Mark? How can I get closer to God?"

He looked up, smiled, and surprisingly invited me in.

We sat on his bed and talked about how I could do more in my service to Jehovah. Since I was somewhere between eight and ten, he said my load wouldn't be too heavy.

"There is so much more you could do to get closer to Jehovah, Bek. Try commenting more at the meetings; add your own personal thoughts when you comment. Go out in field service more, get out on Saturday mornings instead of watching your morning cartoons. That TV is always on and has become your babysitter!"

******

"Field service? As in proselytizing?" Joel asked.

"Yes. He suggested that I miss my Saturday morning line-up of the *Gummi Bears*, *It's Punky Brewster* (the cartoon), *Peewee's Playhouse*, and *Muppet Babies*. He thought I should get dressed up, go out in the cold, and knock on doors all morning. The nerve."

"I gather this wasn't your favorite pastime?"

"No. Never was. I said I *liked* being alone. I *enjoyed* my solitude. I hated going because I didn't like forcing rehearsed conversations with strangers about the state of the world, and what the Bible advises for these *end times*. It never felt like me."

Joel jotted a few notes and nodded at me to continue.

"The panic I felt over the idea of missing Saturday morning cartoons must have been written all over my face, because Mark told me to 'think about all the up-building association I could have with the older ones in the Hall.' Then he pulled out the big guns, reminding me that 'Dad usually meets up with other field service groups, at Brother's Donuts on Main Street, for a coffee break.' Mark knew enticing me with hot chocolate and honey-dipped donuts might work. And I knew that his company was usually bought with biblical discussions, much like my preaching time was purchased with the promise of donuts and hot chocolate. I know he counted time he spent talking to me—"

"Counted time?"

"J-Dubs count their time on field service reports—mini monthly spreadsheets—documenting how many publications are placed with a householder, and how many hours one has spent going door-to-door or conducting home Bible studies. Things like, date, time spent preaching (encouraging your little sister), and any books, brochures or magazines placed, are recorded, and sent to Headquarters."

"Mm-hmm." Joel continued scribbling.

******

IF MARK FELT THE need to police my movie and music choices, an opportunity to *count time* was born.

"What are you watching?" he asked.

I popped a tape from the video rental store into the VCR and said, "*Weird Science*."

I hit play.

"That movie is PG-13. You're not thirteen, Bek."

"I picked it out at Video Vendor. Mom said it was okay."

"She doesn't know any better. If you see something bad, turn it off." And with a disapproving huff, he vanished.

She doesn't know any better? Why? Because she's Deaf, and won't hear any questionable content? Or because she's a woman—the weaker sex—and couldn't possibly understand anything other can cooking, cleaning, and being subservient?

Not more than twenty minutes into the movie, I gasped. My heart stopped. I turned the movie off and ejected the tape after remembering to: *Be Kind, Rewind*. I couldn't believe I had just seen one boy wearing girl's panties, and another boy exposing his bare butt.

Mark came out to the kitchen and saw me in the living room, putting the tape back in its plastic case. "See something bad?"

I ignored his condescending tone and put the tape on a shelf by the door. The scene didn't bother me nearly as much as the thought of Mark seething in the next room did. His idea of an appropriate movie fell more in line with Dad's taste: *The Man from Snowy River, Herbie the Love Bug, The Shaggy Dog*, and any other family friendly flicks.

Living up to Mark's expectation of how every Witness of Jehovah should behave was exhausting. He took all literature and instructions from the ol' GB so seriously, so very life or death. He was fine with being tormented in school. Maybe not so much the day he came home literally seared from the hot poker a classmate branded him with during their Industrial Arts class. Minus the pain, he was proud to be persecuted for Jehovah.

And then there's Luke; the second fruit of my father's loins, and fourth in the Mallory line-up. He created, and cultivated, our unabashed, love/hate relationship. I looked up to him—

idolized him. He had this charismatic way about him. When he walked into a room, you could just feel his power.

Luke and I were close despite the constant push-and-pull of our positions in the sibling queue. He was the baby boy up until the one-and-only baby girl surprisingly came along.

Regardless of the love/hate we experienced in each other's presence, there were so many nights I remember cuddled up in bed with him.

I scared easy.

Terrorizing thoughts of how Armageddon would sweep me away with this *wicked system of things*—and stories of our basement dwelling demons—kept me up at night. I saw fiery orange and blood red every night as I closed my eyes.

Once everyone was asleep, I would sneak into the boys' bedroom with my bear and poke Luke until he woke up. He usually slept on his left side, curled up in blankets, facing Mark's bed across the room.

When I came in and poked him, he'd lift his blanket, scoot his back closer to the wall, and make room for Frederick and me without even opening his eyes. I'd crawl into bed with him and as he threw the blankets over me, pulling me closer, I'd drift to sleep peacefully.

If Armageddon came, or the cellar demons dared to float upstairs, Luke would protect me. I figured if Jehovah planned on keeping Luke, he'd have to keep me, too.

Luke taught me to read at age five while sitting on my bedroom carpet, with our backs against my bed. Mom and Dad knew their English was messy, so they gave us a portable record player and Disney books accompanied by a 45 record.

You know the ones: "*When you hear the chimes, turn the page...*" I loved the whole set so much I wore the records out.

We had *Cinderella, The Three Little Pigs, Lady and the Tramp, The Rescuers*, and countless others. Luke taught me to read using the *Cinderella* book. Once I knew how to recognize and understand words on a page, I became an avid reader; eager to get my hands on anything I was allowed to read.

As well as having an odd fascination for my own pain, I also had a secret attraction to things that scared me. Even though I was frightened, I was enthralled just the same. And the big bad wolf lured me with his evil plans to eat three pigs.

"*Who's afraid of the big bad wolf, the big bad wolf, the big bad wolf?*" sang the three pigs. When the wolf's voice boomed, huffing and puffing, visions of what Armageddon might feel like rattled my cage.

There he is. Almighty Jehovah, up in the heavens, huffing and puffing from his lofty throne. His huffs and puffs blow smoke and fire, destroying all the worldly people. I dodge Jehovah, and the wolf, finding shelter under my bed.

Luke laughed, assuring me the wolf was nowhere to be found and I was safe to come out. He'd been my protector from Armageddon, underground demons, and the big bad wolf since 1977.

But no matter how close I thought Luke and I were, I was often left out of the Luke and Mark club. Those two always had first dibs when it came to Ames purchases—unless it was a doll. Clothes, bikes, roller skates, Legos, and Star Wars toys were always theirs first.

I stared at their Star Wars treasures with envy; Luke Skywalker, Leia, Han Solo, Darth Vader, Yoda, and all their accessories called out to me. I would eventually have my time with them but not until they were used up, and almost ready for the trash.

The *Star Wars* Trilogy were the only movies, besides Disney films from the 1960s, that weren't dubbed demonic in our house. The Force was easily replaced with The Truth. Of course, Yoda was God, and Darth Vader was Satan. So, *Star Wars—A New Hope, The Empire Strikes Back,* and *Return of the*

Jedi were permitted, as were the accompanying toys, and we were all in sci-fi heaven.

The boys ran around in full Star Wars regalia, battling with their plastic, glowing light sabers while I followed them around in my R2-D2 Underoos, trying to get into the act.

The times Mark and Luke excluded me, just drove me further into isolation. They were closer in age; it made sense that they were joined at the hip. I was not only six and seven years their junior but also a girl—rarely included. So, my love of non-J-Dub literature grew rapidly with Amelia Bedelia, Judy Blume, and Apple Paperbacks. Reading in the woods behind our house, alone, was something I always loved.

With whatever book I was reading, I'd sit by the tracks waiting for the B&M Railroad trains. Minutes before they came through, I'd lay pennies on the rails and hope with all my might none would get lost. I'd crouch about twenty feet away from the train tracks to watch it whoosh by. I loved the gust of wind and rumbling sensation I felt as it passed. I kept all my squished pennies as wishes, in a secret collection.

When I wasn't clocking the train, skipping far behind Mark and Luke—trying to keep up with them—or reading, I was lost in an animated fantasy world. I was completely enveloped in the TV shows I *was* allowed to watch; *Inspector Gadget, The Flintstones, Zoobilee Zoo, The Muppet Show, Punky Brewster,* and *Secret City*—a show for young artists. I was completely in love with our television set. I didn't even mind the closed captioning device connected to it because it allowed me to watch TV *and* read—instilling logophilia bit by beautiful bit.

I loved being taken away, far away from thinking about the last days, this wicked system, and Satan's minions living in our basement.

As I got older, *The Muppet Show* and *Inspector Gadget* were replaced with MTV and 80s metal hair bands.

"Bek, long haired guys in a band are the best," Luke said, rattling his Europe cassette tape in my face. He ran into his room, put the tape in the silver boom box above his bed, and turned the volume all the way up.

Deaf parents = loud music.

Luke started jumping around, playing air guitar to "The Final Countdown." And that sure beat Mark's collection of Elvis tapes.

Mark had other tapes at one point, but something in a recent *Watchtower* made him rid his collection of Loverboy. Some stupid song about leading a *double life* was the culprit. Mark wouldn't be caught leading a *double life* or listening to a song about it.

My idol, Luke, prompted me to add to my collection of The Monkees, Debbie Gibson, Huey Lewis and the News, Janet Jackson, and of course, Michael Jackson tapes.

Despite Michael's disfellowshipping and his disclaimer at the end of "Thriller"—denouncing any involvement with the occult—Michael still stole the beat of Mom's heart. And of course, we all hoped he would *come back* to the Truth.

I gave Bon Jovi and Def Leppard a shot. Listening to them didn't seem much different than Europe, so I thought nothing of it. Same groove, same hair, same random beat. Mom and Dad rarely checked my collection and almost never checked Luke's. If the artist didn't look debatable, then it usually wasn't a problem.

But the longhaired guys in my tape collection somehow differed from longhaired guys in Luke's collection. His collection wasn't scrutinized, but mine was.

While Mom was inspecting my Def Leppard tape, she asked about the song "Armageddon It." I explained that it was merely a play on words, and to fully grasp the pun, you had to hear it. Well, she didn't like that one bit—she thought I was mocking her decibel loss.

What's more, she was totally convinced the song had something to do with Jehovah's great day of war—a blatant disregard for his warning. She reminded me that we needed to take heed, unlike the people in Noah's day.

I couldn't help but wonder, *even if they are singing about Armageddon, why is it automatically a bad thing? Maybe they could use a good witness. I'll write them a fan letter to see if they're interested in a possible Bible study.*

As a congregation, we sang *Kingdom Melodies*. Almost every single song contained bible verses, begging for The Great Tribulation and Armageddon to come quickly—

******

"Sorry, uh...the Great Tribulation?" Joel leaned forward in his chair. Eager.

Sometimes I forget how normal this jargon is to me. When I say it out loud, to people who didn't grow up the way I did, I'm reminded that how I was raised was not normal. Whatever normal is.

"The Great Tribulation is a series of necessary world events leading up to Armageddon. First, all false religion and politics will be exposed, then an attack on the one, true religion (J-Dubs) takes place. Next, a judgment of earth's humans, and collection of all faithful believers occurs, *then* Armageddon— the destruction of anyone in opposition to Jehovah—ensues."

"Sort of like the Rapture," he said, nodding.

"Sure? I don't know what that is, but okay."

"It sounds similar."

"Is that what you believe?"

"No. I'm Jewish." He smiled. "Go on."

Is he certain he's not Larry David?

******

WE NOT ONLY SANG songs at the Kingdom Hall dedicated to this event, but prayed fervently before meals, road trips, and of course before and after every meeting.

In each prayer and with every single song—either as a congregation or a family—we implored Jehovah to protect us, love us, forgive us, and asked that his day of vengeance hurry to wipe out this wicked system of things. *So, why couldn't I listen to Def Leppard's, "Armageddon It?"*

Not fully understanding the double standard at play, I vehemently sided with the song's clever play on words and kept signing to my mom, "Song not talk about Armageddon! They say, 'You understand? Yes, understand!'" I fingerspelled I-M-A-G-E-T-T-I-N-G-IT, then fingerspelled: A-R-M-A-G-E-D-D-O-N-I-T. "See? Spell and sound almost same. You not know, you Deaf!"

That did it. I was about to face my own Armageddon, right there in the kitchen with Mom. Her eyes bugged, she charged over to the silverware drawer and yanked it open, trying to locate the wooden spoon.

Okay, okay. Take the stupid tape. I-A-G-O-T-I-T.

I suspected Luke was behind Mom's sudden interest in my music selection. The battle between him and me worsened as I got older. Our relationship drastically changed once I turned twelve.

I chalked it up to sibling rivalry. The more I thought about it, the more I understood that for Luke to engage with me in any way only made it difficult for him to deal with parts of himself he didn't accept. Maybe he saw something in me that made him dislike himself.

Even though we were six years apart, we were more alike than anyone else in the family. I figured whenever he scolded me, he was really battling the mirror's reflection every time. Zeroing in on my bullshit helped him ignore his own. I assumed that my secret epiphany—along with his clout over

Mom and Dad, coupled with his temperamental moral compass—was the catalyst for many of my punishments.

One weekend, a friend from our local congregation, Jocelyn, was at our house for a sleepover. We sat in the living room, innocently listening to Ritchie Sambora's, "Father Time"—a lame ballad about a broken-hearted man.

Luke was in his room with a brother from our Hall until he came barreling into the living room. "Turn off that demonic crap!" he shouted.

"There's nothing wrong with this song!" I yelled back.

"Give me the tape." He grabbed the tape case, studying the lyric sheet. Ritchie Sambora, guitarist for Bon Jovi, was dubbed a satanic threat via Luke's sudden self-righteousness.

The same brother who told me guys with long hair and guitars were sure to be awesome, quickly changed his tune. It usually depended on his mood, recent *Watchtower* articles, how tight the skinny ties around his neck were, or who happened to be within earshot. And maybe looking into the mirror I held up was enough of a reason.

An argument ensued. Dad could always sense when there was a fight; his ears may not work but all other senses were heightened. The stomping that came from the living room caused him to come out and investigate.

Wearing his confused, "Whu hoppen?" face, Dad demanded to know what the problem was.

"She listen bad music. I say off. She rebel," Luke signed.

Dad looked at me. "What music?"

"Not bad!" I signed. "Luke opinion. Not bad."

Anyone who could hear, and was male, often overrode my father's, and most definitely my mother's, authority. In this case, it was Luke and his visiting Christian bedroom buddy.

The squabble continued. It got so heated that Luke's fist plummeted into my stomach because of my disobedience to his older, and much wiser, Christian ear.

Dad stepped in, pushing Luke away, forcing him to stop. "'Nuff, 'nuff."

I fell to the floor crying, gripping my pre-teen tummy in pain and embarrassment—Jocelyn saw the whole thing. Dad remained our referee until we *clammed dawn*.

I stood up to go back into my room with Jocelyn and Luke immediately dropped to his knees, threw his arms around me, pressed his cheek to my belly, and apologized profusely. I put my arms around his neck and just cried. It was so awkward; like a daytime-soap-opera-lover's-spat.

I loved all my brothers madly despite the chauvinism filling the air at home, suffocating me. Nothing I did was right and being me wasn't ever enough.

I wasn't Johnny: the firstborn forgotten outcast that brought a tear to Mom's eye. I wasn't Jesse: charismatically weaving his way into our family's heart, bringing *Good Times*, just to be forcefully cut off repeatedly. I wasn't Mark: spiritually strong as a boulder, gladly persecuted for Jehovah's namesake, and the only *intentional* apple of Mom and Dad's eye. And I wasn't Luke: spiritually balanced, popular at home, school, and the Kingdom Hall.

In that house, I was just Rebekah: last, least, hushed, and insistently tucked away in the shadows, just like Mom.

Many young girls and women are frequently wedged into an uncomfortable position within the *Society's* twisted, religious pyramid; our place is at the bottom, and it started at home.

******

Joel looked at me with pity peeking out between the lines of his forehead. "Why don't we end today with a good memory."

"A good memory…let's see…"

I searched my mind for a minute, as it turned into what felt like forever. Then I got lost trying to remember what forever felt like to me as a kid, and I found my favorite memory.

There was a sunset, I heard music. I saw myself sitting between my parents in the car. I have no idea where we were going or where we might've been coming from. For some reason, I remember New Jersey, and a busy city street.

In the ol' Caprice Classic, I had the perfect view. While the boys sat uncomfortably in the back seat like dry sardines, I sat up front with Mom and Dad. With my butt propped up on the Drinkster—a bench-like seat/car-console that I thought was my own built-in, cushioned high-chair—I sat, unbuckled, with a view of the city streets.

Just ahead of us was a bright orange sunset—the sun looked like it was going to swallow us whole, it was that close. The radio was on playing one of the first songs I remember ever hearing "Arthur's Theme" by Christopher Cross.

I swayed in the front seat as the song sucked me in. Dad glanced in the rear-view mirror a few times, watching the boys mock the song in ASL. Mom sat—looking out the window with a small coffee, two creams, and one sugar—smiling.

I stared at the setting sun, up ahead, caught somewhere between a twinkling moon and New York City.

"Rebekah?"

"Sorry, got lost for a second."

I decided to give him a different memory.

"I caught Mark and Luke peeking at Mom and Dad from the corner of our hallway one day. I snuck up behind them, holding Frederick (I never went anywhere without the bear). The boys were wearing their Star Wars clothes, whispering…"

******

"THEY'RE NOT DEAF. No way," Mark Solo mumbled to Luke Skywalker.

"Yeah, I bet they're Russian spies. Look at Dad!" Luke whispered.

I see Dad sitting in his recliner, struggling to read the newspaper, while Mom hums from the kitchen, hanging over her sewing machine. She looks up, sees us, and smiles.

"Mecky, when I finish you come try on. I fix the hem. You stand on chair, turn around, okay?" she voiced.

I hated hem time. Mom would have me put on dresses she was sewing, stand on a metal folding chair in the kitchen, and turn slowly in one continuous, never-ending circle. She'd crouch down, staring up at the hem to make sure it was straight. When it wasn't, she'd get out those god-awful pins to mark the hem, and accidentally stick me.

"She saw us!" Luke hissed.

"She's not the one we need to worry about. It's *him*. He can hear everything; he's trained to ignore us," Mark whispered.

"Russian spies?" I yelled.

"Shut up, Bek. They'll hear you," Mark whispered.

"Yeah, be quiet." Luke put his hand over my mouth. "They *are* spies. I just know it," he said, pressing his hand into my face.

I wiggled away from Luke's lightsaber-toting, sweaty hand asking, "Why do you think that?"

"Dad doesn't speak English, in case you haven't noticed, dummy," Luke muttered.

I looked up at them both and said, "They're not Russian. Mom is Italian. Grandma said I was supposed to be named Annunziata, but Mom couldn't say it right cuz she's Deaf, not Russian—"

"Shh!!"

Dad looked up from his newspaper, glared at us from the top of his bifocal glasses, and said, "What you do hide for?"

"Quick! Run!" Mark said. The three of us scampered down the hallway.

I don't know if other kids ever suspected their parents of espionage, but the boys sure did. At the time they even had *me* thinking they might be spies. Maybe we *were* caught up in some dangerous *Cloak and Dagger* lifestyle. Maybe there *would* be danger, and we'd have to interpret for them. Except not in Russian.

******

"Did you interpret for them at all growing up?" Joel asked, closing his notebook.

"Oh, shit yeah. All the friggin' time."

Child Labor

"LAST WEEK YOU JOKED about interpreting Russian, but you weren't kidding about interpreting in general, were you?" Joel asked, opening his (*my*) notebook.

"No, interpreting for my parents was pretty much an everyday thing." I kicked off my shoes, lowering myself to the couch. I pulled my knees in and rested my ass on my feet, leaning into my elbow on the armrest.

******

CODAS INTERPRETING FOR THEIR parents in the 80s, long before the Americans with Disabilities Act (ADA) passed in 1994, was an everyday occurrence. The ADA is intended to protect the rights of any person with a disability, ensuring the right to reasonable accommodations, without discrimination.

In theory.

Before this bill became a law, doctors, dentists, lawyers, churches, government offices...etc. weren't required to provide any accommodations to people with disabilities, no matter how reasonable they were.

Accommodations for Deaf people, to have access to qualified interpreters, usually resulted in confusion. It wasn't always refused, but it also wasn't a common request; especially in the small NH town we lived in. "What? You need an interpreter? I don't understand..." It was so annoying.

Rather than explain, ad nauseam, why they needed interpreting services, my parents used us feeling very little guilt, if any. It was routine for us. We didn't know anything different.

Some kids washed dishes, vacuumed, and babysat their siblings—we interpreted. For free. We interpreted doctor's appointments, Mom's house cleaning service interviews, appointments at Community Action, the Social Security office, at home next to the TV if the closed captioning machine was on the fritz, phone calls, and whenever "Billie Jean" came on the radio.

Our hands were up often.

If the boys weren't available, the chore made its way down to me. Being the youngest meant the chore became mine *a lot*. Once my brothers were older, and had acquired their own lives, I was *it* often.

"Bucky, call for me. My lawyer." Dad waved me into the kitchen.

I pressed pause on the VCR. *I* was *watching Flight of the Navigator*. I stood, sighed, and trudged into the kitchen.

I stared at the phone mounted to our kitchen wall. Above it hung a light fixture that flickered every time it rang so Mom and Dad knew someone was calling. *Another strobe light for Club Mallory*.

Telephone calls were rarely private. If an incoming call wasn't for my brothers or me, the god-awful beeps of the TTY would shriek through the receiver damaging *our* ears.

Our TTY, or teletypewriter, was a lightweight beige typewriter with black keys that sat on an end table, covered with a lacey doily. It had a rubber acoustic coupler for the handset to mate with while conversations took place between two Deaf parties. Or, on occasion, between one hearing and one Deaf person using a relay operator as the go-between. The conversation would appear in real-time on a little digital screen above the keyboard, in a green AS400 font.

I'm sure they had their reasons for using us instead of the TTY, but at the time I couldn't think of any.

"We call now," Dad said.

I grabbed the yellow rotary phone off its hook and looked to my father devastatingly. *I'd rather do dishes.*

Dad dialed the law office, inserting the tip of his forefinger into the mini holes of the number wheel. Each number pulsed, swooshing as it went around, communicating with our local phone exchange. With every beat, a little piece of me died.

He'd been battling a discrimination issue. He'd applied for a maintenance job with a manufacturing company, and they wouldn't hire him because he was Deaf. He could definitely do the job—he had the experience—but they refused to hire him, and he was determined to get to the bottom of it, using me as a conduit.

The line rang.

"Hello?" a man answered.

"Hi. This is Bek," I said, "I'm calling for my dad, Mr. Mallory."

"Oh, hi!" the man said, not sounding the least bit surprised hearing a child speak on behalf of her father.

I sat in the hallway on the brown, carpeted floor with the old, yellow phone pressed to my ear, cradling it on my shoulder while signing everything the lawyer said.

Dad wrinkled his eyebrows as the flailing of his hands grew angrier. He tried to keep his voice in off-mode, but the grunts were getting louder as the call continued.

Dad signed the word *discrimination* over and over.

"My dad says that's discrimination," I said. As young as I may have been, I knew and understood the word well. Dad's hands were going at warp speed, and he was so angry, he was repeating himself.

"It certainly does *sound* that way, hon, but tell your dad that it's a liability issue," the man explained.

"What's that mean?" This word I wasn't so sure about.

"If there's an emergency on the manufacturing floor, your dad won't be able to hear any alarms or announcements. And if he gets hurt on the job, the company will have to take care of him. Understand, sweetie?"

"How do you spell it?" I asked.

"L-I-A-B-I-L-I-T-Y." As he spelled, I followed suit, using my fingers. Then I signed the words, *emergency*, *you*, *hurt*, *Deaf*, *work*, and *can't*.

Dad kept signing the word *discrimination* over and over, while shaking his now reddened face. "No! Not right! I sue! Hang up! Hang up!"

I ran toward the phone's wall mount, then screamed "It's discrimination!" into the handset and hung up without saying goodbye. Dad was huffing, and I didn't want to add any friction by disobeying him.

Back to Flight of the Navigator.

I don't know what came of this litigious endeavor. All I know is I yelled at this man, whom I had nothing against, while my father viciously threw his hands about. Once I hung up, my dad stormed into the boy's room to sit at the only desk in the house and brood.

******

"How old were you at that time?"

"Nine, maybe ten? I remember feeling so bad for him. It was hard for anyone to find a job at that time. Factor in being Deaf, people thinking there's something wrong with you, and it's worse. I'm willing to bet most kids that age don't know what discrimination looks like up close."

"I'll bet you're right."

I glanced over at the window, looking for the bird I saw during my first visit. Lost in the memories of many more interpreting scenarios, Joel asked if there were more tales to tell.

"Oh, so many. I don't want to bore you." I smirked, still looking for the bird.

"I'm not bored."

"Okay. How many kids, do you suppose, knew details of their father's hernia operations, and had to interpret 'You can't have sex with mom' in the doctor's office?"

"Um, not many. Go on." He scooted closer to the edge of his seat.

******

A BIT AFTER OUR emotionally charged phone date with the lawyer, Dad was struck with a hernia. He had surgery and was scheduled for a post op visit a week after. None of my brothers were around, so I was *it*. Again.

I usually got a reward at the end of any interpreting chores, so I thought nothing of going to the doctor's office with them; it was pretty typical.

In the office, the doctor asked Dad how he'd been feeling since the surgery. I signed to Dad.

"Fine," he signed back.

"Fine," I told the doctor.

"Good. There's a list of do's and don'ts with recovery: no heavy lifting, no strenuous exercise, no sexual activity."

As he spoke, I signed—*can, can't, no pick up, no lift*, and *no exercise*. I suddenly stopped, hands frozen in midair, when he uttered the phrase: *sexual activity*.

I looked at the doctor. He looked at me. He looked at my dad. Both Mom and Dad looked at the doctor. Then to me. And I started to giggle.

Mom smiled. "Why you laugh?"

"Say what?" Dad signed.

I signed, while smirking and avoiding eye-contact, "You, Mom can't S-E-X."

"Oh boy." Dad hung his head in both hands.

Mom giggled.

My face turned pink, then a deep shade of red. I was hot with embarrassment, riddled with anxiety. The appointment ended and I dragged my remaining dignity to the car.

I felt a bit lighter with the promise of a Happy Meal.

Another time, at Winnisquam Regional Middle School, I thought chatting in the halls with the Deaf custodian had gotten me into trouble the day I was called down to the principal's office.

"The school janitor needs someone to sign for him," the secretary said. "We need you to ride down to the day care around the corner and sign for him."

"But—"

"Don't worry, you won't get in trouble for missing class. You've already been dismissed, and after you're through, you'll get a treat." She smiled, folding her hands on the desk.

"Do my parents know?"

"No, it'll just take a few minutes. We already told your teachers."

******

"Hold on... You were being taken out of school to work?" Joel looked up from his notepad and removed his glasses, brows crumpled.

"Yep. I complied because I wasn't the type to disobey. I was also curious about the treat I'd get upon finishing a hard day's work. So, I rode to the Day Care with the principal and janitor to interpret. When we were finished, they took me to McDonald's and rewarded me with a Happy Meal. It was better than the school lunch, but I had to think my services were worth more than a grey mystery-meat burger and soggy fries."

"Did you ever do any interpreting at the church?"

"The Kingdom Hall? Oh yeah, that stung more than any other setting."

"Why?"

"My mom and dad tried as hard as they could to do what they thought was right. Remember, their first language is ASL not English. They're 'Big D' Deaf, identifying wholeheartedly with Deaf culture; they're not 'little d' deaf, simply accepting hearing loss."

"Mm-hmm."

"They, like many Deaf folks, struggle with written English. ASL is not a dictionary of signs for every English word in existence. ASL is a rich, complex language with its own grammatical structure. Body language, eye gaze, facial expression, eyebrow use, and the many hallmarks of Deaf Culture are weaved in perfectly. If there are subtle changes with *any* of those components, the meaning behind the sign changes completely."

"Wow. I didn't know that. I thought *The Joy of Signing* covered it."

"Ha! No. *The Joy of Signing* doesn't cover it. If you're looking for Signing Exact English, take a time machine back to 1971. You might find it there."

Larry David laughed.

******

MY PARENTS ARE FAR from ignorant or less than. I can't stress this enough. They simply don't use English the way hearing people do. They may even appreciate the English language more than the average hearing person and passed their love of learning onto me.

They often pulled out our blue *Student Dictionary* to look up words I already knew, writing definitions in the margins of that week's *Watchtower* study, beaming with pride. Seeing them do this every week stirred my passion for words, their meaning, and the ability to string them together with pleasure.

Their daily struggle with English, and the fact that the *Watchtower* publications were *in* English, is why it was so crucial to have all meetings and literature interpreted.

The schooling my parents received meant they could utter sound and force a piece of paper to waver. That's it. They weren't taught how to *use* English, and they certainly didn't know what it sounded like.

They were noticeably uncomfortable giving talks in the Theocratic Ministry School (TMS) at the Kingdom Hall but obliged out of their love for Jehovah.

******

"The what?" Joel asked.

"Theocratic Ministry School," I said. "Yeah, I know, lots of things unique to J-Dubs."

Joel began scribbling wildly.

******

THE TMS IS AN opportunity for brothers and sisters in the congregation to practice their speaking and debating skills onstage, resulting in a keen ability to master quick-witted comebacks in the door-to-door ministry.

They're also rehearsals where young ones are trained to memorize scriptural defenses in the face of persecution at school or door-to-door.

The TMS was a thirty-minute segment consisting of short, five-minute biblical talks and demonstrations. Either conversations between two sisters sitting at a table on the platform took place (because women never preach alone from the stage), or quick sermons were given by one brother from the coveted podium.

A congregation elder critiques all TMS speakers on pronunciation, articulation, how well the speaker knows the material—and other components of public speaking—then gives feedback while the entire congregation tunes in. It's like Toastmasters for religious fanatics.

This was challenging for my parents.

Mom adorably used her Miss Piggy voice to mispronounce words. She worked hard at keeping her forefinger on what she read aloud, deliberately pointing to each word, so as not to lose her place. She thought in ASL, and forced the words out in English, just like Dad.

Dad can use English and does well enough for someone who can't hear himself. To this day, I think the man is brilliant. His talks in the TMS were delivered in jagged pieces. While using his voice, he never knew how loud or soft he was speaking. He tried so hard to pronounce words that usually escaped all meaning for him. I often wondered if reading or speaking from the platform brought back any bad memories for them.

My dad longed to be an elder—valued for his wisdom, with an elite position in the Hall—but the ol' GB didn't think he was qualified to serve a hearing, English-speaking congregation. He remained a Ministerial Servant, secretary to the elders in Franklin, but he coveted elder status like David coveted Bathsheba.

As for interpreting, a handful of fellow congregants, in *good standing*, offered their mediocre signing services. I would never call what they did *actual* interpreting. If they weren't available, the duty would be shifted to my brothers and me.

Mark wasn't bothered by it one bit. He reveled in his own glory, sitting across from my parents, diligently representing the word of God from his well-prepared study material in perfect ASL. I admired his ability to interpret with precision and grace. This was no doubt a direct result of him watching himself interpret in the mirror.

I didn't catch Luke signing to himself in the mirror, but he was no slacker. He wasn't burdened and, like Mark, he also harbored a natural talent for it.

Some CODAs can't sign their way out of a paper bag, even if it's the only form of communication they have with their parents (my cousins are prime examples of this). But you better believe my parents knew that they were breeding interpreters.

Brothers who kissed enough elder ass could move up the rungs of the rank-and-file quickly, earning privileges like adjusting microphones for the speaker, handing portable microphones to commenting folks in the audience, queuing the cassette tapes for *Kingdom Melodies*, or standing in the back of the Hall as security.

Interpreting the meeting, songs, prayers, and even holding the songbook open for the person interpreting, was also an earned privilege.

I started holding the songbook at age seven, while whoever interpreted brought songbook lyrics to life in ASL.

******

"What would prevent someone from being in *good standing*, as you put it?" Joel asked, using air quotes.

"Oh, Jesus H, almost anything. Making out, feeling each other up, which is what they call *heavy petting*. Masturbation, fornication (premarital sex), adultery, domestic abuse, loose conduct, homosexuality, smoking, drugs, bad association, acting too worldly, questioning, and doubting the *Watchtower Society*, or being *inactive* (a no-show at meetings). You pretty much had to be too young to have tried anything—like me— or walking the straight and narrow—like my brothers. They did the bulk of the work, and I joined the ranks by age nine, when I became an unbaptized publisher."

"A what?" He raised a brow.

"A publisher is someone who understands basic Bible principles, agrees, counts time on field service reports—"

"Someone who's being groomed for baptism, and in *good standing*?"

"Pretty much, yeah."

"I understand *why* your parents needed interpreting, now tell me what interpreting was like for you and your brothers in that setting."

I shifted my position on the couch. Feet now on the floor, head resting on the back of the sofa, eyes fixed on the ceiling. I could see myself at age ten…eleven…twelve…sitting in a dark blue cushioned chair. Mom and Dad sat in a row of five chairs reserved for our family. The row in front of ours was removed and empty except for the interpreter's chair, which was turned to face Mom and Dad.

I could see it, and them, so clearly even though it had been years since any of us stepped foot inside that Kingdom Hall.

******

BY AGE NINE I didn't do much interpreting. I usually held the songbook and sometimes practiced while interpreting the announcements, or a five-minute talk given by another publisher my age—you know, easy stuff.

With envy, I watched my brothers interpret while Mom and Dad gushed with pride. And when Mark and Luke got busy living their own lives, the chore made its way down to me once again, just like the doctor's appointments.

With each passing year, I was given more time in the Kingdom Hall hot seat. Five minutes became ten, then fifteen, and by the time I was twelve, I was part of the full rotation, sharing the Joys of Signing with a few single sisters who haphazardly flailed their hands in the air.

Mark, nineteen at this time, was grooming himself for a very important post at Bethel in Brooklyn, New York. Bethel's not only a production site but also a communal dormitory. The "Bethel Family" live in shared apartments to be close by and readily available for God's very important work. All Mark's interpreting talent would soon be wasted, doing menial chores for old, unsophisticated, religious writers.

Luke, eighteen at the time, was rarely home. He was spending most of his free time visiting other congregations, looking for a sister to court and marry. He even traveled to Australia for two months to find the perfect mate and came back with vegemite.

When the gaggle of interpreters were absent, I sat across from Mom and Dad—delivering Jehovah's vital messages—alone.

When my parents wanted to comment during meetings, they did so with the voice of a pre-teen. The microphone was handed to me and—as they were signing—comments went from their hands to my brain for split-second processing, out of my mouth, and through the mic, echoing from the speakers.

I couldn't participate as myself while interpreting because I didn't have enough hands. When the Mallory pool-of-skilled-interpreters shared the chore, it was doable, balanced. But when it all fell on me, I floundered.

******

"That sounds like a lot for a twelve-year-old." Joel removed his glasses and rubbed the bridge of his nose.

I shrugged and nodded thinking, *I didn't know any different.*

"I guess so. Day-to-day interpreting bugged me, yeah. But interpreting the meetings, and while out in field service, fucking crushed my spirit."

"What's the difference? Interpreting is interpreting, right?" He put his glasses back on.

"Not necessarily. Each setting comes with its own unique dynamic. Interpreting for my mom at one of her house cleaning interviews—touring someone's home, as they give specific instructions on what to clean and in which rooms—

was different from interpreting someone's disfellowshipping announcement at the Hall. Especially if it was someone you were close to," I said.

"That makes sense. Did you interpret while soliciting the Bible door-to-door?"

"Yes, and even during home Bible studies with interested householders. Sometimes, if it was just my parents and me at a door, I pretended to knock, knowing they couldn't hear my light rapping. My dad caught on to my scam and said, 'Knock hard, Bucky, tap for?' Then, he'd pound on the door himself until someone answered and my plan to breeze through the neighborhood and get a donut was foiled.

"While going door-to-door they tried sharing the *good news* with people who couldn't care less and didn't want any biblical commandments delivered via disabled strangers. I didn't like doing any of it, disliked being at meetings even more, and generally felt sorry for my mom and dad.

"They struggled to fully understand life-saving direction from the ol' GB in English, and I struggled to interpret for them effectively because my heart wasn't in it. I started focusing more on Mom and Dad and less on my own spirituality— which wasn't very strong to begin with."

"Why didn't you think your level of spirituality was strong?"

"It was just something I felt. I knew from a young age— maybe due to all the deep thinking and precious alone time spent in the woods, romancing the Pullman trains—that something wasn't right. The *Watchtower* organization felt like a scam to me. I heavily depended on my own intuition. And it was at constant war with the voices of my fellow brothers and sisters, saying that maybe I 'just didn't have enough faith.' It was exhausting."

"When did you learn to depend on your intuition?"

"I don't recall a specific moment or strike of lightning, I don't know, I can't explain it. I just…*knew*. And I knew the way I was being raised was…*wrong*, somehow."

I stared out the window, frustrated with my inability to express something I felt had been branded to my core since birth. If *that* could speak for me, this would be so much easier.

"What were home Bible studies like?"

"I only remember one mainly because this guy loved my dad, and I loved staring out at Main Street from the giant bay windows in his living room—wishing they were ours. I'd lose myself in thought and envision myself at home watching *Secret City* with a sketchpad and pencil, attempting to draw some obscure corner of the universe. I was usually brought back to the here-and-now by my dad waving his stained snot-rag in my face, prompting me to cover my head."

"Why?" Joel scrunched his face, bemused.

"Women are expected to be subservient to men—we're the weaker sex. And in the presence of any man, especially baptized brothers, a sister was to show proper respect by covering her head if she was needed to say or interpret a prayer, before and after a Bible study. So, my dad signed a heartfelt prayer, and I voiced it with his snot-rag on my head. That's just how it was. Most of the women did it at one time or another," I said shrugging.

"I see…interesting," Joel said, jotting that random fact down. "I just realized, besides your sleepover friend," Joel flipped through his notepad, "Jocelyn, you haven't mentioned any friends."

I thought back and realized that besides my next-door neighbor, Melissa, the only other friend who came in clear was Jax. He was my oldest friend. He was the one who *got me*. No explanation, no questions. We were two halves of the same whole.

"Well, my first real friend would have to be Jax. I don't remember meeting him, he's always just...been there."

"Was he a Witness from your Hall?" Joel looked at the clock on the wall. We were almost at the top of the hour.

My feet danced around, looking for my shoes.

"No. I mean, he was a J-Dub but not from Franklin. When I was about five- or six-years-old, our family started going to Deaf meetings once every couple of months at a Hall in either Maine or Massachusetts. It was nice because there were no crackling microphones, no *Kingdom Melodies*, no interpreters needed, and no talking. It was silent.

"The talks, songs, and prayers were given from the platform in ASL. If someone had a comment, they walked up onto the stage, faced the congregation, and signed. When I was about twelve, the meetings were regularly held once a month. And I liked going because me and my CODA friends were totally stripped of interpreting duties."

"So Jax also had Deaf parents?" Joel scribbled one last note to himself.

"Yeah, and our parents were old friends. So, like I said, I don't remember ever meeting Jax, or his younger sister Gina, they were just always there. Jax used to host these covert CODA meetings in the basement of whatever Kingdom Hall we used that month. We compared war wounds and griped about going home to face more interpreting chores; sometimes we laughed about it all, and sometimes we didn't."

"Were your brothers there, also?" Joel closed his notebook.

"Earlier on, yes. When they were still young enough to enjoy it. They'd never pass up an opportunity to go to The Ground Round."

"The what?"

"After the meeting was over, almost everyone would go to this restaurant to visit all night. Its basement seating area had a movie screen, showing old black and white cartoons. Our families usually stayed until they closed. We CODAs never complained about it. It was our chance to be kids, not interpreters, and we seized those opportunities with both hands. Of course, once the day ended, it was back to the stark reality of being ostracized by worldly classmates, not fitting in, interpreting at home, and at the meetings."

With my feet now dressed to beat it, I stood and grabbed my jacket.

"Same time next week?" he asked.

"Yup." I smiled.

Joel turned around in his office chair to face his desk.

"Joel?"

"Yeah?"

"Thank you."

He turned his head and smiled. "You're welcome."

Pink Suede & Horny Serpents

IT HAD BEEN ONE hell of a week and I couldn't remember where Joel and I'd left off a week ago. By week five, things were starting to blur. One thing was certain: therapy was helping, and the Bible never seemed to.

"Did you ever feel anything more than friendship toward Jax—being as close as you say you were?"

Jax. That's where we left off. Glad he writes shit down.

"No. At least not until later. At twelve, I had a huge crush on someone in the Franklin congregation."

I searched my memory for his face. *Ah, there he is. Trey.*

"You really want to hear this? It's gonna get awkward," I said.

"I'm a licensed therapist, I've heard it all." Joel adjusted his glasses, crossed his leg, and flipped a page in his notepad.

"Okay. Don't say I didn't warn you. I was an incredibly horny adolescent."

"Weren't we all?"

******

WHEN I WASN'T INTERPRETING the meetings, my mind wandered. My eyes danced around the Hall looking for Trey. And once they found him, I fixed my stare on his every move. I paid very close attention to the crossing and uncrossing of his legs, restless breaks he took from his seat to sip from the bubbler, and every comment he made during the meetings.

Trey was sixteen. Older. Wiser. He was spiritually strong, already baptized, and spent over ninety hours each month in field service.

What a catch.

He had blond hair, piercing blue eyes, and a sharp characteristic nose. He rarely got in my way, but how I wished he would. Sometimes when I looked at Trey, it made me feel...funny. I wasn't sure what the sensation was, but I liked it.

Visions of him noticing me, after he sipped water from the bubbler by the Kingdom Hall bathrooms, played out in my mind's eye like a cheesy romcom.

He looks up from the bubbler as if he's never seen me before. Our eyes lock. He takes one step closer, grabbing my face in both hands to kiss me deep and hard. He whispers in my ear, "Be my Shulamite bride." We court until I'm eighteen, wed in the Kingdom Hall, and he lovingly covers my chilly shoulders with his fancy suit coat whenever the ay-kah-geesha kicks on.

These thoughts were more than enough to rouse my randy muff. The throbbing was so distracting, hard to control. I needed a release. I became obsessed with figuring a way to calm the pulse.

Alone in my room, frustrated, I looked for random objects nearby to rub between my legs. I found hairbrush handles, and small blocks of insect-repellent cedar wood from my dresser. Which helped somewhat, but the commotion quaking between my pre-teen thighs was unlike anything I ever felt before. It was electrifying.

While rubbing myself frantically, my breath quickened. When it felt so good, I could barely stand it, I welcomed the paralyzing sensation, thanking God my parents were Deaf. When the flutter softened, I'd close my eyes and exhale. Returning to earth, my vision was always blurry and my head, whirling.

Just about anything made me feel funny down there; it was no longer just fantasies about Trey. Anything on TV even *hinting* at sexuality, or sexiness of any kind, did me in.

Soon enough, I discovered Harlequin Romance and V.C. Andrews novels. I read them in secret, hiding them under my mattress. It got to a point I was retiring to my bedroom a few times a day to feel *it*.

After successfully achieving a blissful high, I'd walk into the living room, dazed. Seeing Mom and Dad carry on was unnerving. He innocently watched TV from his recliner, while she sewed in the kitchen, humming over stitches. I always felt guilty for some reason.

Then, as if by supreme intervention, the ol' GB released a new pocket-sized, blue publication, exposing my guilt in shameful detail—*Questions Young People Ask, Answers That Work*. It was a book dedicated to my age group—dissecting topics such as: "How Can I Talk to My Parents?" "How Can I Resist Temptation?" "Why Am I Afraid to Share My Faith at School?"

And then, there it was. The mystery word of all mystery words, staring back at me from two chapters that grabbed my attention immediately: "What is Masturbation?" and "How Can I Conquer the Habit of Masturbation?"

I asked my friend Jocelyn, "What's masturbation? I saw it in the *Young People Ask* book and it says it's bad, but I don't understand why."

"Um, ask your mom to study that chapter with you." I gathered maybe she was too embarrassed to tell me herself.

I asked my mom about masturbation. I didn't really know what it was, so I fingerspelled it; I didn't think there was a sign for it.

"Oh! Um...that when you feel funny...you know...maybe you...touch self...feel good," she explained while sim-comming (slang for "simultaneous communication"—a way to use ASL and your voice at the same time, like rubbing your stomach and patting the top of your head—doable but annoying).

Suddenly, Trey's face—and all the risqué scenes I'd read in my hidden, romance-novel library—pranced in my head. I'd been feeling funny, touching myself, and I liked it. I didn't understand what was so bad about it.

"When you young, you touch self?" I signed.

"Um, yes, sometimes. Me young, not know."

Mom was always brutally honest with me. These are the kinds of things you can count on in most pockets of the Deaf community, and most definitely in our house—blunt honesty. No prevarication.

"Feel funny," I signed, pointing to my crotch, "bad? Why *Watchtower* say bad?"

"Well, Jehovah no like. Husband wife together touch okay. But alone touch, no," she sim-commed, using her low Miss Piggy whisper.

If I'm not supposed to do it, why do I feel funny even when I'm not touching myself?

The book stated it was because I was in the *Bloom of Youth*. It further cautioned me to stop giving in and pray if I was having a hard time with *self-abuse*. It felt like I was always being told to pray and *wait on Jehovah*. It made no sense to me. If I had the power to start something, didn't I also have the power to stop it?

Mom just told me she let her freak flag fly unabashedly as a pre-teen, and Jehovah's mouthpiece—the ol' GB—said I couldn't unfurl the flag and rub myself with the pole in the privacy of my own room. The idea of Jehovah, and his steering committee, looking down and scolding me every time I went for my hairbrush, felt more shameful to me than the *self-abuse* did.

If the quiver of my crotch snuck onto center stage—for *any* reason—I prayed like a fool. It was exhausting. Fighting a natural urge, accepting guilt-ridden threats from my celestial friend—and subsequently begging him for forgiveness—felt like being robbed of simple humanity. I was beginning to resent him. Them. The whole damn thing.

******

"Didn't you say that from a young age, you knew it all to be a scam?" Joel asked.

"Yes, instinctively. But my world view wasn't in focus yet. At this point I was just starting to see patterns and my doubts were starting to materialize. One thing this After-School-Special-wannabe book said was that 'masturbation is greedy and unnatural, leading to sexual promiscuity and—*gasp!*—homosexuality.' I wasn't lusting after my girlfriends because of my hairbrush handle or spreading myself wide open for anyone who was willing. I was alone. In my room. Bothering no one."

My crossed ankle trembled as I continued.

******

MARK APPLIED FOR BETHEL and once he was accepted, took a vow of poverty, open to any assignment—waiting tables, doing the GB's laundry, housekeeping, printing publications or working on the farm in Wallkill.

One upside to Mark going away to *Watchtower* College, was that his assignment was in one of New York's five boroughs; a far cry from the square-dancing hoedowns in Franklin, NH. Mark was given a very important post at Headquarters: waiting tables for the ol' GB.

The congregation planned a farewell performance for Mark and before I could say no, I was up onstage with the rest of the kids singing, "Goodbye, Farewell, Auf Wiedersehen, Adieu" from *The Sound of Music* wearing a bulky fluorescent Cosby sweater, neon scrunchy socks rumpled over my tight-rolled acid wash jeans, white high-top British Knights, and a horrible mullet.

I looked over and saw Trey snickering with his friends. I was mortified. Trey would surely dismiss me after this humiliating performance, dressed in this horrible outfit. But shockingly, he didn't.

It was sporadic at first. We chatted a bit before and after meetings and were sometimes placed in the same car group for field service. He started calling and my thoughts ran wild. I kept fantasizing he'd court me until I was eighteen, we'd have a beautiful Kingdom Hall wedding, and I could be with my husband like my mother advised, "Husband wife together touch okay."

Then it happened. My parents and I were invited to dinner with a few local witnesses for *good, clean association*, and Trey was there.

At first, we innocently made eyes at each other during dinner. Daring to take it further, we played footsies under the table, and I quivered. I was hot, excited, and felt that familiar pulse between my legs. Trey was driving me crazy. I excused myself and went to the bathroom to take a few deep breaths.

Upon my return, dinner was being cleaned up, and coffee was brewing. Trey led me into a lower-level sunroom down four carpeted stairs. Immediately to my right was a flowered loveseat, pushed up against the wall. In front of that was a Ping-Pong table.

"Wanna play?" Trey asked, smirking.

Yes, I want to play.

We played Ping-Pong for what seemed like an eternity, but I knew we'd barely been at it for five minutes because the coffee hadn't even finished brewing. Every chance he got, Trey slammed the ball to my side of the table with brute force, and it fell to the floor every time.

I thought he just sucked at Ping-Pong, but when I bent down to get the ball for the seventh time, Trey raced to my side and stole an unexpected peck from my lips. I froze. The inner thigh tingle was back—with a vengeance.

No one checked on us as long as the ball could be heard. We tempted fate with the silence of the ball and sat down on the loveseat.

Sitting so close to him felt like a dream. My heart skipped beats, my mouth was dry, my palms were sweaty, and my undies felt unusually tight.

Dreamy-eyed, I looked at him. His wavy, blond hair was perfectly coiffed, and his crystal blue eyes looked deep into my mine. He put a finger up to his lips, smiled, and pointed to a large mirror I hadn't noticed hanging on the wall across from the loveseat. I glanced at the mirror quickly, not wanting to break away from his beautiful face.

"We have to be careful they don't see," he whispered.

Oh, god. Whisper again. Take me. Right here. Right now.

He leaned in closer and kissed me softly on the lips. I trembled. He pulled away for just a second, teasing me. Then leaned toward me again. Just before his lips touched mine, I felt his breath and saw him glance at the mirror from the corner of his eye.

Once in the clear, he pressed his lips hard against mine and took a deep breath in. I felt his tongue flit around my mouth. It circled around my tongue, darting with such force I thought I might throw up. But I was far too aroused to care.

Trey, kissing me with such passion, was much steamier than the fleeting ecstasy I experienced alone in my bedroom. Sure, those moments made me hot, but Trey got me hotter. When I felt his hand slide over my upper thigh, gripping me between my legs, I thought I would lose my mind.

He stopped and I shuddered in my lilac-colored jelly shoes. We gazed into each other's eyes. He pulled back and looked at me.

What an Adonis. Speak, you beautiful creature.

"Not bad. Your breath could be better, though," he said.

The cloud I floated on blissfully—*seconds* prior—deflated and I instantly crashed to the ground. He was a strong kisser. Hot. But once he used his mouth to speak, well, my undies didn't feel so tight anymore.

He spoke again. "What's up with the pin on your jacket?"

My jacket. I absolutely loved my pink suede jacket. It was a fringed, shoulder-padded, trendy gift of perfection from Grandma Nina. It was soft, supple, and smelled like the inside of a new pock-ah-book.

I found myself briefly reliving memories of carefully choosing the jacket with Grandma, at Wilson's Suede and Leather, in Connecticut...

I was surprised Gram could swing it at all since she pinched pennies regularly. I remember how amazing it smelled on the hanger and how it almost felt like the soft, red velvet seats in our ol' Caprice Classic. When Gram bought the jacket, she told me to pick out a pin for the lapel. The only pin that jumped out at me, was the one Trey scrutinized.

"It's just a snake," I said, looking down at the silver reptile—coiled, showcasing his venomous teeth—still insecure about my breath.

"Who else do you know that portrays himself as a serpent?" He raised his eyebrows.

I shifted on the loveseat just a hair and heard the suede of my jacket groan. I looked at him, completely nonplussed.

Trey had staged this Ping-Pong game as a ruse to kiss me with our families in the next room, toyed with my budding sensuality, insulted my breath, and now wanted to discuss a coiled serpent on my jacket?

"You shouldn't wear things that glorify Satan," he said.

The flowered loveseat he leaned his head against while leering at me was suddenly covered in thorns.

I went from high and light-headed, to instantly baffled and loathing myself. I sat there, grappling with the notion that my breath was repulsive, and I was suddenly a clueless Satanist.

I clearly didn't know any better because that didn't stop my infatuation with Trey. I convinced myself he humiliated me because he cared; he wanted to ensure I made it into the *New System* as his wife.

******

"Uh, sorry—New System?" Joel asked.

"A re-creation. After Armageddon, and the bullshit endured there, God's original plan for paradise will be restored. The faithful rank-and-file making it through will live forever, perfectly, in the *New System*."

Joel smirked, writing in his steno pad. "Quick question, are you sure you're okay talking about your...coming-of-age experiences?"

"The racy shit? Yes, and you're about to find out why."

******

TREY CONTINUED TO CALL, and I kept talking to him, despite the fact his hypocrisy was showing. He knew about the dreaded *double life* Loverboy sang about; he was living it.

During one phone call he said, "So, you kissed me. What else would you do?"

"Um, I dunno. What do you mean?" My heart fluttered with the idea that maybe he wanted to get serious and court me properly.

"Well, would you make out with me?"

"Yeah." *We kind of already did that.*

"Would you...give me a hand-job?"

"Um, I dunno?" *A hand-job? What's that?*

70

"How about a blowjob?"

I kept silent. If I didn't know whether I was willing to give him a hand-job, how could I be sure if I was willing to give him a blowjob? At the time, I had no idea what these things were. Judging by his lowered voice, muttering in secrecy, I gathered he was going below the belt. What baffled me was that the coiled serpent on my jacket bothered him more than these lewd conversations.

"Would you fuck me?" he asked.

The words "fuck" and "sex" were used interchangeably at school, and that made it pretty clear to me what he was asking. And while interpreting at the doctor's office, I knew that my parents had S-E-X.

But given all the times I got hot and bothered, alone in my bedroom, I never once thought to *insert* anything, anywhere. I had been perfectly content (until Jehovah started snooping) to rub myself into giddy hysteria, clothes on.

"No. I wouldn't."

That conversation ended quickly, as did our chats and glances at the Kingdom Hall. Everything happened so fast; he noticed me, pursued me, kissed me passionately, criticized my level of spirituality, *then!* wanted me to have premarital sex with him?

Um, no. I wonder if anyone else knows he's a dirty, double lifing liar? How many other double lifers are there?

Feeling dirty, heartbroken, and lonely, I consented to spending the day with my brother, Luke; he was okay to be around when we got along.

He worked as a parking attendant in a booth, collecting fees. We watched old black and white Cary Grant movies on a small TV in the booth to pass the time.

Breaking away from the cinematic magic of the 50s, Luke glanced at me and said, "You know, Bek, this world is crazy, and getting crazier. I worry about you. I hope Satan's wicked system isn't sucking you in. It won't be around much longer. Armageddon's just around the corner."

I nodded, keeping focused on Cary Grant. Armageddon was *always* just around the corner.

"Keep studying, go out in service, and make sure you're associating with spiritually strong brothers and sisters."

I successfully ignored him for a few more minutes. Then I panicked. I thought he might already know something about my tongue-twisted kiss, and secret pillow talks with Trey.

Suddenly I felt dirty. Immoral.

When the time came, Jehovah would check my file and see that I'd kissed someone I wasn't properly courting, had provocative conversations with him while unmarried, and gave in to the thrill between my legs more than once. Maybe I even had AIDS now. *Could you get it from kissing?*

Overcome by my own remorse, I admitted everything to Luke, scared shitless of what he'd think of me. While telling him, I tried to channel the same brother who protected Frederick and me from the big bad wolf, Armageddon, and basement-dwelling demons.

"He said all that to you?" Luke tapped his foot at warp speed. I nodded.

"You know, I never liked that kid," he huffed, "he's such a hypocrite. You know he's leading a *double life.* Why were you even talking to him? You know better!"

Luke was trembling with anger, pacing maniacally in the small four-by-four space we shared. My ears rang and his brotherly scolding bounced off my buzzing ears until his voice faded.

I imagined myself alongside Cary Grant on the tiny TV screen, running behind him. Together, we'd make it; dodging the plane that swooped down over the intersection in *North by Northwest.* Running in the middle of nowhere, escaping villainous thieves.

I'd love an escape route right about now.

Then I heard—

"You know we have to bring this to the elders, right?"

My head jerked when I heard the word *elders*.

"What? Why? I told you the truth. I'm not even talking to Trey anymore. I prayed to Jehovah on my own. I took care of it. Can't we just forget about it?" I hadn't really prayed, but I *had* taken care of it.

"No. He's not going to get away with treating you like that, and you should've known better! It's *porneia*! You would've licked the sweat off his eyebrow if he had more time to talk you into it!" he said.

******

"Porneia?" Joel adjusted his glasses.

"You know, the more I freely use the jargon I grew up with, the more ridiculous it sounds. Porneia is an overused term the ol' GB loves to throw around. Porneia rears its perverted head inside Kingdom Hall walls when *any* sexual immorality is implied or committed."

Joel chuckled.

******

LUKE WASTED NO TIME arranging what would be my very first judicial committee hearing. This committee is comprised of at least two elders who listen to details of wrongdoing and settle on a verdict—like small claims court for immorality.

Everything was all set and happened much faster than my parents could catch on. Mom and Dad were overwhelmed with rearing a teen girl; they knew what to do with boys, but for some reason, I was an enigma.

And with Mark in Brooklyn waiting on the GB hand and foot, Luke tasked himself with keeping an eye on yours truly, stepping in to parent me without hesitation.

But since Luke was technically *not* a parent, the accused, or the guilty, the elders instructed him to wait in the main part of the Hall, where he paced frantically. So, my unnerved mother and father, two elders, Trey, his mother, and I sat in a small room in the back.

There I was—in the *second school* of shame, on a hot summer night—with twelve eyes on me. I closed mine and smelled the July breeze coming from the open window. It flirted with the screen as it bounced lightly against the windowpane. I wished to be anywhere else.

I began pulling at a thread from my blue cushioned chair. I looked up and met the eyes of two elders, one father, two mothers, and a *double lifer*. The elders wanted to keep those present in the back room of judgment to a minimum—no signing brothers or sisters welcome.

Trey, the lucky bastard, shared his account of what happened in one language—English.

And he lied.

He sobbed uncontrollably, carrying on about how I'd seduced him—therefore he lost all control, failing to *keep up the fine fight of the faith* for Jehovah. He was in hysterics over his weaknesses, imperfections, and the fact he was just a victim of *Adamic Sin*. Then he likened me to Eve—the apple-wielding temptress—saying he wanted to please Jehovah, only he failed when pinned up against my feminine wiles. And he repented through fake, rehearsed tears. He'd obviously been in the *second school* before.

For me, being there was upsetting enough. But reliving moments of my very first kiss, subsequent perverse phone conversations, and every dirty detail in *two* languages, simultaneously, was inexplicable.

I also wasn't wired for hypocrisy. I didn't know how to be. Our house was not one of many harbored secrets. The Deaf community holds nothing back, so neither did I.

I bluntly shared my version of what happened, and Trey continued to wail. I was exhausted just listening. I signed *lie* while pointing to him as he burbled his way through a rebuttal.

Dad nodded, silencing me with his hand, and sat on the edge of his blue cushioned seat looking intently at Trey with furrowed eyebrows, trying to lipread through his blubbering.

Trey was going for an Academy Award. It was clear that he had done this before, mastering the art of persuasion and bogus repentance. He had the whole serpent thing down to a science, and no doubt questioned the pin on my jacket because he saw his *own* reflection while gawking at it.

Fine performance. Bravo.

During a judicial committee hearing, if you can skillfully *appear* repentant your slate is wiped clean. I could tell Trey was nowhere near sorry for what he had done or what he said—only sorry he got caught. I *was* genuinely sorry. Sorry I ever noticed him. And sorry I told Luke anything.

We were each privately reproved—a slap on the wrist behind closed doors—and our parents were instructed to keep a closer eye on us.

No need to worry about me dicking around his venom.

******

"That's quite a story," Joel said.

"Understand now why telling you wasn't going to bother me?"

"I do. Telling your congregation elders every sordid detail is..." I could see his mind at work.

"I believe the word you're looking for is *degrading*. Makes telling anyone else easy—almost fun."

"What did you do after this...committee meeting?"

"I spent a lot of time alone—brooding. I went to the only place that still made sense to me."

75

"Oh?"

I closed my eyes, leaned my head back, and saw the birch trees, the brush, and the ferns near the foot trail, leading to my sanctuary.

******

AFTER MY JUDICIAL HEARING, I walked the path leading me to the train tracks behind our backyard.

While perched on two logs, lodged into the ground like nature's sofa, I decided from that point on I would *be me*, whatever the cost. I promised that line of Pullman trains I'd take the pain of living my own truth, rather than conform to someone else's.

I knew what a *double lifer* looked like now, and I had no intention of mastering the art of hypocrisy. I figured, if someone as seemingly spiritual as Trey could fool an entire congregation, whilst trying to get his rocks off, well, he couldn't be the only *double lifer* out there.

Promises made to myself, and the B&M Railroad train conductor, were not in vain. I took them just as seriously as Mark took waiting on the ol' GB in Bethel, and Luke took his Witness protection program.

Luke screened my friends, phone calls, movies, and music. He ensured members of the opposite sex were not within three feet of me. He sat unbearably close to me at all meetings and physically adjusted my clothing, moving thinly strapped tops over to cover my bra strap if it was exposed. He'd even drape his suit coat over me to cover skin. This was not the brother I wanted shielding me from the *ay-kah-geesha*.

I felt stuck. Helpless. Small. I couldn't breathe. I needed to get out.

I pleaded with my parents to let me sleep over Erica's—a J-Dub in our Hall I'd gotten close to. I reassured them her family would, of course, be home.

The moment they said yes was the moment I saw them both a bit differently. I felt like maybe I understood oppression on some level—not the same type they'd suffered, and certainly not for the same reasons—but I was stifled, and they knew it. They understood. They were just as much under Luke's gun as I was, and granting me permission to leave the nest, defied his inclination to lord it over everyone.

I planned to sleep over Erica's on the last night of 1989. A night of mindless crap on MTV and tons of junk food was just the break I needed.

We were up all night, ringing in the New Year with Phil Collins, Madonna, Guns N' Roses, Bon Jovi, and Maxi Priest while wearing confetti-decorated papier mâché top hats and rattling noisemakers.

Erica's parents were *strong in the truth* but graciously gave me what I needed—to feel like a normal teenaged girl, surrounded by *Bop* magazines, MTV, and junk food. They always seemed to know when to loosen the reins, without pissing off the ol' GB. There was no talk of my recent immoral blunder or Armageddon. There were no interpreting duties. There were no older brothers.

Until Luke showed up unexpectedly the next morning.

"You need to *keep on the watch*, Bek. Do you know what's happening?" His whole body shook so much, his Australian black leather hat gyrated on his head.

"What?" I stood, in a papier mâché hat, rubbing my eyes.

"We're prepping for war! Desert Storm is happening right now. And we're just *one* day into 1990. Armageddon is just around the corner! Get your act together. When are you going to get baptized?" He glanced at my head. "And what're you doing in a party hat, celebrating a holiday we don't even celebrate?"

I stood in silence. The music from my clandestine New Year's Eve party faded from memory. The enigmatic vocal talents of Maxi Priest's, "Close to You" suddenly screeched to a halt on the turntable of my mind. I hated Luke, and the GB, for paralyzing my brain with this nonsense.

Desert Storm was now *the* topic of conversation. Luke tied his knowledge of the war in the Middle East to Jehovah's looming battle of vengeance. He was an expert in scaring me just as much as the GB and prime time evening newscasters. He was persistently on me about my spiritual health, and nothing I did ever seemed good enough.

******

"You are good enough, Rebekah. From what you've shared, I see a very caring, altruistic person in front of me."

"Maybe to normal people. But to many in the Truth, I was selfish, weak. A good for nothing slave. A weaker vessel."

"Did you hear that often?" Joel closed his notebook.

"Yeah. At least once a week it was either in a publication, scripture, or said from the platform."

He crumpled his brow and released a disapproving sigh. "Same time next week?"

I nodded.

Young Love

HEARING MYSELF DISSECT PIECES of my life, week after week, made me feel less alone and more certain. I couldn't put my finger on why, but something felt right. Better. Lighter.

"Did Luke ever loosen his grip?" Joel asked, flipping through his notes.

Surprisingly, his notes didn't bother me since everyone in the Truth had a file once they became unbaptized publishers.

"Yes and no," I said, kicking off my shoes, swinging my feet around, tucking them under my ass. "He was spending most of his time with his friends in Massachusetts. When he was gone, I could relax a bit. When he was home, not so much."

"How were things between you and your parents after the Trey situation?"

"Good, actually." I smiled remembering times it was just the three of us.

******

LONG DRIVES TO MASSACHUSETTS for the monthly Deaf meetings no longer fazed me; they were my respite.

"This Michael Jackson?" Mom asked, turning up the car radio. She couldn't untangle the lyrics, but she could usually guess the artist from the beat of the song. And "Billie Jean" was hard to miss.

I nodded knowing why she asked.

As the drum beat and bass guitar found their groove, I put my hands up and they got right to work. "Beautiful queen, movie show-off, who me? Floor, dance, round," I signed.

Not only was I thrilled Luke's shackles would be loosened for a day, but I was excited to go to the Deaf meeting.

Jax—fearless leader of all covert CODA meetings—had blossomed. His deep-set, almost-black eyes, black hair, and one-dimpled smile suddenly drove me crazy. I was incredibly fortunate because he felt it, too. And two CODAs who got each other the way we did, were bound to fall hard.

We knew each other's frustrations, responsibilities, beliefs, and experiences—rarely uttering a single spoken word or lifting one expressive finger. We were just two CODAs, being raised in Deaf-parented homes, mastering the art of ASL inadvertently; for *our* parents, anyway.

Remembering the promise I made to myself on the tracks behind our house—to *be me*, whatever the cost—was easy with Jax. He was the only person who truly saw me without trying.

Our budding romance went mostly unnoticed. We were experts at communicating with our eyes. Jax would look at me during the meeting, then walk to the downstairs bathroom. A few seconds later, I'd follow and find him standing by the water fountain where we'd steal quick, innocent hugs.

When we weren't lucky enough to see each other, we spent hours on the phone. Every chance I got, I stretched the dirty rotary phone wire from the kitchen, down the hall, into my bedroom, and closed the door.

We talked about everything from family and school, right down to how much we agreed or disagreed with what the GB spoon-fed us. Those conversations were highly classified; to doubt the GB in any way was almost worse than accepting a blood transfusion.

The hours we spent doubting our hand-me-down faith was costly, and when the phone bill arrived, my parents went through the roof. Hands flailed and pounded fiercely, while four eyebrows danced passionate tarantellas in both protest and financial desperation.

So, we wrote letters decorated with doodled hearts and bubble-lettered I love you's. Anytime the mailman failed me, I called Jax, demanding to know where my doodles were.

"They're not just doodles, Bek. I love you."

"I love you too, Jax."

We weren't struck dumb by the *Bloom of Youth*, mindlessly bunny-bumping because we happened to cross paths. Being long distance meant we weren't getting physical. And with years of friendship as our foundation, we were able to create something *real*.

As one thirteen and one fifteen-year-old, in the *Bloom of* our *Youth*, we were rarely left alone. Our interest in each other was hardly a threat to Jehovah's almighty sovereignty. We weren't hurting anyone, and since the Deaf J-Dub community is so small and close-knit, all eyes were on us anyway.

And I didn't care what anyone thought because the times I was able to just sit with Jax—I found solace in his presence, an indescribable peace. With him, I was free to be who I'd chosen to be that hot day in July by the train tracks. With him I could close my eyes, feel that gust of wind from the line of Pullmans whooshing past me, and live my life unshackled. Jax always kept knowledge of that safe with him, and I knew he was the one I wanted shielding my chilly shoulders from the *ay-kah-geesha*.

I spent most of one Saturday night in my bedroom, gushing over Jax with Jocelyn, the friend who'd witnessed the dreadful Ritchie Sambora incident. And she wasn't afraid to give me her two cents about Jax.

"You're too young to date. You're not ready for marriage," she said.

"So? We love each other. It's okay to love someone."

"You're *hurting* Jehovah and stumbling *me*."

******

"Stumbling her?" Joel asked.

I sighed. Not because Joel asked for clarification, but because anytime he did, I realized I'd uttered more J-Dub specific lingo. And that made me question the ol' GB even more; the way I did when I was younger.

"JWs are trained to police each other. Tyrannously. If one person is stumbled by the actions of another, they're encouraged to confront that person. If the issue can't be resolved, it moves up the food chain."

"Well, that's life. If you have a problem with someone, address it with them. You'll run across that at work, with friends, in relationships—"

"I get that. *Now*. And that's fine. But how the hell was my talking on the phone, writing letters, and seeing Jax once a month, *supervised*, a stumbling block for anyone?"

"That I don't know. Maybe she was jealous?"

I shrugged. "Maybe? I just remember she wouldn't let it go. And I caved in defeat..."

******

"THE BIBLE SAYS, 'If that right eye of yours is making you stumble, tear it out and throw it away from you.' Jehovah wants the best for you, and he's given you all the guidance you need in the *Young People Ask* book. You're going through the *Bloom of Youth*—hormones running wild—and I don't want to see you get hurt. Neither does Jehovah," Jocelyn said.

"Jax isn't going to hurt me. I *know* him."

Nothing's stumbling me, *so why do I have to tear anything out?*

"You didn't think Trey would hurt you, but he did. You're too young for this to last forever, and if you continue to date him, you could lose Jehovah's favor. Think about all the things we'll be able to do in the *New System*—you could play with lions, and they wouldn't hurt you, hike the tallest mountain, or even swim across the ocean. I don't want you to die at Armageddon."

I sat on my bedroom floor with her, conflicted. I harbored my own doubts about everything she'd just regurgitated, and Jax was the only one who really knew that. Sudden fear crept in, and I gave way to a secret panic attack.

What if Jax and I were wrong? Suppose the Truth really is the truth—then where will I be?

I didn't want to die at Armageddon. I thought about Lot's wife and my heart lost all control. I didn't want to wind up a pillar of salt.

"I love you, and so does Jehovah. I promise, if you wait until you're ready to date, Jehovah will make sure that you're happy. Whether it's with Jax or another brother," she hugged me, and begged, "please, end it."

She shoved me right into a shitty situation. And I let her. I was a thirteen-year-old, unbaptized, spiritually weak girl— taking advantage of my Deaf parents—in the eyes of most J-Dubs. My brothers had moved out and there was no longer that all-powerful, hearing, male presence at home.

Self-doubt became panic and fear. Jocelyn was older and spiritually stronger than I was. But Jax was also a Witness, posing no threat to my relationship with God, or my mom and dad. So, why did I have to choose?

The way I was beginning to see it, Jehovah seemed petty. No masturbating. No dating unless you're ready to get married. Did he *want* his worshippers to be miserable?

I didn't think it was fair that Jehovah and Jocelyn insisted I sacrifice my humanity for their comfort.

Why can't I be anxious about my first kiss with Jax instead of panicked about Armageddon? I'm so sick of hearing "it's just around the corner."

"You know what you need to do," she said softly. She got up and practically dialed Jax's number for me.

My naiveté, self-doubt, and inability to trust myself often drowned in someone else's expectations. Fear and paranoia pumped through my veins, weaving its way around every artery until my body clenched.

J-Dubs are taught from infancy to fear. Fear Jehovah. Fear Satan. Fear your parents. Fear the GB. Fear the elders. Fear yourself.

I felt sick. Standing in the hallway, with the phone pressed to my ear, Jax's line rang.

"Hey!" He sounded happy I had called.

I felt my mouth fill with saliva. "Hi," I said.

"What's wrong?"

I rambled my way through a messy, coached break-up, borrowing some of Jocelyn's one-liners.

He was silent. I cried. Then he hung up.

Letting go of him was like letting a piece of me die. I cried myself to sleep that night while Jocelyn reassured me, I did the right thing. She was happy. Jehovah was happy.

Jehovah's happy? I'm in a pool of my own snot, bawling myself into a pounding headache and God is fucking happy? Fuck him. And fuck you, too, Jocelyn.

The next day I woke with a brick in my stomach. I called Jax after Jocelyn left. Maybe I could undo what I'd done. Maybe we could talk it over and he'd understand how conflicted I was. Only he wouldn't talk to me. Instead, I talked to his sister Gina.

"Is Jax okay?" I sat on the top step of the staircase, winding the telephone wire around my finger. While staring at the cellar door, I realized I was no longer afraid of the basement demons. I was collecting enough of my own.

"No. He's pretty hurt," she said.

I sighed, fighting tears. "I'm sorry. Tell him I'm sorry. Tell him I love him." I hung up.

Giving Gina the message didn't feel like enough. I needed something else.

I kept my eighth-grade Creative Writing teacher after school, to see if she could help me remove the brick from my stomach. We plopped down on a brown, plaid, leg-less sofa in her classroom. With my head feebly resting against the back of the couch, I exchanged my grief for her advice.

She told me to write more. She told me to find exactly where it hurt, rip it wide open, and bleed on paper via ink.

So, I did. I poured my soul onto paper writing songs, poems, novellas, and short stories. I got an A in her class but an F in self-esteem.

I was angry with myself for allowing fear to control me. I feared judgment from an intangible power. I feared that a girl—claiming to be my friend—would tell the elders I'd stumbled her by dating someone long distance.

Having very few people I could befriend in the world because they were *bad association*, left slim pickings at the Kingdom Hall. Tell me how opening up to people in the Truth is supposed to instill trust, when they use their faith as a weapon to bludgeon you with?

At the Deaf meetings, Jax refused to look at me. The unspoken connection and amorous glances we shared were but a memory. It took months before he would talk to me again.

At the Ground Round, Jax, his sister, and I sat at a table together. Old cartoons cavorted on the big movie screen when he told me the news.

"New Mexico?" I asked.

"Yep." Jax looked down at his burger.

"Why?" My voice cracked.

"Dad got a job." He refused to make eye contact.

I was fourteen when Jax and his family moved away. I was crushed. No more CODA club meetings. No more coquettish glances. No more hugs by the water fountain. No more bubble-lettered I love you doodles. All efforts to stay in touch were awkward and sporadic.

I lost the only person keeping me in the Truth. Jax took *my truth* with him when he left.

******

"You're smarter than you think, Rebekah. It's okay to trust yourself and *your* truth. You know how. You just need to give yourself permission. And...I'm sorry you had to experience that," Joel said.

I looked at him and smirked. "Thank you and trust me, I haven't even scratched the surface yet."

Reborn in Providence

"MY FRESHMAN YEAR AT Winnisquam came too quick. I wasn't ready for it. I was spiritually weak in the Truth and no longer cared. Jax was gone and no one filled that void—no one could. I distanced myself from friends in my congregation, even ones at the Deaf meetings. I didn't trust anyone—"

"Well, how could you? With someone always ready to snitch or be stumbled," Joel said, opening his notepad.

Wow. Yeah...how could I?

"Good catch. I shied away from most of my classmates, too. I didn't connect with anyone, and I saw no point in getting swept away by anyone or anything. I ignored *new light* and *spiritual food* the GB fed us, and willingly sat alone at school by the Star Wars mural during lunch. It would all be for naught soon enough since Armageddon was always just around the corner."

"*New light?*"

"Sorry, new *information*. Any doctrinal changes within the organization were called *new light*. It meant the light—the GB's understanding of scripture—was getting brighter. My god, that sounds fucking ridiculous out loud." Joel scribbled feverishly. "Anyway, high school was weird for me. I felt like I didn't fit in with anyone and I was suddenly getting attention from worldly boys. My little boobs were full-out, developed breasts and I guess they noticed. It wasn't like Trey, who'd picked me out of the four-girl-line-up at the Kingdom Hall, or Jax who loved me for me. It was a whole different experience."

I sighed, remembering how awkward my freshman year was.

******

IT WAS PURE HELL. But one guy stood out above the rest—a seventeen-year-old redhead who pursued me relentlessly. He piqued my curiosity. We snuck around school during classes, searching for dark corners to make out in. Our secret romance, heavily influenced by studying Romeo and Juliet in English class, stirred me. And knowing my parents wouldn't approve, aroused me even more.

A huge nor'easter swept through NH and dumped the customary foot of snow. School was cancelled. My parents braved the storm to do one unavoidable cleaning job.

Teen horniness, angst, and my blatant disregard for all spiritual codes uttered at the meetings culminated into one courageous act of defiance—I called the redhead.

"Come over," I dared my modern-day Romeo while wrapping the curly telephone wire around my forefinger nervously.

I had no idea what I was doing. The furthest we'd ever gone was a very *heavy petting* session at my worldly friend Jamie's house around the corner. While making out on her bedroom floor, I felt something hard poking up from his tight acid-washed jeans. I rubbed against it until I Bloomed in my Youth. He was much more fun than the handle of my hairbrush.

All of a sudden, one seventeen-year-old redhead—sporting a feathered mullet—stood at my back door. I quickly shelved the memory of our recent, make-out rendezvous at Jamie's and led mullet boy down the hall into my bedroom. I didn't want to talk, I only wanted to do what I knew he'd come for, even though I wasn't entirely sure what that was.

We started making out on my bed and I grinded on him again, rubbing up and down. Once my breathing increased, and uncontrollable moans penetrated the air, our clothes came off. I was about to lose my virginity and there was no stopping it even if I'd wanted to.

I was totally clueless and scared as hell. He didn't use protection or ease gently—he almost forced his way inside. I wanted to scream. I threw my arms around his neck and pulled him closer; I didn't want him to look at me. The smell of our sex was completely rancid. The pain and swooshing fluids inside me felt repulsive.

He kept mostly silent, breathing in rhythm with his back-and-forth pumping. While climaxing, he shouted, "I love you so much!" then stopped and collapsed on top of me—out of breath and sweaty. I wasn't that impressed, and I didn't understand why it was over so quickly. I lay there shaking in utter disbelief of what I had just done.

My virginity is gone, I've now had premarital sex. Jehovah saw that and is wagging his heavenly finger at me.

The redhead kissed my mouth as if he'd done it for years, jumped up, and began to get dressed. I quickly joined him since I had no idea when my parents were due home. I didn't think to use the bathroom and check myself at all. I was in a hurry to cover my lady lips—I wanted to mask the smell of our nasty *porneia* as soon as possible.

We walked through my back yard, keeping in line with each other's footprints. We used my in-ground, all-natural, log sofa as a stool to climb over the rusty, wired fence that ran along the railroad tracks.

Walking the tracks was the safest route to take in case my parents drove through town and saw us together. Just before hitting civilization, we kissed, parted ways, and I walked to my friend Jamie's house.

"We just did it," I told her, going up the stairs into her bedroom.

"Oh, my god!" Jamie closed her door. "Are you okay?"

"Yeah, but it felt weird. It smells funny. I feel gross." I shrugged. "Wasn't what I expected. Is that *really* what people want?"

"With the right person, yeah, it is," she said.

Red and I had sex two more times after that; I had to be sure he was the wrong person. And those times were equally as impressive as the first—it was over quickly, smelled foul, and he didn't even try to satisfy me. Maybe the hairbrush handle *was* more fun.

It was certainly more loyal. Because Red, the feather-haired-mullet-boy, broke up with me and started sleeping with my friends.

I was hurt but in no way broken.

With very few people to talk to, I stupidly told a couple of my J-Dub girl friends about Red, immediately regretting it. Panicked, I decided to tell on myself before anyone else had a chance to do it for me. Trust is not a two-way street with most J-Dubs. So, I told my mother.

I just didn't know which Muppet I was going to get. Miss Piggy's temper? Kermit's caring character? Rolf's practicality? Animal's wild and unpredictable personality? No, wait, that's Dad.

I sat on our kitchen table before a Thursday night meeting, nervously dangling my legs. I gave her brief snippets of what happened and how I was sure my virginity was gone.

"You okay?" she signed.

Phew, no sign of Miss Piggy. I nodded.

Using ASL, she asked if I'd gotten my period by raising her eyebrows and puffing one of her cheeks full of air.

Rolf's sensible approach, I can handle that.

I nodded again and she exhaled with relief.

"He hurt you?"

Oh, Kermit, there you are!

I shrugged. "No. He mean. He break up with me and sex my friends," I signed.

"Worldly boy only want one thing," she said, shaking her head.

Go away, Piggy.

How quickly she'd forgotten about Trey. He wasn't worldly; he was a baptized pioneer asking for hand-jobs, blowjobs, and straight up fucking.

I chalked her counsel up to the fact that the education JW teens received—via the *Society's Young People Ask* book— only covered abstinence. It was poorly written, antiquated advice, backed by scriptural misuse of their shoddy Bible translations. We were not educated about safe sex, STDs, or pregnancy. Their guidelines were (still are) impractical.

Direction given by the ol' GB, mirrored Mom and Dad's schooling. At ASD, they'd received severely misguided lessons; they were forced to exaggerate words, lip read, and regurgitate information ad nauseam—it was all the same.

Worse yet, Mom broke down and told Dad. I was completely shamed. Daddy's little girl had been deflowered. Instead of talking with me, he lost his temper.

"We tell you over and over no worldly boy or friend! He use you sex! That is whore!" Dad raised his belt high toward the ceiling and whipped me on the hip. Again, and again.

When he finally stopped, I lay on my bed sobbing in the fetal position. My hips, and my ass were throbbing. While choking on my own tears and snot I thought, *I know it was wrong to have premarital sex, but why am I getting hit for it?* I had come clean only to be met with Dad calling me a whore, while beating me into submission.

******

I came out of my trance and saw Joel waving a tissue at me. "Rebekah. Here."

"Sorry," I said taking a soft tissue.

"It's okay. Were the beltings frequent?"

I wiped my eyes, realizing I'd cried my way through that memory.

"Um, yeah, I guess. It didn't feel right though, even if the Bible did say 'Spare the rod, spoil the child.' I asked a friend at school if he ever got belted. When he said no, I questioned J-Dub doctrine even more. I didn't think asking would prompt him to get too concerned, but it did."

"What do you mean?"

"When I confided in him, he told the school counselor, and I was called into his office."

******

THE GUIDANCE COUNSELOR MOTIONED for me to take a seat.

I sat across from him and looked at the top of his head. Light brown stripes of hair grazed his balding, freckled melon. He wore a wedding ring, a thick moustache, and liver spots.

"One of your classmates came to me this morning, concerned. Is everything okay at home, Rebekah?"

"I guess. Why?" I shrugged.

"Are you experiencing any type of...abuse?"

I sighed. "My parents discipline me."

"Discipline you?"

"Yeah, you know—*the rod of discipline*."

He scrunched his face.

"From the Bible?" I said.

He pursed his lips and nodded. "If this is true, it needs to be reported. Can I record this conversation?" He pulled out an old tape player.

I didn't think I could tell him no; worldly or not, he was my elder. I nodded and sat on the edge of my seat, playing with my sweaty hands as I explained, *in detail*, that my father used his belt until my hips welted; it wasn't the first time, and probably wouldn't be the last.

This resulted in a home visit from DCYF, which was an incredibly humiliating experience; I was so thankful my brothers weren't there.

Sitting around the kitchen table, notes were passed, and I sporadically interpreted. When I saw the words "Foster Home" written on one of the notes passed, I spoke up.

"No. I'm not leaving. This is my home," I sim-commed. "My friend was just worried. He doesn't understand us." Then I told them again, just in case they didn't hear me, "I'm not leaving."

******

"I don't blame you for wanting to stay but...were you at all curious about life outside of the Witness community?" Joel asked.

"Oh, always. But in that moment, none of the J-Dub shit mattered."

"Why? Wasn't that the source of your angst?"

"Yes. But ask almost any CODA, and they'll say they feel the same obligation to their parents as I do mine."

"You still do? Though your relationship is now severed?"

"Oh, yeah. I'll always feel a sense of obligation to protect them from this...*hearing* world. And sore ass or not, I was obligated. Period. *Especially* then. Their Deafness often kept them out of the loop, and if they found solace in some overprotective religious sect, so be it. I wasn't about to leave them alone. I knew they were doing the best they could and who would take care of them if I had to leave?"

"You didn't think they could take care of themselves?"

"It's not that they couldn't. They could and they *do*. It's hard to put into words... If I could be around to stop someone from taking advantage of their Deafness, or defend them when someone was being an ass, then I wanted to be. I still want to be."

"That's very altruistic. I also find it interesting."

"Oh?"

"You'd had premarital sex. Which meant, according to Witness doctrine, you were selfish. Yet, what these elders and Governing Body members in the Witness community didn't see, is the selflessness of a teenage girl. Especially when it really mattered."

He was right and the ol' GB was so busy writing drivel, publishing rules upon rules, and overwhelming local elders with *new light* that there's no way any of them could possibly know—or care—about the rank-and-file buried at the bottom of their religious pyramid.

"What happened next?" he asked.

"I made sure nothing more came from the meeting with DCYF. I wish I could say the same about my judicial committee hearing."

"Oh, not another one." Joel shook his head.

"And not the last."

******

THE JUDICIAL COMMITTEE HEARING was held at our house, around the kitchen table. And unlike the DCYF visit, my brothers were informed beforehand. Mark drove up from Brooklyn to interpret because I'd been deflowered. This was serious.

There we sat—two elders, my parents, Mark, and me. Not only did I have to tell everyone present the details of losing my virginity, but now, the DCYF visit was also on the table.

Mark's face haunted me. Although we'd never really been close, I could see his heart cracking. He pursed his lips and his brown eyes refused to meet mine the entire time. Worse than recently sim-comming my way through that first judicial hearing with Trey, was now watching Mark interpret.

Mark heard, processed, and churned out the details of his little sister sneaking a seventeen-year-old into her bedroom and spreading eagle for him. In graphic ASL. It was a sick and twisted kind of shame.

Losing my virginity was punishable, whereas being belted was not. Most Witnesses use the *rod of discipline*, so, no biggie. I was privately reproved and stripped of my Kingdom Hall privileges. I couldn't hold the songbook, or comment, or interpret during the meetings. I was to go and sit quietly.

Having a break from interpreting was most welcomed, but I felt bad for my parents. They now had to suffer through half-assed interpreting attempts via an unmarried sister who was learning ASL. They painfully grimaced during meetings as their native language was being butchered. They deserved real interpreting. So, I did what I had to do.

******

"What did you have to do?"

"Bow to the Golden J-Dub Calf."

Joel wrinkled his nose.

"I started studying for all the meetings before attending and went door-to-door on Saturdays *willingly*, in order to earn my privileges back."

"Is that what it takes?"

I nodded. "The elders need to see that you're making a sincere effort."

"Did you get your privileges back?"

"Yeah, but not in time."

"In time for what?"

"To be in Luke's wedding."

"Oh, he met someone! Wait, why couldn't you be *in* the wedding?"

"Because I was *spiritually sick.* I could attend, that's it. Anyway, Luke's fiancé was in his new congregation, which included a small group made up of the same Deaf folks we saw once a month when Jax lived in New England. They were almost large enough to qualify as a small congregation, and shortly after Luke's wedding they did."

"Did this change anything for you?"

"It changed everything. My parents and I, along with our files, were transferred from the Franklin congregation to the sign language congregation in Massachusetts after all their meetings were firmly established. Everything was in ASL. No more interpreting, holding songbooks or suffering through mediocre signing. All the speakers were Deaf or really knew ASL.

"My parents flourished; they found the confidence and belonging they lacked in our previous congregation, and undoubtedly, for most of their lives. My father was finally dubbed an elder and my mother found a close network of friends. The only strain was the long drive from New Hampshire to Massachusetts and the deafening silence at the sign language Hall, which often put me to sleep."

"Did you make any new friends?"

"Yeah, a couple. And I was still close to Erica—hostess of our clandestine New Year's Eve bash. She had this *way*...confident, true to herself, cooler than anyone I knew. And she was getting baptized at the next assembly. I figured if she was getting baptized it meant she knew something I didn't. I was determined to walk on her Led-Zeppelin-loving-studying-the-*Watchtower*-while-*21-Jump-Street*-played-in-the-background path. She mixed worldly and spiritual into the perfect cocktail. She was my idol."

"Assembly?" Joel scribbled again.

"Assemblies are large semi-annual gatherings, dubbed 'circuit' and 'district' assemblies, sometimes held in sports arenas. At the time, ours had a designated Deaf section near a small, raised platform on the ground floor, with a dark blue cloth background. Interpreters who volunteered were all baptized brothers and sisters, in *good standing*, with tremendous skill. These interpreters, or 'terps, were either CODAs or people who had spent *years* in the Deaf community.

"Right next to the Deaf section was a place designated for Deaf/Blind folks, using tactile interpreters. While resting their hands on top of the 'terp's hands, they'd either sit in front of or right next to the 'terp, and that's how they communicated. There was a lot to see at assemblies, lots going on, but I only wanted to see one thing."

"Which was?" Joel looked up from his notepad.

"Erica's baptism. I stood by the velvet ropes separating the pool from the crowd, nervously wringing my hands. She sauntered around the pool, wearing a white t-shirt over her one-piece bathing suit, unfazed by it all. She walked into the pool, flashed a smile, and approached one of the brothers waiting to dunk her. She plugged her nose with her left hand, cuffing her right hand around her left wrist. The brother, wrapped his left arm around her shoulder, placed his right hand on top of hers, and asked her a question. She nodded yes. Under she went and up she came. Everyone clapped. She stepped out of the pool and wandered around the corner toward the bathroom."

"What did the man baptizing her ask?"

"I don't know. She never told me. I was too busy wondering if she felt something after her baptism. Something deep. Something special. Maybe she felt more mature or more spiritual? Seeing Erica take the plunge, I thought there just had to be a way to balance it all. Erica showed me it was possible to be you and still love Jehovah. She didn't scold me like Jocelyn, and she wasn't a *double lifer* like Trey. She made being a J-Dub almost cool. So, I thought it was time."

"Time for what?"

"Time to get baptized. An older sister started studying publications with me, I was going door to door regularly, and soon enough my privileges were given back. Then, two elders scheduled a time to go over the baptism questions with me. And if, while going over the questions, one showed they not only knew their stuff but believed it wholeheartedly, anyone could get baptized—it didn't matter if you were nine or ninety."

"Is it some sort of test or—"

"Sort of. The elders quiz baptismal candidates on Bible principles, and everything that's unique about being a J-Dub. Being a born-in makes these 'tests' pretty easy to pass."

"A born-in?"

"Someone raised in the Truth. Answering the questions was the easy part. What puzzled me was the lack of sentiment I experienced. I thought a talking donkey, burning bush, or tiny flame above my head would appear."

"And when it didn't?"

I leaned my head back on the sofa and closed my eyes, remembering a time I doubted nothing; a time when the talking donkey paled in comparison to the B&M Railroad. I smiled.

"Rebekah, what do you see?"

"Me. I'm standing at the tracks, in my brothers' hand-me-down clothes—that god-awful 70s tan, yellow, and brown striped shirt we all wore at one time, with flared denim bellbottoms to match. My ponytails are flapping wildly. My dirty, little playing-outside-all-day hands are eager with sweat, waiting to get hold of the pennies I laid on the track. My heart is uncontrollably mad with excitement. The bells ring, the train horn bellows, and a line of Pullman trains whoosh past me. The ground rumbles and I smell dirty summer.

"Once the B&M trains pass, I hop the rusty, wired fence to collect my wishes. The smell of burnt copper is strong. I scoop up my pennies, inspecting each one. Although every penny is squished to my satisfaction, they all look different; like little copper snowflakes. Lincoln's face took on a different shape for each penny. I squeal with delight, running through the backyard, feeling whole. Complete. And never more like myself."

A tear streams down my cheek and I open my eyes.

"That sounds like an exciting way to spend time." Joel smiled.

"It was. I'd give almost anything to go back to that time. Alas, it's not possible. Where were we?"

Joel looked over his notes. "Talking donkey."

"Oh, yeah. I didn't see one after going over my baptism questions, which forced this gut-jabbing, never-ending doubt. But it didn't matter because the elders praised my ability to pass the organization's test, and I was on my way to getting baptized at the next assembly."

******

AT THE PROVIDENCE, Rhode Island Civic Center I sat in the baptism section proudly with other anxious brothers-and-sisters-to-be for our special dedication talk. At the sermon's end, the speaker asks all baptismal candidates to stand and answer two questions:

"On the basis of the sacrifice of Jesus Christ, have you repented of your sins and dedicated yourself to Jehovah to do his will?"

"Yes!"

"Do you understand that your dedication and baptism identify you as one of Jehovah's Witnesses in association with God's spirit-directed organization?"

"Yes!"

Once our resounding *Yes!* was heard by hundreds, the brother then delivered a long prayer full of advice and guidance. At the time, I dismissed the fact that a sixteen-year-old girl (me) and ten-year-old boy (kid sitting next to me) could make this kind of life decision and commitment *to an organization*. Yet, there we stood, signing our voices over to Ursula the Sea Witch.

After this long-ass oration, a special baptism song was sung. During the last verse, baptismal candidates walked to the bathroom in single file. With wide smiles, clutching duffle bags containing modest bathing suits, we passed our families who were beaming with pride.

Once I was in my acceptable one-piece, I left the Civic Center with other aspiring sisters and walked to a nearby hotel. My family followed, snapping picture after picture of me in the street, barefoot and wrapped in a blue towel.

As I approached the indoor pool, I took one last look at my family. My parents, Mark, and Luke were huddled close together, smiling, snapping pictures and waving.

My heart beat out of my chest but not the same way it had anytime I stood waiting for the train. This time it beat with anxiety. And panic. Saliva sat in a pool under my tongue. I wanted to run. But I didn't.

One of the brothers in the pool motioned for me to come closer. Dazed, I stepped into the lukewarm pool and slowly walked toward him. He put his left arm around my shoulder, instructed me to plug my nose with my left hand, and cuff my left wrist with my right hand, just like I'd seen Erica do. And just like Jesus had done.

He rested his right hand on top of mine and asked, "Is this your first time being baptized?"

"Yes," I answered. *How many people do it* again*? And why?*

Under I went. Up I came. It was quick and painless; nothing spectacular happened. I was hoping for a dove or some holy-spirited, warm blanket of God's approval. But I was just wet, half-naked, and in the arms of a strange man.

He smiled, loosening his grip. I wandered toward the steps, exiting the pool, shocked at what I'd just done.

******

"It doesn't sound like you wanted to do it, so why did you?" Joel asked.

I shrugged. "Approval? My family was relieved. I mean, I'd really raised their blood pressure as soon as I turned thirteen and I guess I felt I owed them?"

"But you didn't buy into any of it, did you?" Joel adjusted his glasses and crossed his leg.

I smirked. "You already know me so well."

"Did you and your family find the relief you were looking for?"

"For a little while. It felt odd for all of us to be at peace—not in a judicial committee hearing or warding off DCYF. My dad started introducing me to baptized brothers he had already stamped with his approval."

"At sixteen?"

"J-Dubs marry young. Remember, most of them—the spiritual ones—wait to have sex. You can imagine how hard it is for a teen in their *Bloom of Youth* to wait. So, they get married as soon as they're of age."

"Jeezaloo. Did you like any of the suitors your father chose?"

"Nah. I was still stuck on one person I knew my parents had already approved."

"Jax?"

The Bloom of Youth Betrays

YES. JAX.

My feelings for him had not waned, regardless of any redheaded, feathered mullets that once distracted me. Time spent with anyone else had been short-lived. Unimportant. A mistake.

Time had allowed Jax to forgive and move forward from previous heartbreak because he planned a trip home to New England, and Dad and I were getting him from the airport.

Overflowing with exhilaration, I told Rene—a sister my age at the Franklin Hall I'd gotten somewhat close to after Erica's family moved to Tennessee. Rene knew how I felt about Jax, knew intimate details of our history, and the devastating heartbreak following our breakup. She knew how much I loved him.

And all those feelings came rushing back when I saw Jax walk out of the airport's secure area. My heart stopped. He looked the same and wore the same goofy, deep-dimpled smile. His jet-black hair and deep brown eyes were like home. The *Bloom of Youth* had been good to him.

I walked closer and hugged him, afraid to let go.

"Hi!" He squeezed back.

"Hiya Jax," Dad voiced, slapping him on the back. "Good see you."

While my dad and Jax exchanged small talk—waiting for his luggage to make its way around—I ogled him, in total disbelief that he was once again within reach.

At home, Jax was welcome to sleep in the boys' old bedroom or on the living room couch; wherever he was comfortable and, more importantly, in whatever room I wasn't occupying.

The next morning, we drove an hour and a half to the meeting in Massachusetts. While sitting beside him, during the meeting, I entertained fantasies of us being engaged.

I could see it now...

The ay-kah-geesha kicks on and he covers my chilly shoulders with his suit coat. I'm snuggled into him; we're sitting the way serious, engaged, J-Dub couples often do. And while sharing a Bible, we point to certain passages, and make brief eye contact, falling into doctrinal agreement.

Curse the meeting's end; it took him away from me. He'd hitched a ride with some other Witnesses, planning to spend his first week in the Northeast visiting his childhood home in Maine.

That week felt like a year.

When he came back to NH, the rules my parents set forth that first night were back in full swing: separate sleeping arrangements, doors remained open, and during the day we were not to be alone, if possible.

We were alone for short periods of time while my parents tended to their cleaning jobs. The four of us agreed to keep this to ourselves. No need to advertise his stay and potentially *stumble* anyone.

******

"So, you and your parents had established some trust, then?" Joel asked.

"Yeah. It was nice. Things felt normal for the first time. Jax being there reminded me of the train tracks and the promise I'd made to myself—*be me*, whatever the cost. Jax's presence always helped me with that."

"How did the visit go?"

I smiled, remembering details of another favorite memory...

EVENING THUNDERSTORMS DURING A NH heat wave had always been one of my favorite things.

"Let's go outside!" Jax jumped up and headed toward the back door.

I bounded to his side. As we ran down the back-porch steps, the screen door slammed behind us. We were suddenly two little kids who'd just heard the ice-cream truck go by. We ran into my dead-end road and stood in its center as heavy rain drenched us and thunder shook us.

He looked at me, opened his arms wide, then looked up to the sky, smiling. I wanted him to kiss me. I wanted to keep him with me forever. Little did I know then that the thunderstorm symbolized the tumultuous turn our friendship was about to take.

Trusting us a little more each day, my parents allowed us to be home alone after we promised to find local brothers and sisters our age to associate with.

"Oh! We could call Rene and her brother Finn! They go to the hearing Hall I grew up in."

"So, call 'em." Jax hit me upside the head with a couch pillow.

I called and fifteen minutes later Rene and Finn came in through the back door.

"Hi!" I said.

"Hi. I gotta make a quick phone call." Rene waltzed through the living room to the old rotary on the kitchen wall.

She picked up the receiver, rotating the numbers on the dial. As the line trilled, she flipped her long, flowing, red hair. Her light, green eyes danced around the room. Her long lashes flittered while she wound her finger around the grimy, spiraled phone wire.

And Jax caught it all in slow motion; like a lion, just waiting for the perfect moment to pounce a gazelle.

Rene put the phone on its plunger, came into the living room, and said, "Hi."

"Hi," Jax said, glassy-eyed.

Rene immediately noticed how enamored he was; he responded to every word she said and each subtle move she made. The attraction between them was as instantaneous as a car crash.

"We have a pond in our backyard, paddleboats, and a small dock. Let's go to our house and go swimming!" she said.

"Okay!" Jax jumped off the couch.

As if Rene prancing around my house in Daisy Dukes and a tank top wasn't enough, now she'd be slithering around in a two-piece.

Driving in tandem to a murky pond in Northfield, I felt a sudden distance—an uncontrollable tension—between me and Jax. Whatever cable we had connecting us, *just moments ago*, had been snipped with industrial-strength shears.

"Rene seems cool," Jax said, blushing while looking out the passenger window.

"Yeah."

I switched the radio dial to ease the tension rising in my mom's little Colt. "Hey, Jealousy" by The Gin Blossoms played. Its timing, impeccable.

While wading in swampy pond water, paddle-boating, and eating Rene's dad out of house and home, my place was clear. I was now the annoying, dreaded third wheel—unworthy of throuplehood. My blood boiled seeing how comfortable they were together. The teasing that was mine, just hours ago, bounced effortlessly from me to Rene. What should've been an innocent afternoon in mixed company—to satisfy the anti-stumbling-J-Dub-chaperoning code—swiftly mutated into me watching Rene, the hungry serpent, tease her unsuspecting meal.

When evening came, Rene batted her long lashes, flashed a smile, and said, "Come over tomorrow."

"Definitely." Jax's dimple now adorably indented for Rene.

That evening, while Jax and I were watching *Say Anything*, Luke's weekly phone call to check on the family came through. He quickly ascertained that Jax was staying with us, and immediately urged us to have him stay elsewhere.

"It doesn't look good for him to be at the house with you two unsupervised," Luke said. "It could stumble someone. He needs to find somewhere else to stay."

My heart fell right into my lovesick stomach. I felt like I had already lost Jax to Rene, the hair-flipping serpent. Losing him to the stumbling factor—because of how it *looked* to other J-Dubs—just pissed me off. I cared about Jax and wondered if asking him to leave, and stay elsewhere, would stumble *him*. But Luke didn't care about that. The decision had been made. Jax had to leave.

My parents submitted to Luke's suggestion, yielding to his orders, fearful of the turbulent storm that would occur if they didn't. For the rest of his time in NH, Jax stayed at my recently reinstated brother, Jesse's, in Franklin.

******

"Reinstated?" Joel asked.

"Jesse had been disfellowshipped, and when he proved he was repentant enough, was reinstated."

"How does one do that?"

"A disfellowshipped person needs to attend all meetings— showing remorse and a strong desire to be back in the Truth. Then, they write a letter to the elders and a private hearing is scheduled. If everything lines up, an announcement is made, and they're welcome back to the congregation with open arms."

"How...*conditional*." Joel shook his head. "How did the rest of Jax's visit go?"

******

JESSE HAD NO PROBLEM letting Jax stay—he was rarely home. And I had no problem going over Jesse's to see Jax, unchaperoned.

One night, in Jesse's absence, we each had a beer from the fridge. While sipping this horrid tasting ale, I noticed that with me, Jax was suddenly cordial; comfortably bored. The bond was barely there, and it felt like we didn't know each other the way we had just a couple of days prior.

Rene had already bewitched him. But I didn't care. I planned to tell him I still loved him. I wanted to share the fantasies I had to date long distance again, until I was eighteen. When I turned eighteen, and he, twenty, we could get married. I'd move to New Mexico, or he'd move back East. My plan was fool proof. We had years of history. How could he say no?

I'd drafted a whole speech, resting it on its own special shelf in my head, aching to be released. I waited for just the right time to broach the subject. And I thought I'd found it until the strange brew I drank sloshed in my unsullied belly. I felt queasy. My courage had quickly turned into nauseated cowardice. I cursed my weakness as he walked me to the door.

"Call me to let me know you got home okay."

I nodded, belching and exhaling.

Once I got home, I called, as promised.

"Made it home."

"Good." Jax yawned.

I decided to rip off the Band Aid.

"I need to tell you something. And I don't know how so...just gimme a sec..." I hesitated, then closed my eyes and blurted, "I still have feelings for you. They're stronger now. I don't know how you feel, but I'm sure about how I feel. I still love you, Jax."

There was an awkward silence. It felt like forever before he said anything.

"I love you, too," he said.

I knew it. Step aside, Rene.

We said good night and hung up. I rode to my bedroom on a cloud, snuggling with my bear into a heavenly night's sleep.

The next morning Jax called.

"Come over. We're having breakfast," he said.

"Ok." I yawned. *Wait, what?* "Who's we? Is Jesse home?"

"No. I'm at Rene's. She picked me up. Come over to Rene's."

"Come over!" I heard Rene shout in the background.

******

"What was he doing there, and without you?" Joel asked.

"I wondered that, too. He told me he loved me and then found his way to her place—first thing in the morning. Being at Rene's unchaperoned was no different than being at our house unchap—"

"Were you...perhaps...*stumbled*?" Joel raised his brows and smirked.

Holy shit, I was. I'd been taught that *I* always needed to be careful. *I* needed to worry about what people thought of me and my level of spirituality. Not once did it seem anyone concerned themselves with *my* feelings.

"Joel, you're a genius. Yes. Yes, I was fuckin' stumbled."

******

JAX AND I HAD years of history—family clambakes, and hikes to Maine lighthouses, Deaf culture, CODA bitch-sessions, and even a past relationship serving as a foundation. What did Rene and Jax have besides one paddleboat date on a filthy pond and a poorly cooked breakfast?

I got ready in a hurry and trembled while driving to Rene's. When I arrived, Jax, Finn, and Rene were sitting around the kitchen table with a breakfast spread. Standing in the entryway to the kitchen, I lost myself in fantasies of shoving Rene's face into a plate of scrambled eggs, then straddling Jax, and kissing him passionately in front of them both.

"Bek? Bek!" Rene shouted.

"What?"

She snapped her fingers in my face. "What do you want to drink?"

"Oh, whatever."

"Where were you just now?" Jax asked, shoving a forkful of pancake into his mouth.

"Dazed, I guess."

Fantasies of kicking Rene's ass, and Jax carrying me off into the sunset, continued all day into the evening.

We all walked to the beach at the end of Rene's street, around the time the sun and moon dance briefly together in a dark blue sky. Stars were twinkling, the sun was setting, and a crescent moon hung over the pond.

Rene and Jax sat at the shoreline, shoulder to shoulder, pants rolled up, feet barely touching the water, talking. As they looked out over the pond, it glistened with early stars from the twilight sky.

I wanted to die.

The image of them, shoulder to shoulder, seared itself into my brain, branding itself to my forehead. Rene had stolen my story. Jax was supposed to be leaning into *my* shoulder and whispering in *my* ear.

I'd already spent years feeling less than—at school, the Kingdom Hall, and in my own family. I'd always felt different, like no one could possibly understand what my core was born already knowing. Jax was my anchor. If anyone could even *begin* to try and understand me, it was him.

"You don't seem yourself today. You're super quiet. It's not like you," Finn said.

"I'm fine." I took in one last look of Rene and Jax sitting closely, their toes in the dirty pond. I leaned back, lying next to Finn on the sand, and stared at the stars that were now wide-awake. Tears streamed down my cheeks.

"Did you see that? It was a shooting star." Finn pointed at the sky.

"Mm-hmm." My voice quivered.

Finn and I stayed there for what felt like forever, until the sound of Rene laughing brought me back to a cruel reality. I reluctantly glanced over and saw Rene chasing Jax. He ran from her playfully. As Rene gained speed, she reached out and grabbed his shirt, tearing it.

"I'm so sorry!" Rene laughed herself into a giddy frenzy, holding a piece of Jax's shirt in her hand.

"You owe me a new shirt, brat!" Jax said, tickling her.

Gross.

We walked back to Rene's, said our goodbyes, and I gave Jax a ride to Jesse's, dumping him at the front door.

The night before Jax's flight back to New Mexico, I wore a crushed velvet, skin-tight, emerald-green Bodycon dress—right out of Tori Spelling's closet. In a desperate attempt to get his attention, I brushed my blossoming, shapely body against his whenever the opportunity presented itself. He barely noticed.

Game over.

I wanted Jax to leave so I could start getting over him. I also didn't want to let him go. The mental images of Rene gripping her claws into my childhood love were excruciating. Maybe time and distance would bring Jax and me closer, putting a wedge between him and Rene. *Maybe.*

Our goodbye was bittersweet. I knew Jax felt my pain. He could fool himself all he wanted with Rene, but no one would ever know him like I did. And vice versa.

We exchanged a quick, clumsy hug. He wandered toward security, turned, pursed his lips, flashed the *I love you* sign, and vanished. My anguish was interrupted by my sweet father—who was clueless about all that had transpired in just two short weeks.

He turned to me and said, "You enjoy?"

I nodded and headed for the parking garage. I went into hiding, coming out only for food and meetings. Until Rene called.

"Hi! Where have you been?" she asked.

"Around. We go to meetings in Massachusetts now—"

"I know, but you haven't called or come over. We're going shopping. Wanna come?"

"Sure," I said, uninterested.

"Okay. We'll come get you in a few minutes."

Wandering Sam's Club, Rene gravitated toward the men's shirts. "I need to send a shirt to Jax."

"Why?" I scowled.

"The night I ripped his shirt on the beach, he said I owed him a new one."

"He was kidding, Rene." I rolled my eyes, left her standing there—comparing obnoxious Zack Morris shirts—and went to find Finn.

I couldn't listen anymore. Rene knew how I felt about Jax long before he flew out. I had talked about him enough. She knew. And Jax wasn't off the hook, either. As soon as Rene popped over in her Daisy Dukes, I was benched—forced to watch a game they'd never let me play.

We left Sam's Club with a hideous, silk, collared, button up shirt for Jax, and I went back into hiding. I buried myself in *Watchtower* publications, longing for school to start so I could further distract myself.

Rene popped by, unexpectedly just before school started, and we took a walk. We wandered down my quiet, half-residential/half-industrial dead-end road toward town.

"What's up?" I asked.

"Well, I kinda wanna talk to you about something."

We continued walking. I kept silent.

"Jax and I have been talking. A lot. We like each other. I told him I didn't want to start courting until I talked to you first, Bek. We want to take things slow. Being long distance will take the pressure off us getting physical, or needing chaperones..."

Her voice trailed off, the synapses in my brain started to misfire, and my body began to tremble. Words no longer made sense; everything was garbled. My plan to date him long distance had become her plan. It was like being given the starring role in a play—night of the big show rolls around and I'm excited, more than ready. I've rehearsed all my lines and suddenly I'm replaced by my understudy, just before the curtains go up. No rhyme or reason.

All the years of friendship, secret CODA meetings, Deaf meetings, long phone calls, letters, mixed tapes, our break-up, heartache, and family visits—including this one—gone.

I stopped listening and started walking faster. She stepped up her pace. I looked at her and spat the first thing that came to mind. "Don't you dare hurt him."

"Do you mean you don't want either of us getting hurt?" she said, practically chasing me.

"I meant exactly what I said." I turned around, left her in the road, and walked back home.

Once I reached the back steps, I flung the screen door open and let it slam behind me. I heard her start her dad's station wagon and leave. I stopped talking to both of them that day. One of them played games with my heart, and the other disregarded my pre-existing intentions to feed her own ego.

My junior year at Winnisquam was a much-welcomed distraction. Schoolwork, and attending meetings three times a week in another state, took up a good chunk of time.

But somewhere between school and meetings, Rene wiggled her way back into my life—

******

"She did?" Joel raised an eyebrow. "Why?"

I sighed. "I knew you wouldn't let me skirt past that. Self-flagellation?" I laughed.

He didn't.

I cleared my throat. "I thought I deserved it. I had a lot of time to brood, and I decided that being angry and unforgiving wasn't a good look for me. It was downright exhausting; I felt like a *double-lifing* hypocrite. And at the time, I really *was* trying to walk the straight and narrow regardless of any Pullman train promises."

"How were things between you and Rene?"

"Well, I kept my guard up. I'm not stupid—"

"Good girl."

"I knew not all J-Dubs were like Erica—that perfect mix of spiritual and sass you could trust. And unfortunately, our friendship was reduced to written letters, random phone calls, and mixed tapes once she'd moved to Tennessee. As for Rene... We resumed trips to the mall, mid-week sleepovers, and rode to school together.

"In a toy store at the mall, a man with long, dark hair and a goatee approached me, asking if I wanted a job. He handed me an application and I took it home to fill out. The only thing Rene wondered on the drive home was why he hadn't asked *her* to fill out an application."

"How did that make you feel?"

"Like what we shared wasn't true friendship. I felt like a stepping stone she balanced herself on while looking off into the horizon—plotting to take whatever she could get her hands on."

Part of His World

A WEEK AFTER BRINGING my application back to Kay Bee Toys, I was hired. The goateed manager must have noticed something about me that I missed. Time spent there was another welcomed distraction from the void Jax once filled, and I loved the discount; my Disney movie collection was growing.

"*Little Mermaid* okay?" I took the VHS tape out of its ornate Disney case.

"Yeah, but I don't like the Sea Witch. She's demonic, casting spells, using magic. You can either fast-forward her part or I'll leave the room," Rene said.

I snickered to myself while sliding the tape into the VCR.

******

"You're talking about the Disney cartoon, right?" Joel asked.

I nodded and said, "Rene had it in for Ursula and all things supernatural. The ol' GB had her well-trained, and she was a pro at denouncing all evil. Even Disney characters."

"Interesting that her sensitive conscience didn't poke her once while stealing your childhood beau."

"Right? Exposure to satanic Disney magic was cringe-worthy but betraying my trust and swooping in to steal Jax wasn't. I started noticing a lot of things J-Dubs did that just didn't align with what I thought Christ-like behavior should be."

"I have no doubt," Joel said, opening a new steno pad.

******

THE OLD YELLOW ROTARY on the kitchen wall shrieked, flashing like a nightclub strobe light. I jumped up to hush it.

I was greeted by a familiar voice. "Hey, Bek!"

Danny was from Franklin. We'd met at the Hall when some J-Dub friends witnessed to him. He feigned interest in the Bible, and had come to quite a few meetings, to try and date one certain J-Dub; a common occurrence that leads most worldly boys somewhere between being on deck and first base, waiting for what usually doesn't happen.

"Whatcha up to?" I asked.

"Nothing. What're you doing?"

"Homework, watching *The Little Mermaid*."

"*Little Mermaid*, huh?"

I heard a shuffling in the background as the phone made its way to someone else.

"*Little Mermaid*! What part?" an unfamiliar voice asked.

"Who's this?"

"Which part?" he said.

"Um, Ariel's singing, 'Part of Your World.'"

"Sing with me!" he said.

"Who is this?"

"C'mon! Just put the phone up to the TV and sing!"

"Who are you talking to?" Rene asked, looking up from her history book.

I looked at her, shrugged my shoulders, and started singing.

Ariel's song ended, and what turned into a seven-hour conversation began. Rene went to bed around 11:00pm, but I was too intrigued by Dean, *The Little Mermaid* fanatic, to hang up just yet. I waved good night to Rene as she vanished down the hall into my bedroom. I knew it was late, but I was wide awake as Dean rambled on, ripping into my recycled faith.

"It's a total cult!" he said.

"No, it's not. Everyone says that, but it's not."

"Typical response from someone *in a cult*. Could you leave if you wanted to, without any consequences?"

"Sure. Anyone is free to leave whenever they want." I half-lied. I knew what the consequences were for abandoning the Truth.

"At what cost?" he said.

"Well...you get disfellowshipped." As soon I said those words, I felt Johnny and Jesse leaving home after their announcements all over again. It still hurt. Especially Johnny since he'd never come back.

It's almost like Dean knew—before he even asked—that leaving came with an expensive price tag.

"Do you masturbate?" he asked.

I flashbacked to my horny pre-teen self, rubbing against hairbrush handles in my room. I used to masturbate, but now that I was older, baptized, and had some level of self-control, I could definitively say no.

No, I don't masturbate. I kicked that habit.

"No."

"Why not? It's a healthy release."

"We aren't supposed to. It's...uh...an unhealthy...selfish habit... It's self-abuse." I wasn't even equipped to defend my own beliefs to a strange man. My dedication to Jehovah had an unstable foundation at best. Theoretically, I should have been high on the holy fumes coming out of God's ass, but I wasn't. *Hang up, Rebekah.*

"You aren't *supposed* to? *Self-abuse*?" he asked.

"The Bible says—"

Dean scoffed. "Tell me where the Holy Bible uses the word *masturbate*."

"Somewhere toward the back, maybe Galatians?"

"It really doesn't matter. My point is, darlin', only a *cult* would be so prescriptive and controlling,"

Every time I was ready to hang up, he posed another intriguing question. I was stupefied. Come 4:00am he was still talking my ear off.

"I gotta go to bed. I have school in a couple of hours." I yawned.

"I hope to talk to you again, darlin."

Click.

My heart slid into my stomach. I couldn't breathe. Air wasn't passing through the brick in my chest. This unfathomable character had taken every one of my beliefs—safely balled up in my brain where the ol' GB had put them—and proceeded to unravel them like double-stranded DNA. Once the double helices were outstretched, he uncovered the very backbone of the *Watchtower* organization by pointing to every fictitious pillar they built upon. He exposed them for the low-lying worms I'd suspected they were years ago.

Maybe it was all a dream. Maybe I just needed to sleep him away. I dozed off for what felt like a minute.

"Get up," Rene said, waking me. "We're gonna be late."

I forced myself out of bed and got ready, barely awake.

"Did you talk to that guy all night?" Rene asked as we pulled into Winnisquam's parking lot.

I yawned and nodded.

"Be careful. You don't know him, and he could be one of Satan's tools," she said.

Oh, shut up and go buy another hideous Zack Morris shirt for Jax.

******

"Satan's tools?" Joel asked.

"Human temptation is often, almost always, chalked up to Satan and his busy minions. Beelzebub, Mephistopheles— whatever you wanna call him—lures people away from Jehovah using their biggest weaknesses."

"How was Dean your weakness?"

I was officially stumped and scared to answer. Just *hearing* Dean's name sent a permanent shiver down my spine. Dean was the Sid to my Nancy, the Manson to my Van Houten. Dean was irresistible; inscrutable. Dean was the toxic poison my parents told me not to touch, the worldly boy who "only want one thing" that my mother warned me about. Dean wasn't necessarily my weakness. Dean was more an overpowering strength, wielding influence over anyone within a twenty-foot radius.

"I don't know how to answer that," I finally said.

"He still a thorn in your side?" Joel rested his chin on the palm of his hand, intrigued.

"A thorn? I guess. A thorn I'll probably never be able to remove."

"Why is that?"

"For everything Dean was, did, and coaxed me to do, he gave me...*life;* an indescribable drive that's helped me over the years."

"Go on." Joel surprisingly put the notepad down.

******

DAYS WENT BY and I comfortably settled into a Dean-filled fog. Every day I stepped further and further into the dark tunnel he led me through. With each step toward his lair, my mind opened a bit. I wanted to be part of his world. The idea of Jax and Rene courting, slowly began to fade away. This was about *me*. Dean wanted *me*.

The only thing troubling me then was, I couldn't stop admonitory scriptures from prancing around in my mind. One particular passage was on repeat, thanks to *The Little Mermaid*. John 17:16: "They are no part of the world, just as I am no part of the world." Why, when Ariel sang about it, did the scripture seem less forbidding?

It didn't matter. I had already been sucked into a world where Dean's probing questions were like a feather tickler. And I was indeed tickled. I justified talking to him. I even thought that doing so would strengthen my shaky faith. If I could learn to defend it, and stick to my convictions, I'd be stronger spiritually. And maybe being tested by Beelz wasn't such a bad thing. Maybe my doubt could be useful.

I had no idea what Dean looked like; we hadn't met in person. I only knew I was drawn to him. When he was no longer satisfied with secret phone dates, he came to see me at work the very next week.

Standing before me, at the Kay Bee Toys entrance, was a six-foot-two giant towering over my five-foot-three petite frame. He was wearing a black leather jacket, dog chains wrapped around his wrist, and an ominous gaze. Long, stringy, strawberry-blond hair flowed past his shoulders, and his piercing blue eyes looked right through me. He looked like Keifer Sutherland with much thicker skin. His formidability shook me...and drew me closer.

I hugged him and he softened like play dough. I handed him my journal—a request he'd made on the phone the night before. He smiled and became softer still.

We were on the phone whenever possible. When our conversations came down to beliefs, lifestyles, love, sex, and of course religion—the impetus for it all—I fell deeper and deeper. And there was no going back the night he seduced me over the phone, persuading me to give in to the thrill betwixt my thighs once again.

Masturbating, I was familiar with. And up until meeting Dean, I was able to dismiss the flutter on occasion. But he had other plans. Suggesting mutual masturbation, phone sex, was definitely a first. I had plenty of fortuitous moments as a horny young girl in the *Bloom of Youth* and followed each one up with an appeal. But moaning and groaning on the phone with Dean, absolved me of my sins somehow.

I didn't use a hairbrush handle, or a block of old cedar wood from my dresser. I bravely used my own finger and found a sweet spot that I never even knew existed. Playing with this little bump introduced a new way to masturbate. I was throbbing and wet with *something* in unexpected places. We gave way to quick, shallow breath and sweet, simultaneous release.

Being completely captivated by Dean was like being in love with God's archenemy. His claws gripped mercilessly. I reached out, clasping his monstrous talons with my puny hands, and said, wide-eyed, "I love you, Satan." I was hooked.

"Do you still talk to that guy?" Rene asked pulling into Winnisquam's parking lot.

"Sometimes." I shrugged.

She didn't buy it and there was only one way to appease her—Danny. Rene was not a complex creature. Regardless of her loyalty to Jax and Jehovah, she was easily distracted by a wink and a complement. Attention from boys—J-Dub or worldly—was a tool Satan used on her.

As Danny and Rene spoke on the phone, he reassured her that the few conversations Dean and I had were nothing but insignificant chatter. She unclenched. Rene was easy to sidetrack, and Danny was just the guy for the job. It even went further than I'd anticipated.

"Danny says we should take a drive to Dean's sometime after school to say hi," Rene said, hanging up the phone.

"Oh?"

She hesitated, then said, "We probably shouldn't, but if we make it quick, I don't see the big deal."

And we did just that.

We went to Dean's three-bedroom apartment located in one of the worst parts of Franklin. When we turned the corner onto Spring Street, the scenery drastically changed.

It went from Norman Rockwell, picturesque, small-town New England to a sketchy side street—unsavory, overrun with dilapidated houses, and dirty kids running amuck.

We parked my mother's little white Mitsubishi on the street in front of Dean's apartment. I prayed nothing would happen to it while we were inside. Funny that I prayed to the same God I was now brazenly showing my middle finger.

I knocked and Danny answered.

"Hey!" He hugged me.

"Hi, this is Rene," I said as we entered the apartment.

A wall of cigarette smoke hit us as we stepped through the entryway, leading into the living room.

My eyes were immediately drawn to the flimsy, veneer wood paneling that covered the top half of Dean's walls. The bottom half was covered with sandy-brown, light, mauve-colored bead board, separated by a white chair rail.

An eclectic group of posters decorated the paneling. A velvet black light poster, a half-naked girl, and a poster of Jim Morrison were tacked up above a beat up, salmon-colored armchair pushed up against the wall.

Next to the shabby chair, an upturned, milk crate served as an end table where an open beer sat all alone. A TV, directly across from the armchair, set on a worn-out particleboard stand with a VCR on the floor underneath.

Brown and tan shag carpeting covered the floor and looked like it had been there since the 70s; maybe earlier.

Next to the TV, a particleboard shelf housed books like *Paradise Lost and Paradise Regained* by John Milton, *The Necronomicon, The Satanic Bible* by Anton LaVey, Edgar Allen Poe, Nietzsche, and Jim Morrison biographies. I liked that Dean was an avid reader.

I heard a pair of combat boots excitedly stomp through the apartment and stop in front of me.

"Hey, peanut! Welcome to my humble abode." Dean bowed, wearing a devilish Kiefer Sutherland-like grin. His eyes were glazed over and slightly bloodshot. His lips were pink from the chilled beer he just triumphantly chugged.

"Hi." I smiled.

"C'mere, I wanna show you something." Dean grabbed my hand, leading me through the living room, leaving Rene and Danny in the entryway to chat. I followed him, taking in the rest of the apartment.

To the left of the living room was a large, dark, empty space. The hardwood floors, decrepit. And the walls—which were coincidentally painted the same mint green color as my house—were heavily plastered and met with another white chair rail which was connected to more sandy-brown, light, mauve-colored bead board, extending to the floor.

"What's that room?" I asked quickly passing by.

"Dining room," he said. There were no table or chairs. It was empty.

We passed through a tiny hallway with an open food pantry on the left. Shelves were lined with Ramen noodles, instant mashed potatoes, and boxes of quick, easy meals. Directly across from the pantry was a small, carpeted bathroom with a stand-up shower and freestanding sink—both filthy.

We entered the kitchen. Opposite the tiny hallway was a stove, alone, no neighboring counters or cupboards. Every wall was plastered, and mint green, right down to the grungy linoleum.

Behind me was the kitchen sink and only counter-space in the apartment. Above and below the counter-space were white, vintage, leisure metal cabinets. A white, 50s style Frigidaire stood alone to my right, backed up against two large windows. It looked like it hadn't been maintained *since* then.

Two open doorways on either side of the isolated stove, piqued my curiosity. The one to the right was another dark, empty room. The one on the left was where Dean brought me.

A full-size bed set atop a metal frame, a beat-up dresser was in the far corner against the wall blocking the only window, and a box fan was on the floor next to the bed. On either side of the bed were more upturned, milk-crate side tables.

Dean turned to me, pressed his thumbs into my underarms, and picked me up as if I were a child. He stood me on his bed to meet his height. "I'm glad you came."

With no warning, he pulled me closer and kissed me. His tongue fiercely searched for mine. It was the first time I'd ever tasted cigarettes and beer. I ran my hands over his long, stringy, blond hair, found the back of his neck and cupped it, pulling him closer. My heart raced as his hands found my tits. He forcefully massaged them, breathing heavier, the way I heard him breathe over the phone a few nights ago.

My hands moved down to meet his and I slowed them. "We can't stay long," I whispered.

He sighed. "You better be back." He stuck his pointer finger in my face, wagging it, rattling the dog chain wrapped around his wrist.

I hopped off his bed, wiped the recycled beer from my lips, and left the bedroom. Walking toward the door, I noticed *another* almost-bare room, sharing a wall with the entryway. This room had a huge bay window facing the street, beaten-up hardwood floors, a twin bed on a metal frame, and a few posters of half-naked women.

"Whose room is that?" I peeked inside.

"My roommate's," Dean said from behind me.

In my mom's car, Rene and I quickly discovered that the cigarette smoke—coupled with the stale air in Dean's apartment—was pungent. Once home, we ran into the bathroom and immediately hopped in the shower to avoid any parental interrogation.

Dean was more than a sixteen-year-old, sheltered, and clueless J-Dub girl like me could handle. I didn't care that he was ten years my senior or not a Witness. I didn't care where he lived, or where he worked. My only thought was, *When will I see him again?*

Dean quickly grew bored on the phone, daring me to swing by his place after I finished work. As weeks went by, I stayed later and later.

I'd make myself comfortable on the beat up, salmon-colored armchair, while Dean and Danny sat on the shag carpet, beers in hand.

It was 1993—the age of grunge and alternative rock. Bands like Stone Temple Pilots, Soul Asylum, Red Hot Chili Peppers, Nirvana, Gin Blossoms, and Pearl Jam permeated the musty air in Dean's apartment.

Whenever we grew bored with MTV, Danny strummed his acoustic guitar and the three of us sang while Beavis and Butthead, or random grunge videos, played on Dean's muted television.

Dean and Danny sang, "Tommy's Down Home" by Tesla while I interpreted, per Dean's request. This was the night I lost track of time.

I pulled into the driveway at home much later than 9:30pm, and it did not go unnoticed. I figured my mother was dozing in front of the TV, the way she did every night. I thought I could enter at any time, undetected. Unfortunately, Mom had trained herself to awaken the very second headlights flashed through the kitchen window.

It was 11:30pm.

"Mecky, where you?" she voiced while rubbing her eyes.

"Work," I signed.

"No, you no work late. You home usual 9:30, sometime 10:00," she sim-commed. If she's sim-comming, that meant the Muppets were waking up. Any second, an angry Miss Piggy was going to surface.

"I smell cigarette, where you go?" *Ugh, Piggy.* Thank god Dad was in bed. It was too late to watch four furrowed eyebrows dance a tarantella tonight.

"Stay late, store mess. Soon holiday," I signed.

This tamed her temporarily, but I realized late night jam sessions had to stop. I laid low, playing the good girl—attending meetings, reading *Watchtower* publications, and studying for school. I understood why some opted for that *double life* because I fell right back into Dean's lap two weeks later, boldly staying later.

My parents caught onto my lies about working late, and the battle for independence began. I'd lost the interest and energy required to soldier on as a Witness, and they knew it. Coming home wearing Dean's black leather jacket, random dog chains, and a yin yang charmed necklace made it obvious I'd been spending late nights with someone who showered me with unchristian gifts.

******

"How much time had passed since meeting Dean?" Joel asked.

I looked to the ceiling, trying to remember. "Maybe a month, a month and a half?"

Joel's eyes widened. "A month?"

I looked down shamefully. "I know how it seems—"

"It seems like an older man flimflamming a young girl." Joel really *was* like an uncle.

"It *seemed* that way to everyone else; it wasn't that way for us. I felt like I'd lived a thousand lives before meeting Dean, and he saw that. He saw *me.* He made me feel special, darkly unique. I swelled with self-importance at the thought of *him* choosing *me*. Plus, I guess… I wanted to prove I could handle it, handle *him*."

"How do you mean?"

"My brother Luke was so overprotective. I felt like he thought I was just 'cute, clueless, little Bek, who had to constantly be shown the way, because she couldn't possibly handle things alone.' I felt Jax and Rene shrugged me off much the same way. People either felt the need to care for me, policing my every move, or found it easy to take advantage of my kindness. But not Dean. I welcomed Dean. He challenged me, saw in me what no one else did because they hadn't bothered to look. He gave me what none of them could."

"And what was that?"

"Attention. Interest. He was mesmerizing, intriguing. He knew things. He looked *at* me, he didn't see past me the way everyone else seemed to."

"Okay," he sighed, "go on."

"Well, my parents went through the roof…"

******

"BUCKY, HE WORLDLY!" Dad yelled. "Why you go his house for?"

"Mecky, I told you—worldly boy want one thing!" Mom sim-commed.

I rolled my eyes, knowing that was an ol' GB lie because Dean and I hadn't had sex.

"Make-ay! No make face me!" Mom yelled. *Uh-oh.* I was no longer Mecky. When she was angry, I became Make-ay.

Then, the up close and personal drug checks began. My father would hold my face, squishing it between his thumb and four fingers. Then, drag me under a lamp and force my head into its light. Looking into my eyes, he voiced, "You take drugs?"

"No!" I wiggled my face away from his grip. I wasn't on drugs unless you counted Dean's hypnotizing persona, his knack for exposing the vein of a cult, jabbing it with a needle, and injecting logic.

I was forced to attend meetings. Everyone at the Hall knew I was fading, and fast. I no longer cared how I presented myself, what I wore, whether anyone was stumbled, or who I hurt. During meetings, the loving glances and sympathetic stares from my spiritual family came at me full force. Ignoring them, I'd slouch in my chair, wearing Dean's dog chains and a grimace.

Luke and his new wife kept me close during the whole debacle. Luke sat next to me at meetings, handing me that week's *Watchtower* study article saying, "Follow along."

I'd take it, glance, and toss it into the aisle, rolling my eyes.

Whispers about my *spiritual sickness* became a topic of conversation and I received several phone calls from brothers and sisters in *both* Halls, pleading with me to "think about what I was doing." They advised that my "involvement with a worldly man would pull me away from the Truth." The pull to be with Dean, and immerse myself in his dark, tangled web of sin and degradation, was stronger than my desire to identify as a Christian.

******

"Would you say you were honoring the train track promise to yourself?" Joel asked.

"Yes and no. I was finally paying attention to the gut-jabs I'd always felt about the ol' GB and being a J-Dub. But I was also caught in *Dean's* web, not my own. I didn't know it at the time, but he was—in many ways—almost like another overbearing belief system that I'd been sucked into."

"You're much more astute than you give yourself credit for." He scribbled wildly in his notepad.

"If I only knew then what I know now."

******

IT WAS CHRISTMAS TIME, and the mall was packed.

The sales crew at Kay Bee Toys were expected to dress for the season. During Halloween, my goateed manager respected my wishes to dress as myself and allowed me to tell any customers who asked, that what I was wearing, *was* my costume.

During the Christmas season, I didn't ask for any special treatment because I didn't give a fuck. I rang the Christmas bell outside the store, proudly wearing a Santa hat, shouting, "Merry Christmas!"

Dad came to the mall, saw me decked in Pagan yuletide, and stood outside the entrance to the store, threatening me in ASL. "Jehovah punish you for that," he signed. "Jehovah mad. You be punish."

As my father spat ill-intentioned J-Dub hate all over me, I glared at him thinking, *Yeah, I want to spend eternity worshipping a petty God that can't contend with any opposition—the God that will punish me, forever holding a grudge, because I wore a fucking red, fluffy hat.*

I finished my shift and left the mall with Dad.

As he drove erratically down Route 106, he voiced his condemnation for my recent choices to disobey God, get involved with an older, worldly man, and borrow Santa's hat.

"Jehovah hurt now. You hurt him. You hurt me mom, too!" he shouted.

Unlike Mom, Dad did *not* sound like a temperamental Miss Piggy you could easily dismiss. When he screamed, storm-like ocean waves roared in your ears, violently crashing, over and over.

"I feel like kill myself! I kill myself and kill you!" he yelled swerving into the oncoming lane, nearly taking us off the bridge we were on. He roared with anger, weaving back and forth on the road, *barely* missing oncoming cars. I gripped the car seat, shrieking.

Then suddenly, we were home in the driveway. I shot out of the car, scared for my life. I ran inside terrified. I raced past my mother toward my bedroom. Once on the other side of the door, I tried to lock it, but my fingers fumbled, and it was too late. Dad had kept up with my speed.

He pushed on the door from the hallway. I pushed back from the other side. A seesaw effect took hold. I felt him using all the hypocrisy I'd seen over the years and push it up against every intuitive belief I'd held onto from the first time the line of Pullman trains blew past me at the tracks.

He flew in screaming, "You will die at Armageddon! Jehovah kill you!"

Instinctively, I grabbed a pair of scissors from my bureau and threw them in his direction. They missed his cheek by a hair. Time warped. I watched him in slow motion, dodge to the side. He looked behind him to see what I'd thrown. As he turned to face me, his eyes widened, and he lunged. In real time, he threw me down on the bed. The full weight of his body was on mine. His hands tightened around my throat, his legs straddling my waist.

Mom appeared in the doorway, ran in, and peeled him off me. I sat up on the bed, hands around my throat gasping for air. I looked up at him and charged. Mom broke it up once more, pounding on me for bulldozing him. The cycle of lunges and screams continued until we all grew tired. I collapsed on the floor in defeat. They left me there wailing and closed my door.

Trapped.

I couldn't trust anyone in the Truth, and surprisingly, I was still leery of worldly people. The things I'd learned through

Bible verse and personal experience were in an un-ending battle.

Lying on the floor, I wondered if the B&M Railroad trains even blew past our backyard anymore. I hadn't heard them in years. To jump the train and go anywhere would've been my saving grace.

I called the only person I could think to call. I cried and it only made him angry.

"Just fuckin' do it, Bek," Dean said.

"Do what?" I sniffled.

"Disfellowship yourself. Once you do that, they'll shun you and you can just leave."

"And go where?"

"Move in with me. I'll take care of you. Write a letter to the elders and just be done with all this bullshit. Say, 'In light of recent events, and a change in my religious stance, I wish to disfellowship myself from the Kingdom Hall of Jehovah's Witnesses. I don't feel the need to justify my reasons...'" His voice faded.

He was verbally writing my letter based on things I had told him—rules, religious tenets, and looming consequences. The only thing making any goddamn sense during this emotional catastrophe was that Dean was tangible, and God was not. That was all the reason I needed to write the letter, and I used Dean's speech almost verbatim.

The Sunday I handed my letter to the elders I said farewell creatively. During the same old forty-five-minute talk of impending gloom and doom, the importance of remaining in God's love during these *end times,* and resisting all temptation, I went into the ladies' room. I made myself comfortable in one of the stalls, hiked up my flowered, ankle-length skirt, found that sweet little bump between my legs, and masturbated to climax.

******

Joel cleared his throat. "Well, that was quite the exit. Since you wrote a letter excusing yourself, did that still require a judicial hearing?"

"It did. They came to the house, we sat around the kitchen table, and I think I scared the elders."

"How so?"

"In a moment of Dean coached lunacy, I sat at the table, closed my eyes, and chanted some nonsense."

"What nonsense?"

"I don't remember. Something from *The Satanic Bible*— which I don't put much stock in besides the believe-in-your-own-power-and-here's-how parts. Anyway, the elders didn't like that one bit and left the house shortly after."

"Not surprising."

"No. And I didn't attend the meeting to be present for my disfellowshipping announcement, which sent a message to the congregation—"

"And that was?"

"I. WILL. NOT. REPENT. In English, the announcement is: 'Sister Rebekah Mallory has been disfellowshipped from the Christian congregation of Jehovah's Witnesses.' And in ASL, it's a bit more callous: 'Sister Bek kick out.'"

"How did that feel?"

"At the time, liberating. And scary. And sad. And nerve-wracking. And exciting. It didn't stop me, though. I shrugged it off thinking, *Here's my middle finger. You guys are a bunch of zombies kowtowing to the Watchtower Society.* I moved out at sixteen. My move out wasn't at all like Mark's—with a going away party, poorly rehearsed skits, and a family road trip to Brooklyn, New York to set up a Bethel dorm room. My move out experience came complete with Luke at the house yelling, 'So this is it? You're just gonna leave? Fine! Go! Go move in with your twenty-six-year-old boyfriend, you slut!'"

Joel pursed his lips in disappointment. Or disapproval. Or both.

"I walked out with a bag of clothes and a box of Lucky Charms. My own stubbornness and refusal to *double life* it, like some J-Dub hypocrites do, barred me from rethinking my decision. I pigheadedly stomped down the road.

I could feel my dad creeping slowly behind me in his red Toyota Corolla. I felt his remorse from the driver's seat. I looked ahead and just cried, remembering a time when I was Daddy's Little Girl, which wasn't that long before the whole shitstorm."

"What did you remember?"

"I had just received my first moving violation, a $72 ticket for not coming to a complete stop on a back road. I slithered into the living room and found Dad sitting in his recliner. With ticket in hand, I sat on his lap and snuggled him, resting my head under his chin. He asked what I had in my hand, pointing to the ticket. I sighed and handed it to him, batting my eyes. He glanced at the citation and whispered, 'I pay; no tell Mom.' I hugged him tight, signed *thank you* and flitted to my room."

I shook the memory and looked up. Joel waved a tissue at me and said, "Let's pick this up next week."

A Babylonian Harlot

"HOW HAVE YOU BEEN since last week?" Joel asked.

"Okay. And you?"

"Good, thanks. But we're not here for me," he said, flipping through his notepad. "I can't imagine it was really okay for you—a minor—to live with a man ten years your senior."

Ah, yes. Dean—my messiah and my assassin.

"It wasn't, but I'd been officially disfellowshipped. Which meant—just like Johnny and Jesse—I had to go. Where else was I going to go?"

"A valid point. Your family's decision to fall in line with the Witness creed, left you no other choice, really. It's just…" Joel slightly shook his head.

"That's just how it was at that time—"

"Have things changed since then?"

"Not really. But the GB's *new light* flickers; they change their stance on things when backed into a corner. At this time, 1993, I was out on my ass."

"How was it living with Dean?"

"Fine. I'd been there for five days when two officers showed up on his doorstep, summoning me home. Dean and I stood at attention, baffled, but I gathered my things and left with them. I panicked sitting in the back of that police car, wondering if something had happened to Mom and Dad—"

"Still protecting them even after everything you'd been through."

"Yeah, I guess I was." I hadn't even thought about that.

A CODA's work is never done.

******

134

PULLING INTO THE DRIVEWAY, I saw Dad standing on the back porch, arms crossed. I got out. One of the officers escorted me up the porch steps. I kept my head down, refusing to make eye contact.

I trudged past my dad and walked into the house. I glanced over at Jesse sitting calmly at the kitchen table, hands folded, not uttering one single word. He was there as a buffer. Even with opinions and worries written all over his face, he didn't make a move, or say a thing.

Once I heard the officers leave, I wandered down to the basement, found an old pushbutton phone, and plugged it into the phone jack by the washer. I dialed. The line rang once before he answered.

"Make them regret bringing you back," Dean said. "Find something in the house to destroy and destroy it."

In the same basement where the demons used to play, I unleashed the one living inside me.

Leaning next to the woodstove, I noticed an axe. In the main part of the basement, where we once hosted weekly Bible-book studies, an old coffee table ate up empty space. I shifted my gaze between the two objects and grabbed the axe. I walked to the coffee table, heaved the axe above my head and cracked a slit down the center of the table. I wiggled it free, brought the axe above my head, and let it kiss the table again. I grunted, crushing the table over and over, until my grunts became screams.

Jesse flew down the stairs, rushed toward me, grabbed the axe from my hands, and tossed it across our old book-study floor. He threw his arms around me in a half-hug/half-restraint and demanded I *clam dawn*.

My head throbbed. My body shook. I sobbed uncontrollably.

After hours of exhausting negotiation, using Jesse as our mediator, it was decided: I was moving in with my wayward brother, Johnny, in the next town over. Johnny conceded to my parent's suggestion and once I arrived, rules were firmly established.

"You will have a curfew. You will clean up after yourself. You'll watch your nephew when we need you to, and you'll get your schoolwork done. You're not gonna be out, staying up all night, got it?" Johnny said.

I agreed.

Johnny, my sister-in-law, Lisa, and my six-year-old nephew, Sean, lived in a three-bedroom trailer. It was small, clean, and cozy. I slept in Johnny's weight room, on the mattress of a twin cot with a pillow and a sleeping bag. I used an antique chest for my clothes and tried to keep to myself.

I got rides to school with Lisa's sister, Stacie, and they allowed me to see Dean with a few restrictions. There would be no sleepovers, my curfew was 9:00pm on weekdays, and 11:00pm on weekends.

Dean came to visit a few days after I settled in. We went into my room and sat on the mattress, backs up against the wood paneled wall. With his hands in my lap and my head on his shoulder, he said, "We need to talk."

I listened while playing with the dog chains on his wrist.

"Your dad called the cops and told them I was raping you and selling drugs."

I froze, stopped fiddling with his dog chains, and stared ahead, fighting tears.

Dean continued, "I want this to work, but it's getting too intense. I can't lose my job over this *lie*." His sullen voice trailed off, and before my brain caught up with the pounding of my frantic heart, he was gone.

******

"This is the first sensible thing I've heard, Rebekah."

I could've been upset. Irate. Pissed even. But I laughed, because what Joel said was so true once I pieced together the puzzle of my own story thus far.

"It's funny?" he asked, half-smiling.

"Well, when I think of it like a Disney movie, yeah. Picture it: baby girl is born into a fated plan. Girl grows up wanting something else. Girl meets a sordid character that shows her a whole new world. Girl forges her own path despite her family's desires—"

"Does this girl live happily ever after?"

"Did any of *them*? We'll never know. Their stories stop."

"What happened after Dean broke it off?"

"He didn't." I waited for Joel to look up, anticipating a jaw drop. *Three...two...*

"What?"

One.

"Surprisingly, Dean decided I was worth the risk. He said he was really into me. He loved the fact that I was 'old school,' as he put it. Regardless of his reasons, it meant the world to me. Trey threw my seductive, Eve-like ass under his self-righteous chariot the second he was pressured during my first judicial hearing. Mullet boy, the virginity thief, had fucked my friends as soon as he was through with me. And Jax dismissed me as soon as Rene flipped her hair in his field of vision."

"Didn't Dean care about the statutory rape charges?"

"Oh, he cared alright. Which was another good reason to stay at Johnny's for a month—to let things cool down. Dean made me feel like I was more than just a disfellowshipped nobody. He proved it by driving from Franklin to Belmont, in his beat-up old Mustang, to see me on his days off. He sat uncomfortably with my brother, sister-in-law, and their friends just to share space with me."

"Why just a month?"

"My sister-in-law didn't like him, and I didn't like that."

"Oh?"

"One day after school, she laid into me. She said he wasn't welcome there. She didn't like the way he 'knocked me around.' She said he was too old for me, and a man that age just wanted a little girl to manipulate."

"What did your brother think?"

"He sided with her. So, I left. And this time, no one had the energy to stop me."

"What was it like living with Dean the second time?"

******

WITH DEAN I WAS free to do what I wanted. Allowed to make choices. I exercised free will in ways I never thought I would. Being with Dean was what I imagined being with Charles Manson might've been like. Dean was my mentor—sexually, emotionally, and psychologically. He guided me through his nefarious world, showing me its ominous underbelly—leading me into the dark, disturbing rooms that held space in my own mind.

He encouraged me to confront the Devil himself while looking through drug-covered lenses—as long as I didn't do any without him present and my homework was done. My mind was a dizzying cloud of sex, drugs, anarchy, and anti-religion.

Everything I thought I knew about sex was mere child's play to Dean. He not only knew where the fun, mysterious, little bump between my legs was, but he massaged it—with his tongue. This was definitely *porneia* and it blew my sheltered little mind. With verbal tutorials, and Dean's collection of porn videos, he taught me how to return the favor. And then I could most assuredly say, I knew what a blowjob was.

When it came to sex, Dean didn't just thrust repeatedly until he was inspired to drown me in fake I love you's. He made sure my experiences with him were unimaginable to the door-knocking masses I'd left behind.

Regarding religion, Dean had a personal vendetta against all types of tyrannical, fanatical Christianity. He most certainly had issue with Witnesses and got into long debates with them when they knocked on his door.

"Peanut, it doesn't matter if you want to worship a head of lettuce, as long as you hurt no one in the process," he said, sipping his beer. "And J-Dubs hurt people. Maybe they don't mean to, and maybe some don't, but the upper echelon sure does."

"I don't know what to believe now," I said, looking through his library of books. I pulled down a book by Edgar Cayce, hoping to find some answers.

"Believe in yourself," he sipped again, "get to know who you are."

A sheltered sixteen-year-old—heavy-handedly bullied by religion and her family, used as a conduit for other people's words and emotions with little opportunity to feel her own—is not likely to develop a strong sense of self. I felt like I was missing something.

The swift journey through our dark, perverse tunnel slowed down about two months later. The influx of drugs (pot, acid, mescaline laced pills, 'shrooms and a one-time meet-and-greet with cocaine), nights spent waxing philosophy, and engaging in gritty, porn-like fucking fiascos that would leave Ron Jeremy proud came to a screeching halt.

My schoolwork, and Dean's job, now boldly headlined the top of our to-do list. He worked overtime, frequently stressed about money. The shift from live-in boyfriend to parental figure happened so fast, it went overlooked. Dean burdened himself with paying my way, and once we both finally noticed it, reality hit like a bitch.

On nights Dean was able—he drank. Like a fish. I preferred the times he smoked pot to the times he drank a twelve pack of cheap beer. When he smoked, he mellowed, talked, and philosophized. When he drank heavily, he became someone I hadn't met yet.

"I'm hungry. Make me a bologna sandwich with extra mayonnaise," he said, sipping his seventh beer.

I shot up from the dirty, shag carpet and went into the kitchen to play short-order cook. He was a demanding beast when he drank, especially if he was hangry. I came back from the kitchen, handing him a sandwich.

He took a bite.

"Not enough fuckin' mayonnaise!" he said, giving it back to me.

As I smothered the bread once again, I heard him mumble, "I said *extra* mayonnaise, you deaf fuckin' bitch."

My shoulders dropped. I knew I could be a bitch and was on several occasions. But no one had ever called me that after I'd made and handed them food. With tears in my eyes, I gave him the sandwich and headed into the bedroom.

"Hey, Peanut! Where ya goin'?" He took a bite, moaning with pleasure.

"I'm tired. I'm just gonna go lie down."

Dean drank himself into a cantankerous spell a few nights a week. I was usually able to tell what kind of night I was going to have when he came home from work. If he held a twelve pack of beer under his arm as he walked in, my walls went up, and I was careful not to step on the eggshells he scattered all over the nasty, shag rug. And on those nights, I remembered, *extra* mayo.

The nights I fought back were nights verbal abuse switched to physical abuse. I guess it was just a matter of time. It didn't take much to set his teeth on edge—insufficient mayonnaise on a sandwich, questioning points made during any of his long-winded tangents, incorrectly rolling a joint, or simply casting a shadow at the wrong time usually did it.

I considered myself lucky when all he did was holler obscenities and insult me. On one cold, winter night I was less fortunate; it went much further than it needed to.

"What did you say to me, cunt?" Dean said.

"Fuck you!" I screamed, running for the bedroom.

Shit. Why'd I have to say anything?

I heard his combat boots storm after me. I felt his hand grab the back of my head. He forced my forehead into the white chair rail that ran in a strip around the bedroom wall—the one I'd noticed the first time I visited. I wished we could go back to that day, insanely infatuated with each other.

My head, throbbing in pain, begged to be coddled. I slowly stood up and immediately placed both hands over the bump on my head, trying to comfort myself. It was growing by the second. Dizzy, I stumbled into the bathroom, and as I looked up into the mirror, I couldn't believe what, or *who*, I saw.

I saw a young girl with long, thick, curly, dark hair. Her faint olive skin was becoming dull, her full lips were turned down. Her brown eyes, cradled beneath her thick, black eyebrows, focused on the swelling knob protruding from her head. I didn't recognize her. Tears welled in her tired eyes, her lips quivered, and her forehead wrinkled. I had to take care of her. I owed her that. I bundled her up and left.

It was nearly 1:00am when I left. I walked down the hill to the 24-hour convenience store and stood at the pay phone, staring at it. I didn't think my parents would answer. If they were in bed, the strobe light flashing above the mounted rotary phone at Club Mallory wouldn't faze them. My brothers certainly wouldn't answer if I called—those bridges had gone up in flames as soon as my disfellowshipping announcement was made; they were quick to discard me.

I stood at the pay phone crying. I couldn't bring myself to ask anyone for help. I told the girl that I saw in the mirror she would have to suck it up; we had nowhere else to go. She hesitated. I was able to *clam* her *dawn* and we negotiated. I'd go back to Dean's when I was sure he had either settled or passed out by the time I returned. She agreed.

I walked into the store to pass the time. The bell above the door rang and the cashier behind the counter looked at me.

"How ya doin'?" he asked.

"Fine." I shied away from his gaze, wandering down the snack aisle.

"You sure?" He raised a brow.

"Yes," I said, peering over a bag of Doritos.

"That's a pretty fuckin' big blow on your head. Can I call someone for you?"

I stood before him, with nothing to purchase, refusing to meet his eye. I shifted nervously with my hands in my pockets. The deafening silence felt eternal. I shook my head and left.

Dragging myself up the hill, my heart sped the closer I got. I turned the knob quietly and entered slowly. The lights were off. I closed the door, turned the deadbolt, and snuck into the bedroom.

Dean was out cold on the bed. My heartbeat returned to its normal rhythm. I undressed using light from the street coming through the window, turned the blankets back, and gently nuzzled in next to him.

I wanted Dean to be the guy he was before—the guy who vowed to protect me from the evils lurking within organized religion. But now, I needed protection from *him*. He was a stranger to me, much like the girl who leered at me in the mirror.

With no one I trusted enough to call on, I welcomed anyone that came through the door. Their company served as a buffer. Except when Dean used anyone present as pawns for his twisted, erotic fantasies. I was content to keep fantasies during our fuck-sessions as fantasies and nothing more.

He wasn't.

An acquaintance, Jones, stopped over to see if any of his friends were loitering at Dean's. Which was usually the case any given Saturday night; most of the derelicts in town usually stopped over at some point.

After one beer, and a few tokes from a bowl had transpired, I could see by the shiftiness dancing in Dean's eyes that he was bored. He escorted me to the bedroom, leaving Jones in the living room.

"Know some of the things we've talked about when we…you know…" he whispered, stroking the side of my face. I missed his tenderness. My body shuddered as he softly grazed my cheek with his hand—the same hand that had forced my head into a chair rail. I looked into his eyes and saw a savage beast, behind his baby blues, trying to claw its way out.

During many of our X-rated moments, he'd go into detail about things he wanted to do to me while others watched, things he wanted other people to do to me while he watched, or simply what type of narrative he wanted to hear afterward. I was never really a fan of dirty talk, but it was usually over within minutes and most of the time, I'd just let him ramble on.

"You mean the dirty talk?" I asked.

"They're *fantasies*," he chuckled, bringing his face closer to mine. "They could become a reality, if you let them."

I felt his hot breath on my neck inhaling and exhaling. I longed for his love and attention. Maybe if I satisfied his insatiable libido, he would ease up, scream less, stop hurting me, and we could return to where we were just a week ago.

"What do you want me to do?" I wrapped my arms around his neck and drew him in closer.

He whispered a slew of amoral tasks I could choose from, then disappeared into the living room. I sat on the edge of the bed and didn't dare to move. I was embarrassed, anxious, and shamefully curious about what Dean would be like once his cravings were satisfied.

Would he be softer?

From the bedroom, I heard Dean ask, "How come you never come around with a chick? Do you have a girlfriend?"

"Nope. No chick," Jones said, holding his breath in after taking a hit from the bowl.

Dean teased Jones, suggesting maybe there was no chick because he was gay. Jones laughed, denying it, saying he'd prove it when he started dating one worth his time. Dean challenged him to "prove it tonight—right here, right now."

"Wait...what? How?" Jones asked.

Jones shied at first, but Dean's charismatic cajoling worked. Before long, Jones appeared in the doorway and cast his shadow before me. I looked up at him, welcoming him inside with my eyes and nervous smile. He stepped closer. He sat on the edge of the bed and leaned into me.

"Are you sure you're okay with this?" he whispered.

I hushed him, knelt on the bed, rested my hands on his bony shoulders, and pulled him closer. He started to kiss my neck. He exhaled hints of beer on my skin. I shuddered when my desire for Dean's beer-breath was met with a stranger's.

"Whaddya want me to do?" he asked, slobbering on my neck, boldly rubbing my t-shirt armored tits.

He was already talking too much, and it annoyed me. I just wanted it to be over.

"Jerk off."

This would make a thrilling newsreel for Dean, allowing Jones to prove himself and all I would have to do was *be there.* He pulled out his dick and began stroking himself. He grabbed my hand and moved it onto his so I could feel him jerk off. His dick was puny, bumpy, and small; it felt like a gherkin.

No wonder he doesn't have a girlfriend.

"Here I go," he muttered between shallow breaths. He came all over my t-shirt while quietly grunting. His breathing normalized, he zipped his pants, jumped up, and scampered out of the bedroom. I heard the guys exchange a few words, the door opened, closed, then I heard Dean lock it.

Dean's combat boots charged madly through each room until he got to the bedroom. He flipped the light switch. I looked up at him with the remains of Jones' heterosexual proof all over my shirt. To squash the awkwardness, I giggled, knowing it would drive Dean mad with passion.

Behind my laughter, I felt like the Harlot of Babylon. All I needed was a seven-headed beast to straddle, a leopard-print dress, and a glass of red wine. One slut, coming up.

I guess Luke was right.

Dean stripped in a hurry, pouncing down on the bed next to me. I drowned him in kisses and a spicy narrative, hoping my willingness to do the unspeakable quenched his thirst, and served as payment.

******

"Did it?" Joel asked, removing his glasses, wiping them, not meeting my eye.

"No. He was master of puppets, and I was his favorite doll."

I felt stupid. I looked out the window, searching for some sign to tell me I wasn't.

"I'm not going to ask why you allowed that scenario to play itself to the end. It's clear, given your upbringing, you were impressionable; sixteen, dating a twenty-six-year-old." He put his glasses on and set his notepad down.

I nodded. "Yeah. I guess it was easy for Dean to mold me." I looked down, feeling stupid.

"Rebekah, your Witness programming didn't foster independent thinking. You were used to being told what to do, how to think, what to believe. You couldn't doubt your indoctrination, and you definitely weren't licensed to ask any probing questions. Now, Dean's beliefs, behavior, and values differed greatly from your upbringing, but still, you didn't question him, and you learned not to challenge him. Whether it was a religious organization or a one-man show, you were easily manipulated. And that wasn't your choice for a long time. Not your fault."

I nodded again, then said, "I always hoped my compliance would appease Dean's beast, but those hopes were all in vain because he was a salivating, sex-crazed savage; nothing tamed his insatiable impulses. The more I gave, hoping his hunger was satisfied, the more he demanded."

"He really was Mansonesque, wasn't he?"

"Well, I never killed anyone or anything, except maybe my own spirit. We did have some good times. Especially when Danny moved in. Until it got weird."

"Oh?"

******

OUR MUTUAL PAL DANNY moved in with us the latter part of my junior year at Winnisquam. Not only did this relieve Dean financially—my little part time, after school job at a local day care contributed a mere pittance—but Danny's presence took the edge off.

Once again, it felt like the times we'd had when I used to stop by after shifts at Kay Bee Toys. We played music, sang, drank, smoked weed, debated, waxed philosophy, nihilism, and everything in between. And the night Dean brought home a fluffy, black kitten sporting a little white patch on her chest, I knew things would be better.

Sid Vicious, the Amazing Pussle Kittle, had the biggest, most beautiful green eyes. She became my little attitudinal partner-in-crime. I dressed her in a mini studded collar and envied her for being the badass I knew I wasn't.

Saturday mornings were for wake n' bakes with sugary breakfast cereals, *X-Men,* and *The Tick.* Times I could click the TV on and hear the *X-Men* theme song, made me appreciate Dean working as hard as he was to ensure we could always wake n' bake with our favorite animated characters.

I was passing all my classes, Dean's schedule was just how he wanted it, and Danny's contribution—both financially and personally—helped tremendously. We were a throuple, we were *Three's Company* flipped. Things were beginning to feel somewhat normal, and just when I thought it was safe to relax, the uninvited creature behind Dean's blue eyes appeared once again.

It slowly folded its claws over top of the room I'd built to protect me and Dean. It pulled itself up—peering over the edge, snarling—eyes widened, teeth gnashing, and drool oozing from its mouth. It used the flimsy walls I had erected as leverage to leap into the bedroom and attack. It stomped around my protective enclosure, swatting its tail viciously, demanding to be fed.

Dean, having drank himself into another horny stupor, used Danny's intoxication to lead our threesome to the next level. Dean shooed me into the bathroom, told me to put on some make-up, and closed the door.

I heard them whispering while dressing my face to match that of a Babylonian whore. I sat on the toilet, staring at the mint green plastered wall, wondering if Danny was drunk enough to accept Dean's offering.

Did young maidens in biblical times feel this cheap?
"I offer my daughter for two goats and a calf."

"A fine offer. I accept."

I heard Danny stagger to his bedroom, mumbling.

Dean's boots landed just outside the bathroom. I opened the door and peeked through the crack. My lips were painted red, eyes heavy with black liner, and my crop-top-exposed tummy was in knots.

Dean shook his head. "He isn't into it, said it would be like messing with his sister."

I was relieved. And angry. With myself. Apparently, I needed a drunken friend to say what I wanted to say—no.

The next morning not a word was spoken. Danny and I shared uncomfortable glances. From those alone, I could tell he pitied me and maybe even felt responsible since he had introduced us.

Danny moved out shortly thereafter and financial stress took his place. This made Dean anxious and, when he could afford to, he came home with his precious twelve pack. Usually around beer number eight, an argument ensued for some reason, *any* reason, and my head was the target once again—same chair rail, same spot on the head.

I had reasons to stay. If I went back to Mom and Dad's, I'd be forced to squeeze my boundless spirit into the ol' GB's straitjacket. Going home just to be kept safe in a J-Dub group-think bubble with no escape, didn't appeal to my anarchist soul.

Also, I held fast to the idea that Dean—the enigmatic man who piqued my curiosity months ago—still adored me. We'd had good times I couldn't shake any more than I could the bad times. So, I stayed. Again.

The start of what would have been my senior year at Winnisquam was met with opposition. Living out of district, I was required to pay tuition I didn't have to walk with classmates I'd known since the first grade. Finishing out my senior year at Franklin High was not an option since I had not been properly emancipated from my childhood home.

Frustrated, I racked my brain for a solution. I was not about to forgo my diploma. I remembered my idol, Erica, home schooled. Attempting to ride her one-of-a-kind coattails again, I saved my small pittance and bought the materials needed for Intro to Psychology, Social Civics, Art: Drawing People, and World Literature. I completed my assignments and sent all correspondence via USPS, acing every class. I received my high school diploma just eight months after my classmates at Winnisquam.

To celebrate earning my high school diploma, Dean ordered in. He said Ramen noodles and fried bologna sandwiches weren't special enough. So, we had buffalo wings with ranch dressing and pizza, while sitting on the shag carpet watching *Commando*.

"Hand me one of those wings with some dressing," Dean said, keeping his eyes on Arnold Schwarzenegger.

I pulled the skin off the wing, dipped it in ranch dressing, and handed it to him. Only he wouldn't take it.

"What'd you do that for? Did I say I didn't want the skin?"

"No, but I like mine with—"

"I don't fuckin' care what you like."

I sighed, looking down at the wing in my hand.

"I can't ever just have a good fuckin' night with you, can I, Bek?"

I couldn't keep quiet this night. This was *my* graduation party, and he should've let me have this one night, since I'd sacrificed myself to him in more ways than I cared to count.

"Maybe it's not always me. Maybe it's you!" I stood up, tossing the skinless chicken wing into the take-out container.

"Me!?" He grabbed the chicken wing and stood up, towering over me. He flung the naked buffalo wing in my direction. Then, meeting my eye, he bent down and grabbed her.

"No!" I screamed. "Don't!"

He picked Sidney up off the floor and squeezed her until her little, pussle-kittle voice yowled.

"Stop it! Give her to me!"

He threw her down and she scurried away. I stood between the living room and empty dining room. Time slowed. Fire blazed in his eyes and smoke blew violently from his ears. He used the same psychotic glare Keifer Sutherland had in *Lost Boys*, and I knew I needed to run. But I didn't want to leave Sidney with him.

Within a split second, I decided to bolt into the empty dining room and accept whatever was coming to me. I avoided running near the chair rail, so my head wouldn't suffer a third time. He lunged, pushing me with such force that I instantly fell to the floor. With nothing in the room to break my fall, the weight of my entire body fell onto my right shoulder. He spat on me, his black combat boots stormed past my head, and he charged through the kitchen to the bedroom. I heard him light a cigarette and sigh.

I lay still on my right side in a fetal position, afraid to move. Any movement would have set him off, calling him back to finish what he'd started.

A little over a week ago, I polished this dining room floor until it fucking shined. Hands, knees, rags, a bucket of diluted Murphy's Oil Soap, and an hour of elbow grease did me proud. And here I am—face planted on the cold, hardwood—kissing it. I'm glad I scrubbed it.

I shifted my feet and stopped as soon as I heard my boots grinding against each other. Then, an indescribable pain shot through my right arm all the way to my neck. I wanted to scream but didn't want him to come back.

Don't move. Don't sniffle. Don't cry. Don't breathe. Just, don't. Focus on something else.

I looked around without moving my head. My direct line of sight was the hardwood floor. *Damn that's clean.* From my vantage point, I could see the ceiling, the living room in front of me, and the tiny fibers of the ugly, shag carpet. Past the fuzzy threads of the rug, I glanced up and could see Arnold Schwarzenegger still on the warpath looking for little Alyssa Milano.

I started searching the room for *my* little one. I wondered where she found refuge. Since I didn't see her anywhere, I assumed she was safe.

My left arm hung across the front of my body. My forearm was pressed against my chest and the top of my hand touched my right cheekbone. A tear fell to the knuckle of my forefinger. I sniffled quietly. I shifted once more, trying to sit up, but I couldn't without straining my right shoulder.

Deep breaths. Try again.

I took several deep and controlled breaths as I pushed myself to sitting a position with my left palm. I winced in pain as I looked to my left arm and saw spit mixed with buffalo sauce.

I planted my left palm on the floor next to my ass. Steadying myself, I set my feet firmly underneath me and pushed myself up. I didn't care what he heard anymore; I knew something was broken.

I walked into our dank, nasty bathroom. I turned on the light and looked in the mirror. And there she was again. She looked worse than before.

Her hair was still long, curly, and dark. Her lips were even fuller from crying. There were bags under her beautiful brown eyes and her thick, dark eyebrows took on the shape of worry. Her skin was no longer faint olive but pale as a ghost, and her right shoulder was off. There was a bone visibly out of place—dislodged, dislocated, broken. *I need to get her out of here.*

I bravely did the unthinkable.

"DEAN!"

"What?" He was audibly irritated.

"Something's wrong." I walked into the bedroom and turned on the light. "My shoulder, I can't move it."

He had surprisingly *clammed dawn.*

"Lemme see." His bloodshot eyes danced between my right and left shoulder. He tried to inspect me thoroughly, but he was completely wasted.

"I think it's broken." I sniveled.

He sighed, looked down and said, "You need to go to the hospital, and I can't bring you."

I looked up at him in disbelief, tears streamed down my face. He wouldn't meet my eye. He sat down on the bed and lit another cigarette.

Broken, in spirit and bone, I walked into the living room and picked up the phone. I dialed and the line trilled. I waited anxiously, no clue what to say if anyone answered.

"Hello?"

"Mom!" I shouted loud enough for her to hear me.

"Hello? Mecky?"

Aw, it's Piggy.

"Mommy!"

"What matter, Mecky?"

"I hurt myself! Pick me up! Pick me up!" I repeated myself to ensure her meningitis-stricken ears heard me at some decibel.

"Pick you up now?"

"Yes! Now!"

"Oh, okay. I get Daddy, we come."

I was surprised at how amenable she was.

I draped my winter coat over my shoulders carefully, left Dean in the back bedroom to think about what he'd done, and waited on the front steps for my Muppets to rescue me.

They took me to Franklin Hospital. From the backseat, I explained that I'd fallen in the dining room, which was true. I signed all this left-handed; it wasn't easy. It's like writing with your non-dominant hand, sloppy. Not really a problem for English speakers since you don't have a dominant side to your mouth.

After the x-rays, and repeatedly telling nurses that it was an accident, I was discharged with a cushioned sling for my shoulder that wore like backpack straps. No pain meds were given since I was under eighteen.

Mom and Dad reluctantly brought me back to Dean's.

"Why not come home now, Mecky?" Mom asked with severe concern in her eyes.

I looked at her sadly and shook my head no. I opened the car door and stepped out. I walked up the two busted steps leading to Dean's apartment and gave them one last pathetic wave before going inside. Hearing them drive away, a little piece of me died.

Once inside, Dean greeted me at the door, apologizing profusely. "I'm so sorry. I won't ever drink again. I won't ever hurt you again, I promise." He hugged me.

I didn't believe him. I wanted to, but I didn't. For every shitty thing he said or did, he had a warped way of building me back up, and I fell for it every time. He knew he could inflict pain and be the only one there to comfort me. His finger flipped that goddamn gaslight incessantly, and I started to wonder if even *he* was fully aware of what he was capable of.

The girl in the mirror started showing up every day, and every day she asked, "Why?"

I needed to make her understand why I stayed. I knew why I didn't want to leave, but I couldn't remember why I wanted to stay.

I carefully drove Dean's grey, beat-up, old Mustang—his precious punk-mobile—to my parents' house.

I went home hoping for some kind of revelation, hoping the girl in the mirror would finally get why we were at Dean's.

Dad and I sat in silence, and unbroken eye contact. He knew Dean was the reason my clavicle bone was broken and never said one word about it. I knew he knew. His worried eyes told me so.

He reached for me, pulling me onto his lap like he did when I was small, and softly voiced, "Why not come back, Bucky?"

I shrugged my one good shoulder and my eyes welled up with tears. I broke eye contact. I knew I'd lose it if I held onto his gaze.

"No cry, Bucky. You need smile me. Come back."

Smiling was hard because I knew what *come back* meant. It wasn't just *come back* home but *come back* to the Truth, like the Prodigal son. In one house, it's do or die for Jehovah, and in the other it's do or break for Dean. I wanted to go home, but I didn't know where home was anymore.

I stood up and signed, "I need go now."

"You think about it," he sim-commed.

Going home meant admitting defeat and being subject to the ol' GB again. Sure, I'd be welcomed back with open arms, the network of J-Dubs who shunned me would smother me in conditional love once again after I successfully submitted for the appropriate amount of time. But the very core of who I was would suffer and eventually wither away in a mindless crowd of sheep, wandering toward the *New System* in perfect group-think harmony. I just couldn't.

Going to Dean's meant a certain kind of freedom I wasn't granted at home, but there were limitations to that freedom as well. In either place, what I wanted didn't matter. The immeasurable desire I had to feed my soul with all the wondrous things I imagined I would once I left the Truth, were met with blows to the head, broken bones, and incredible sexual favors.

Not knowing then which was the lesser of two evils, I took my chances and went back to Dean's. The girl in the mirror came kicking and screaming.

Mommy Dearest

"WERE YOU ABLE TO appease the girl in the mirror?" Joel asked, flipping through his steno pad.

"I wasn't, no. But my mother was."

"Oh?" He grabbed a new pen from his desk. I imagine my stories, thus far, had worn out his writing utensils.

******

I WAS SHOCKED TO see my mother standing on my busted front steps, smiling. I let her in.

She sat across from me in the living room and shared her concerns about my broken clavicle. Word of me showing up at home, where Dad and I shared a tender moment, must have gotten back to her. But that wasn't why she stopped by.

"I soon disfellowship," she voiced.

My eyes widened. I stared at her incredulously while she relayed the experience of her own judicial committee hearing.

Welcome, mother. I've been waiting.

We swapped stories of humiliation and waxed disgust about our respective experiences in the dungeon of shame. I was both enthralled and nonplussed. I mean, there were no recognizable Muppets anywhere.

"I go back work now," she said, standing up. "I come again sometime."

And with that, she vanished, leaving me with a million questions.

Once Mom's disfellowshipping announcement was made, the Mallory men had no problem drawing a line in the sand, standing to one side with stones in hand, ready to cast them at us both—the *weaker vessels*.

They even came to my underprivileged neighborhood and stood at my trashy front step, accusing me of being the reason she was now exiled; her disfellowshipping was somehow my fault. They charged me with being the *bad association spoiling* her *useful habits*.

Dean, still feeling remorse over breaking my clavicle, made a real production out of Christmas that year. On his tight budget he spoiled the shit out of me.

The empty dining room that had served as scene of the crime earlier that year, became Santa's Village. He got a tree and dressed it to the teeth, surrounding it with presents.

And my sinful Muppet was there for all of it. Never in a million years could I have imagined that my mother would come, bearing gifts, and celebrate a Pagan holiday with me. But she did.

With my shoulder strength slowly improving, Mom hired me to help her clean houses a few days a week, assigning light-duty tasks she knew wouldn't cause pain.

Spending almost every day with her, I realized that her disfellowshipping wasn't merely centered around her own unrepentant, daring rebellion—it was an opportunity to keep me as close as she could. She was forfeiting her one shot at everlasting life for her only daughter. Guilt free.

******

"Why would the men in your family blame you for your mother's disfellowshipping?" Joel asked, looking up from his notes.

"Easy target, I guess? They were wrong because I'd had no opportunities to influence her."

"How was having her in your life again? With both of you 'out?'"

"Liberating. We freed ourselves from the austere tenets we'd been forced to follow. We rebelled against everything the men in our family expected."

"What specifically?"

"Their expectation that we'd continue to submit, handing over pieces of ourselves little by little until there was nothing but the shell of a woman left. That's how the ol' GB likes their women—subservient, docile, and meek. Unfortunately..." I looked down at my socked toes wiggling on Joel's therapy couch. "Rebellion doesn't *fix* anything. It feels good while you're doing it—and we were having a blast. But after so long I noticed that it didn't rebuild anything. The exhilaration I felt, even at the zenith of our coupled apostasy, couldn't possibly repair all the years of squashed womanhood. Our rebellion was just a distraction. We were still broken."

Joel nodded in compliance. "But you got closer, yeah?"

"Oh, yeah. Especially when my aunt Kathy drove to New Hampshire for the weekends. I wasn't twenty-one but Mom convinced the bartenders, of whatever bar she felt like going to, that I wasn't drinking and was her designated driver. They always let me in when they saw she was Deaf and adorable."

"Your mother brought you to bars with her?" Joel's eyes bugged.

I nodded. "I told you—we revolted."

He shook his head, half-smiling.

******

THE MOTHER-DAUGHTER INSURGENCE duo crossed state lines. Dancing in bars had turned into road trips. Every other weekend we drove to Gaylord Towers, in Connecticut, to visit Grandma Nina once she was diagnosed with breast cancer.

Just Grandma, Mom, Aunt Kathy, and I together—no men anywhere—was invigorating. Without the usual overbearing, masculine energy bringing us down, we softened.

The sound of *I Love Lucy* reruns, our hysterical laughter, and the garlicky aroma from homemade Italian dinners brought life to Grandma's lonely, dark, little apartment. Visiting extended family for more food, Bocce ball games, and dancing to Dean Martin's, "That's Amore" made the weekends shorter but more fun.

That lasted about a year.

Then Mom went back.

Back to the Kingdom Hall.

Back to a life of servitude.

Back into miserable bondage.

The free, strong-willed woman Mom showed me she could be, rapidly morphed herself for the ol' GB's approval. I lost her to the life-saving Christian belief of an everlasting existence in paradise, surrounded by The Stepford Wives.

An empty pit in my stomach replaced the bond we had. I felt like I had been hit by a truck—lying in the road, gasping for air, left for dead. I wasn't prepared to lose her twice.

And that's when the panic attacks started.

Regularly, fear pulsed through my veins, sending my heart into a fast-paced fit. I'd search the room for something to feel familiar, only to realize that I was floating above it, watching myself break. Seeing myself unravel, unable to come to my own aid, I tried desperately to scream—only nothing came out. Pure frenzy took control as I heard my heart pound in my ears. Sometimes, I'd rock back and forth on the floor, hands over my ears, until it stopped.

Drugs helped.

By this time, I'd become a joint-rolling pothead. I'd had my fill of LSD, pills, and alcohol. Weed was the only thing that hushed the basement demons perched comfortably inside my head.

A toke a day keeps the ghouls away.

My ghosts resurfaced for Halloween later that same year, and I decided to face all my shit head-on. I dressed as a dead Jehovah's Witness, wearing a tattered and torn ankle length floral skirt and a shredded, solid colored blouse. I soaked myself in fake blood and applied a generous layer of zombie make up.

At a party given by one of Dean's co-workers, I gimped around, dragging a foot behind me, trying to pawn off the latest *Watchtower* and *Awake!* magazines from my old black, leather book bag. Using my best zombie grunt, I asked partygoers, "Would you like to hear the *good news*?"

"Sure. First come over here and shotgun this joint with me," one of Dean's co-workers said.

Clutching my magazines, the way I used to, I stopped zombie-ing and plopped down next to him. He moved his face closer to mine and blew smoke into my mouth.

"Okay, lemme see your...*literature*." He flipped through the *Watchtower* magazine, shaking his head. "Opiate for the masses. How do you feel now that you're out?"

I was taken aback. No one had asked me how I felt in a very long time, and naturally, I wasn't prepared to answer. I sunk into the couch, inhaled the sweet smell of my favorite anti-anxiety medication wafting throughout the room, and searched for the right words.

I felt... Angry. Afraid. Ashamed. Stupid. Naïve. Sad. Happy. Excited. Anxious. Hurt. Unsafe. Lonely. Imprisoned. Free. Calm. Excluded. Disoriented. Paralyzed. Lost. Abandoned. Betrayed. Weak. Exploited. Abused. Insignificant. Doomed. Orphaned. Wrong. Worthless. Behind-in-life... Train Gone.

"I don't know," I finally answered.

"C'mon. How do you *feel*? Like, what do you believe now?" he pressed, passing the joint to someone in a cow costume.

I feel like yanking on one of those cow's udders.

Instead of voicing that, I just shrugged, falling deeper inside my head. It was the only place I ever felt safe.

The party around me continued. I successfully ignored the question, and the needle of my mind's turntable caught the groove of a Marilyn Manson song. I drifted away, letting the concert play within.

Manson got me. His words spoke to me, comforted me. As scary and blasphemous as he may have been to the masses, to me, he was a true poet. Another tortured soul with stories to tell and broken pieces to forge back into place. His music saw me through many painful experiences. The more I listened, the more in tune I felt with myself. His autobiography had me convinced we were kindred spirits; we had a lot in common.

Dean and I saw Manson for the first time at a small Rhode Island dive, Club Babyhead, during his *Portrait of an American Family* tour. And four more times after that for his *Antichrist Superstar* tour.

Manson didn't just release albums that tickled my ears; he quieted the lonesome desperation fidgeting within my soul. He introduced me to what became an obsession with true crime.

I loved learning about the minds of Charles Manson (who technically wasn't a serial killer), David Berkowitz, Richard Ramirez, John Wayne Gacy, and Henry Lee Lucas. This led me to other celebrity killers like Ted Bundy, Albert Fish, Ed Gein, and a new killer surfacing that very year—Andrew Cunanan, the Versace Killer. I closely tracked Andrew's killings, saving newspaper articles, placing them in my scrapbook.

My very first credit card purchase was a stack of Serial Killer Trading Cards. The front of each card was decorated with a deranged drawing of a well-known murderer, and a summary of their triumphant kills was on the back. I kept these safe in a trading card binder, with plastic loading pockets, gawking at them often, wishing I knew more.

"I wanna learn more. Maybe I should go to college and become a serial killer psychologist, work in a forensics lab, or something," I said, rolling a joint to perfection.

"Do it," Dean said.

"I'm getting sick of the Nursing Home."

Dean, Sidney the Pussle Kittle, and I were doing better. We'd moved from Franklin to Tilton, into a one-bedroom, and acquired actual furniture.

It seemed that once I turned eighteen, Dean's unspoken guilt about dating a minor dissipated, because there was less tension between us.

But something inside me *still* felt off. My soul was aching for answers to questions I hadn't asked.

Licking the edge of the paper and rolling the J tight but not too tight, I thought about how working in the field of Human Services, like Dean, had strengthened our bond. But it didn't take long before I grew tired of wiping old, saggy ass at the nursing home and living for our weekend laundry pile. I wanted more. But I didn't know how to go about finding a college—let alone apply to one.

Being raised a magazine-pushing *good for nothing slave* didn't prep me for college or even a 401K. What it did was force me into a chair three times a week, spoon-feeding me fictitious doctrines, while stealing my essence and instilling fear that Armageddon was just around the corner.

A post-secondary education wasn't necessary and wasn't encouraged. The only valuable information we needed came from Jehovah, via the good ol' GB.

We were told to utilize our spry energy knocking on doors full-time, gathering all interested sheep to grow in number while waiting for Jehovah's great day of vengeance with bated breath. There was certainly no need to go into student debt or associate with worldly people any more than was necessary.

Living with Dean hadn't fostered a studious environment. Sure, he kept on me about schoolwork with the promise of doobies or hits of acid upon completion, just long enough to get my diploma, but beyond that—nothing.

So, for many months working at the Nursing Home was rewarding enough but was also a constant reminder of the one senior citizen that stood above them all—Grandma Nina.

"I thought you were coming to visit with your mother," she said when she called to see why I wasn't in Connecticut one weekend.

"No. I'm sorry, Gram. I had to work." I half-lied. Mom would no longer let me ride down with her after she was reinstated, and I didn't have the heart to tell Grandma Nina.

"Oh," she said, "but I saved you a banana, and a *Lucy* special is scheduled to air Saturday night."

"Thanks Gram. Maybe I can come down next time."

There was no next time. My aunt Kathy called in the middle of the night to tell me Grandma was gone.

I was allowed to ride to Connecticut with my parents for the funeral once their elders had sanctioned it. The four-hour ride was eerily quiet.

I walked into the funeral home and saw the extended family Mom and I spent all those weekends visiting. I heard Dean Martin's, "That's Amore" in my head as I slowly made my way up to the open casket.

I stood before Gram and tears welled up so quickly, my vision blurred. I gave in and sobbed, shoulders shaking, face scrunched. I saw pans of lasagna, *I Love Lucy* episodes, bowls of corn flakes swimming in skim milk, and a lonely banana that never made it to my mouth.

I felt someone come up beside me.

"She doesn't look like herself. I kissed her," Luke said hugging me. It felt weird for Luke to be talking to me, *hugging* me, but I welcomed it.

A woman pastor walked to the front of the funeral home. We took our seats, and the service began. She stood next to Grandma's casket and started her eulogy.

Sitting in the front row with my family to one side, and Aunt Kathy on the other, I noticed no one was interpreting.

I leaned over Mom, looked at Mark, and whispered, "Why isn't anyone interpreting?"

Mark's conscience keeping him rigid, and he barely even acknowledged me. "Ask Mom and Dad," he whispered, not meeting my eye.

I sighed and rolled my eyes.

"Who interpret?" I signed to my parents, furrowing my eyebrows into a question mark.

They told me not to worry with their faces, while hushing me with their hands.

I sat quietly, perplexed.

The pastor shared a story about Grandma's driving history. When she was younger, her brother Peter had given her a driving lesson. During that lesson, she missed a turn, panicked, and hit a tree. That was why she never drove and always rode the city bus. Everyone laughed.

Except my parents.

When the service was over, the entire family went to a nearby restaurant. Mom's side of the family was huge, filling more than half of the restaurant. I took my mother aside and asked why no one interpreted.

"Mark and Luke say not good idea because Grandma different religion, and talk from woman priest wrong," she signed.

I'm gonna lose my ever-loving mind.

"Your mother funeral! You not need agree her religion," I signed. It was now *my* eyebrows' turn to dance a tarantella.

"Boys say not good idea," she repeated.

"You miss funny story, Grandma drive hit tree." And I told her the whole story.

******

"They couldn't have the service interpreted because of a difference in religious beliefs?"

I nodded. "J-Dubs are hell bent on not exposing themselves to other doctrines. It doesn't matter if you're at a wedding or a funeral; subjecting yourself to false religion only welcomes Satan, planting seeds of doubt."

"A funeral," Joel removed his glasses and massaged the bridge of his nose, "especially one for your own family," he sighed, "is a way to honor someone—say goodbye." I could see him struggling to understand J-Dub logic.

"Well, not to J-Dubs. Their funerals aren't really about honoring the deceased. They're a way to showcase Jehovah and the resurrection."

"I don't see how anything said at a funeral, or any other service, plants seeds of doubt." Joel massaged his temples.

He was really working overtime with this, and sadly, it was all too easy for me to explain, and if I had to—defend.

"I've thought a great deal about this. And here's what I've come up with: the J-Dub's entire belief system is based on the doubt of one man, Charles Taze Russell. He doubted the legitimacy of eternal hellfire, abandoned his own beliefs, and became an Atheist. He then doubted Atheism. So, he taught himself Greek and Hebrew, translated the scriptures on his own, and after several tweaks, a publishing company..." I smirked, "I mean...a *new religion* was born."

"Interesting. Where'd you learn this?"

"Pastor Russell's history is in one of their publications, minus my sarcasm. I guess he's allowed to doubt, but no one else is. Not even a sad Deaf woman, mourning the loss of her own mother. Somehow stories about her mother's driving blunders were off limits, especially when delivered via the lips of an evil woman pastor, baring the marks of false religion."

"What happened after the funeral?"

******

BACK HOME WITH DEAN, I was freed from nonsensical damnation but enslaved by his carnal fascination once more. Dean and I were on our way to pound-town, *alone*, when he suggested I go wake his unconscious friend—who'd crashed on our couch, after one too many drinks and hits from the bong.

"Go wake him?" I asked, hoping he didn't mean what I already knew he meant.

"Yeah. You know...go *wake* him," he said, with a longing in his voice that spelled it out for me.

To quell his overactive sex drive, I tried waking his friend myself to no avail. *This bastard is out cold.*

I snuck back into the bedroom, relieved, and said, "Sorry, he's out."

"Like hell he is!" Dean said, jumping out of bed.

Dean—not willing to let this opportunity slip by—forcefully woke his friend, telling him what I was willing to do. Now wide awake and ready, my very own wild seven-headed beast was in the dark, waiting on the couch.

Exit Bek, enter the Whore of Babylon.

I slipped into the living room and wasted no time sitting on his already hard, Hanes-covered cock, wrapping my legs around his waist, and rubbing myself on him in rhythmic motion. I threw my arms around his neck and pulled him into a kiss. He was no one I was attracted to, but I grew tired of being shoved into these precarious set-ups, getting very little out of them.

I inhaled forcing my tongue into his mouth. His tongue twisted around mine and I pulled away in playful haste, only to thrust it further in again, surprising him into a mini gag. If he was okay with using me, I was okay with using him.

And I did, until I came.

As my breathing slowed, he whispered, "Suck my cock."

I moved my head away from his neck and looked him in the eye, wantonly. I slithered my way down to the floor, resting on my knees between his legs. I tugged at his Hanes with my mouth and slid my hands up his thighs. I found the waistband and pulled them down. I looked up at him. He smiled as I wrapped my mouth around him. It was rock hard, bigger than average sized. I sucked and stroked with the effort of a porn star, looking up at him occasionally.

"You're so fuckin' gorgeous," he whispered, looking down at me.

I continued, gasping for air between vicious, energetic sucks and strokes. I sucked hard, soft, fast, and slow. Only, he never came. I looked up again. He moaned and stopped me.

"Just watching you, and feeling you, is enough. I've thought about you more than once since we met at the Halloween party."

That satisfied me.

Since Dean and I had been together, I was in constant competition with his porn collection. I knew I'd never be as beautiful or as airbrushed as the lustful bunnies he salivated over. I knew no matter what I did to quell his ravenous appetite, it would never be enough.

Hearing one man say, "watching you was enough" was *my* enough.

I smiled, wiped my mouth, and stood. I waltzed into the bedroom where a sex-greedy Dean lay on the bed awaiting a narrative. He came as I unfolded every detail. It was far too easy for me to go into porn star mode with no forethought.

******

"I have to ask, Rebekah, why did you do these things if you didn't want to? This is technically *abuse*." Joel rested his notepad on the desk and his eyes pierced my very soul.

I sighed, looking out the window, dissatisfied there was no playful bird to watch. Then I looked down, searching for something to distance myself from the mirror Joel held up. I didn't know I was being abused at the time.

I said the only thing I knew for sure. "I loved Dean so much it physically hurt. I had such a fierce, irrational love for him that it grew teeth and got stupid. It ate whatever he fed me. I was hypnotized by the way he protected me from everyone but himself."

"He sounds...radioactive."

"He was. But that didn't stop me from loving him. I guess, if you think about it, the same could be said about my family. Especially Luke."

"How so?"

"Luke was just as overbearing. My mother and I were repeatedly backed into corners, outnumbered, in that house. The way I forced myself to feel a faith that lay dead inside me from the very beginning was the same way I hung onto Dean's every word."

"Of course, you'd bend to Dean's whims—you'd already done it for the Governing Body, and your family's approval. It only makes sense you'd find someone to fit the mold your family showed you." Joel grabbed his notepad and started scribbling.

I guess that mirror wasn't so bad to look into; my gut already knew what he'd just said, long before setting foot into his office. That rationale had lodged itself somewhere in the back of my mind years ago, and I knew I'd been avoiding that place—the place where my head and heart meet—for a long time.

"Yeah, I'm a chameleon—accustomed to slipping on personalities that don't belong to me. At the time, Christian, interpreter, and porn star were only a few."

Joel nodded and looked at me, waiting.

******

SHORTLY AFTER I REACHED burnout at the Nursing Home, I got a job at Cumberland Farms—a convenience store within walking distance. I still had no car of my own. I filled shifts during the week and worked weekends at a tattoo shop on the Weirs Beach strip in Laconia—a city in the Lakes Region, buzzing with summer fun.

Weekends at the tattoo shop were my favorite. I was hired on as the face of the shop—booking appointments, drawing up tattoo stencils, prepping the stencils, washing needle equipment, and other random errands.

During the week at Cumby's, I saw many familiar faces and it didn't take long for the face of Dean's buddy to find me there, asking if he could come by to debrief about "that hot night" on my couch.

Request granted.

"Hey," he said, walking into the apartment.

Something immediately felt off, but I couldn't place it. We sat at the kitchen table, and I lit a cigarette.

"What's up?" I took a drag of my Camel Wide.

"May I?" He grabbed my cigarette, slipped it between his fingers, took a drag, and said, "I've been thinking a lot about that night. I don't know if you totally get how I felt."

I took my cigarette back, raised one eyebrow, and thought, *Rock hard schlong in my mouth? I think I get it.*

"I want you to know just how you made me feel. Maybe we could pick up where we left off." He took my hand and placed it on his growing stiffy. I jerked my hand back and jumped up.

"You need to go," I said, "now."

He stood, smiled, and said, "Can't blame a guy for trying," then left.

I felt like an unpaid, stupid whore. All afternoon I paced the apartment, chain smoking, unsure of what I'd tell Dean.

Should I tell him that his friend stopped by for round two? They weren't just friends but co-workers. And why could I tell his friend no but never say no to Dean?

When Dean came home from work, I tore off the Band-Aid and just told him. I expected him to be my knight in shining armor, come to my defense, fight for my honor, and confront his friend. He didn't.

"Can't blame a guy for trying," he said, cracking a beer open.

"You're not gonna say anything to him?" I said, standing before him, arms akimbo, ready for a knock-down, drag-out fight.

He sighed, looking down at his beer calmly. "No. We work together, and it would make things uncomfortable."

I sure wished his work ethic made its way to our apartment. Pissed, I stormed into the bedroom.

"Peanut, will you come back out here?"

I walked back into the living room and found him sitting on the couch. I stepped closer and sat on the coffee table across from him, placed my legs between his, folded my arms, and waited for an apology.

"I didn't mean for this to happen," he said.

Good. An apology.

"Just a few months ago, we got a new resident aid. I didn't think much of her when she came on staff, but we've been scheduled together a lot lately and… Peanut, you gotta believe I didn't mean for this to happen. She is just this…" I could see his mind hard at work searching for the right word, "*enigma* to me and I've just gotta know. I need to know if there's something more. I'm sorry."

It was an apology alright, but not at all for what I expected. He'd met someone else. My eyes welled up with tears and I pursed my lips together to avoid crying.

"I've gotta know if it's worth—"

"Breaking up over?" I finished, tears now streaming down my cheeks.

Four years. Four years of religious exploration and debates, rebellion, anarchy, scandalous sex, Marilyn Manson concerts, domestic abuse, drug use, tattoos, piercings, my first holiday celebrations, my mom's wayward year, my grandma's recent death...all of it faded away in seconds. I stood up, went into the bathroom, and looked in the mirror—shocked by who I saw and what I felt.

I think I know her.

She wiped a tear from her big brown eyes and flashed a half-smile. She flipped her long, curly, dark hair, raised one eyebrow, and slightly tilted her head to the side, parading the characteristic profile of her Italian nose.

She was free.

Free from domestic abuse, Dean's never-ending Hall Pass, his drunken tantrums, and emotional terrorism. She vowed to hold onto the good parts of the relationship, the things she learned. She was definitely keeping her unending curiosity for all things outrageous—she had always been drawn to them. She planned to pack the jagged pieces of her dignity and reshape them. She remembered to pack the softer parts of her heart; they were still good.

I was finally getting her out.

There was a knock on the bathroom door. I cracked it open, feeling lighter than when I went in, and I smirked at Dean, standing in the doorway.

"Can I come in?"

I opened the door and stepped aside, making room for him.

"This is weird to ask, but...could you trim the hair on the back of my neck? It's driving me crazy." He rubbed the little hairs under his long ponytail.

"Sure."

I wiped a tiny, runaway tear and grabbed the clippers from under the sink.

Yeah, her heart's still good.

A Misfit's Grand Climax

☺

"YOU SEEM TO KNOW yourself pretty well, Rebekah," Joel said, skimming last week's session in his notepad.

"Why do you say that?" I kicked off my shoes.

"You loved Dean, much to your own peril, but you took the break-up in stride."

I shrugged. "Yeah. We'd been together about four years, and I guess I knew it had come to an end."

"How did you know?"

"I don't know, instinct? Even before he told me about the *enigma* he worked with, something felt off. I knew before we broke up that it was coming," I shrugged, "I just knew. I'll always love Dean, but I think because I never felt him at the tracks, I knew he wasn't *the one*."

"Do you believe in *the one*?"

"Oh, yeah. We'll get to him."

"So, where did you go after Dean ended it?"

"I stayed with Dean for another month after we broke up. I had nowhere to go and had no clue how to be on my own; I lingered. But I figured out how to be on my own pretty quick the night he brought his new girlfriend home. I lay motionless on the couch while they carried on in the bedroom—*our* old bedroom. I knew I had to get the shit outta there, and fast."

"I'll bet!"

******

A WEEK AFTER DEAN'S sleepover, I found a place. I brought my now *two* black cats, Pogo the rat, and the little furniture I owned into a one-bedroom apartment in Laconia. I asked a friend from high school to room with me, and I was on my own for the very first time.

Being carless didn't stop me from finding a way to work. Not only did I now have rent to pay, but work was also a nice distraction.

I sat on the steps of the tattoo shop, crying.

Laz, the body piercer at the tattoo shop, sat with me. He was a tall, large, bald man, pierced everywhere. He looked scary but was just a big teddy bear, disguised as a huskier Anton LaVey.

"You should come over and hang out sometime," he said.

He lived in an apartment just a few houses down from mine. I was only a few steps away from spending most of my free time with him and Amanda—his best friend and co-piercer.

I walked over that evening and later that night found myself handcuffed and hogtied on the floor of Laz's bedroom. As all the D&D-Final-Fantasy-Lost-Boy characters paused in the doorway to gawk at the peculiar creature cuffed to her own limbs on the floor, Amanda said, "We're tying her up for the fuck of it."

And that's when I met Carter—on my back, disarmed.

Carter was shadowy, reserved, and dark. He had long, straight brown hair falling to the middle of his back, a frowzy beard, and long lashes drawn around his gorgeous, green eyes.

He intimidated me with his intellect. He knew things and read books I hadn't by authors like Cervantes, Orwell, and Dostoyevsky—all a far cry from the very unsophisticated, *Revelation Its Grand Climax at Hand!* I thought he was too good for me, too smart, too *something*. To my surprise, he was just as intrigued with me as I was with him.

Somewhere—between a few awkward conversations we'd had about our Tamagotchis and him loaning me George

174

Orwell's *1984*—he managed to sneak in a few kisses. Then he vanished. He was obscure and intriguing.

Although Carter had temporarily disappeared, the gang I'd befriended at Laz's kept me close. Finally, I belonged. Laz got me a job at the Mobil Mart in town and the timing was perfect. It was closer for me, and just about everyone in and out of Laz's apartment also worked there; transportation wasn't an issue.

When we weren't working or dawdling in the Mobil Mart parking lot all hours of the night, we loitered at Dunkin' Donuts armed with piss-poor coffee. If we grew tired of those locations, we either went to Laz's or to my apartment, which I heavily decorated with noosed baby dolls, Marilyn Manson posters, my Pet Monster (Louise), and random James Dean tapestries serving as curtains. Wherever we were was home as long as we were together.

Thanksgiving came fast that year and I suddenly found myself alone. Where my fellow misfits had plans with their families, I stayed home with a bowl of Ramen. Until a surprise visitor stopped by.

"I just wanted to be sure you were doing okay," Dean said, standing in my empty kitchen.

"I'm okay. Thanks?" I tilted my head to the side, stumped by his social call.

"I only have a few minutes. I just wanted to check on you and say I'm sorry about before, about all of it." His head hung low.

"Shit happens." I shrugged.

I didn't want to rehash our recent past. It was bad enough being alone for the holidays. I was willing to fake holiday mirth if the opportunity presented itself, but it hadn't. Standing before Dean, I longed to be alone with my sad bowl of Ramen.

"You were a big part of my life and I want you to know I'll always love you," he said.

I looked at him and realized a painful truth—I still loved him, madly. He offered an unearthly type of stability I knew and found comfort in. His presence somehow satisfied my persistent grief in an oddly consolable way.

"Can I come back tonight?"

I nodded, unsure why I agreed, hoping the girl in the mirror would understand.

He came back later that night as promised.

"You brought your guitar." I smiled, closing the door behind him.

"Yeah, thought we could have a jam session like we used to."

He set a six-pack of beer and a four-pack of cheap wine coolers on my counter. We sat on the living room floor, drinks in hand, while he tuned his guitar.

"Why aren't you with your girl?" I sipped my wine cooler.

"We're going through a rough patch, I guess."

I stared at Dean fiddling with his guitar strings. As his fingers busied, plucking and tuning, I suddenly saw *myself* as strings—rigid but yielding.

Watching him, I realized something. I allowed people in and out of my life, freely handing them opportunities to bully me softly and tune me to their liking. If I was able to cast a shadow of someone they needed, I was useful. Whether that be a good, Christian interpreter; a stepping-stone for planned boyfriend thievery; a punching bag; a slutty nymphomaniac; or a defiant daughter—perfectly positioned to accept the blame for Mom's own moral blunders—I could bend until almost broken.

But not quite.

I was glad I let Dean come over. It opened my eyes, it gave me closure, and insight. The revolving door of people tuning me, demanding their favorite songs, had to stop. Dean stayed the night, we shared one last intimacy, and he left the next morning.

******

"Did Dean's visit resolve anything for you?"

Anytime Joel held a mirror up, it didn't hurt nearly as much as when *I* held it up. He had this way of knowing when I was ready to look.

"It did, and it was a bit jarring."

"How so?"

"Well, I've always hated conflict—even if I was the reason for it—but if I could quietly slither into my chameleon suit, to diffuse a situation, I would. And I realized I'd spent four years doing that with Dean."

"Why couldn't you do that with your family and the Witness community? There was enough conflict there to allay, enough reasons for you to slip into your chameleon suit."

Shit. He's got me there.

But even I wasn't prepared for my own answer.

"I think, maybe, because my keen sixth sense trumps the chameleon suit," I said.

"Explain." He set the notepad down and crossed his leg, looking at me intently.

"I can wiggle my way through most situations by adjusting to my environment for short periods of time. Because I didn't want to go home—and wear the J-Dub straitjacket—I quickly understood that to live peacefully with Dean, I'd have to do his outlandish bidding.

"And that was okay, my gut somehow knew we wouldn't last forever; we were temporary. As far as being a J-Dub—that *is* forever. Like, paradise on earth *forever*, according to *their* will. Their suit wasn't one I could slip in and out of as easily. Their forever hurt. And my gut, the one formed at the tracks, was stronger than my J-Dub chameleon suit. Does that make sense?"

"Yes. You can't wear the suit if your gut is conflicted. Your instincts have the final say," Joel rephrased to the ceiling, making sure we were on the same page. Then he asked, "But wasn't your gut conflicted with all Dean's sordid requests?"

"Yes, but oddly those didn't jab me nearly as much as the J-Dub lifestyle did. Sorry about taking the scenic route to my point, I swear I have one. I blame having Deaf parents."

"No worries. So, Dean is now out of the picture. What next?"

******

CARTER EMERGED LIKE A whack-a-mole, long enough to be seen and gone just as quickly as he came. He faded into the background at a safe distance, but I noticed.

When Christmas came around, he'd left a note, taped to four king-size Twix bars, at the threshold of my apartment. I picked it up and opened the door.

"I saw that and left it for you to find," said Eric, a fellow Mobil Mart misfit.

Eric and my roommate were together so much that he practically lived with us. He was a spikey-haired, bleached blond freak, sporting athletic swishy pants and candor that was refreshing. He was real. He filled a brother void for me.

I opened the package, took a bite, and unfolded a note from "Satan Claus." *I like this guy.*

"To my dearest Rebekah,

First, I would like to say thank you for the wonderful kisses. I do so enjoy them. It is 1:00am Monday morning and I hope you appreciate the fact I am giving up my cigarette break to write to you. I look at it as penance for the sin of kissing you, but that's because I'm demented... I've missed seeing you these past two nights... I don't know why you like me enough to kiss but I feel horrible. I'm leaving the 26th. You're only the fifth girl I've ever kissed. I don't mean to sound conceited but feel privileged. I don't let anyone kiss me, or touch me for that matter... I wanted to let you know how special you are because you are. This isn't just a physical thing for me, but it can't be love. I'm trying hard not to make this a love thing... I hate you for doing this now, but I like what you're doing, and I like the pain that will come after I've gone. I hope you feel the same because least of all I don't want to hurt you unless you ask.

Sincerely, Carter"

I was taken aback and suddenly excited at just the mere thought of Carter. It was quite a sincere note for a couple of random kisses. I'd done more with Dean's friends. I wasn't about to let this mystery-man slip away.

I kept the note with me, wearing it out—unfolding it, reading it, refolding it. Then again—unfolding, reading, and folding. Unfolding, reading, and folding. It was nuts. I was desperately trying to wrap my brain around what fascinated him, and me, so much.

It was New Year's Eve, 1997. My roommate and Eric were tongue-tied by midnight. Nauseated and bored, I read Carter's note again. And again.

Come 2:00am, a long white Cadillac parked in front of my building. I opened the door to my second-floor apartment just in time to see a black trench coat flapping up the stairs. The winged beast landed on my doorstep.

"Where've you been hiding out?" I stepped aside to let this creature of the night in.

"At my mom's drinking firewater!" Carter pulled a bottle of Aftershock from his trench coat. "Want some?"

I coughed after taking a swig from the bottle. "Jesus! You've been drinking this all night?" It tasted like the numbing liquid my mom used to spray in my throat when it was sore.

"Hey, let's go in the other room." Carter grabbed my arm and led me toward the only bedroom in my apartment.

"Wait! Carter, I have a question for you," Eric said. "I heard that when you've been drinking, and someone even *mentions* being naked, you—"

"Naked!" Carter squealed.

A huge smile ate his face and he quickly stripped down to nothing. Hooking his fingers onto the doorframe, between the bedroom and living room, he hung upside-down like a monkey—hairy balls swinging to and fro.

Once Eric was satisfied with Carter's acrobatic striptease, Carter dressed, and we went into the bedroom.

There we were, on the bedroom floor, in the dark, and I suddenly remembered it was well past the 26th of December and he was still in Laconia.

"I've been listening to a lot of Nine Inch Nails lately cuz of you." He hiccupped.

"Me? Why?"

"It's really hard not to fall in love with you."

I was speechless. We had mutual friends, had kissed a few times, and he'd left a cryptic Christmas note taped to a package of Twix bars—that was it. *In love with me?*

My feeble, deformed identity was riddled with black, jagged pieces of shame and lewd, dangerous sex, exploitation, abandonment, fear, and betrayal. There were *some* tiny shards of love and affection haphazardly lodged in obscure places—a bit harder to find—but still there.

I still slept with Dean's memory every night, and I wasn't ready to fully appreciate the colorful mosaic Carter was beginning to piece together.

Carter rarely spoke, rarely expressed much emotion—remaining this dark, secretive creature—but he showed an obvious tenderness. Thankfully, cynicism hadn't rooted itself in too deep and I was able to spot authenticity peeking through his jaded, green eyes.

We spent every waking moment together after his New Year's Eve confession. Working the same graveyard shift hours made seeing each other easy. Nights off, we were with the crew, wherever that happened to be, or having private sleepovers.

Carter was different.

Sitting on the edge of my pull-out sofa one sunny afternoon, in the living room of my apartment, he showed me just how different he was. He started singing, "Crash." As I watched his lips move in unison with the music, I still couldn't believe that this Dostoevsky-reading-Nine-Inch-Nails-loving-trench-coat-wearing-shadowy-nineteen-year-old knew Dave Matthews well enough to sing along.

He had a soothing hopelessness. His loneliness looked like mine. He leaned in closer and kissed me. His tongue ring danced in my mouth as we undressed each other.

Until Carter, I'd only been fucked. Red, the Mullet Boy, simply ran off with my virginity, pleasing me not even once. Dean and I fucked like the cameras were always rolling, and when circumstances allowed, I played the role of human cum collector/provocative news reporter.

But not with Carter.

We spent the afternoon in a passionate haze while the song he surprisingly knew so well played on repeat, cheering us on. I had no idea I could achieve a toe-curling shudder from thrusting alone. It stirred a wave of emotion that bubbled forth, transformed into shallow breath, and brought a tear to my eye. It was love.

Weeks later I found myself shivering nervously in the passenger's seat of Carter's old Cadillac. He pulled into the driveway of an adorable, grey, raised ranch, and turned the car off. He looked at me and smiled.

"You ready?" he asked.

I took a deep breath and exhaled. I wasn't ready. I'd never done this before. Memories of appeasing Dean's needy libido seemed less nerve-wracking.

"It'll be painless. I promise," he said.

Standing on the front steps of this raised-ranch was a tall, dapper fellow with brown hair, a thick moustache, and dimples—eager to make my acquaintance.

"Hello!" he said as we came up the walkway. "Carter! I'm so glad you brought your girlfriend for dinner! Come in!"

"Hey, Phil. This is Bek. Bek, this is my stepdad, Phil." Carter introduced us as we stepped inside.

"Hi. It's nice to meet you." I extended my hand, and Willem Dafoe's look-alike pulled me in for a bear hug.

"It's so nice to meet you!" He squished me excitedly. "Paula! Come meet Bek!"

Phil took my hand, leading me through the living room. The smell of a home-cooked meal hit me, and I almost teared up.

A petite lady with brown, shoulder-length hair and a beautiful smile emerged from the kitchen, wiping her hands on a towel.

"Hi!" she said, hugging me. "It's so nice to meet you!"

"It's nice to meet you, too."

Are worldly people, parents, *really this nice?*

She smiled. "Dinner's almost ready. Phil, why don't you show her the bar?"

"Good idea, c'mon!" Phil guided me through the house, leading me to the top step of the basement.

I took in the neon bar signs that decorated the wall as I glided down the stairs. Standing at the bottom step I scanned the room. A sectional couch, coffee table, TV, VCR, fireplace, karaoke machine, and dartboard filled the space. At the fully stocked, hardwood bar, barstools set in a perfect line. It was almost like Aunt Kathy's, and nothing like the vacant demon-possessed basement I had envisioned.

Once we were upstairs, Phil taught me something very important.

"Now, Bek, if you and Carter are going to be together for a while," Phil said, eyeballing Carter and putting his arm around my shoulder, "there's an important thing you need to know how to do."

Carter walked up to the counter, rolling his eyes. My curious gaze shifted between the two of them.

"You need to know how to make my drink." Phil grabbed a bottle of Johnnie Walker Black. "I always use an old-fashioned cocktail glass, a little ice, and as I pour my whiskey, I count to four," he said, pouring generously. "One...two...three..."

"You're counting pretty slow, Phil," Carter said.

"Four... the slower, the better." Phil winked.

"Dinner's ready!"

Sitting next to Carter at the table, I felt lost.

It had been years since I had dinner at the table with my own family, and this was far removed from the times Dean ordered wings and pizza, or we had fried bologna sandwiches *with* a side dish, while sitting on the shag carpet. This was a real meal. I couldn't remember the last time I'd had one or the last time I sat at a table with people and cloth napkins.

Phil grabbed a platter and began serving himself. As the platters of food were passed around the table, Italian-style, he asked, "So, Bek, what religion are you?"

My eyes widened. Carter caught on immediately and looked frantically between me and Phil.

I wasn't sure how to respond and I didn't want to be rude.

"Um… I was raised a Jehovah's Witness." I looked down, poking at a broccoli pastry puff with my fork.

"That's a Christian religion, right?" Phil asked.

Carter reminded him that religion wasn't good dinner conversation. He was ignored.

"What do they believe?" Paula asked.

The tension in the room was growing. My heart beat faster. I fidgeted in my seat and asked for the pepper. Carter passed it. I peppered my prime rib and thought about how to answer the question. I remembered wanting to pull on a drunken cow's udders the last time a question like this was posed. Only there weren't any drunk cows around to distract me.

I can't just sit here, thinking, then blurt, "I don't know." She asked what they believe…

******

"Hadn't Dean armed you with all the rough edges needed to feel comfortable with the subject?" Joel looked up from his chicken-scratches.

"You mean, was I Teflon? Not then, no. As repulsed as I was (and am) by organized religion, I didn't like talking about it. And I knew I couldn't say what I really wanted to say."

"Which was?"

"The truth. *My* truth."

"Well, let's have it." He put his pen down and waited.

"The GB manipulate their flock with deep-seated, fear-mongering mind control. They refuse blood transfusions, and I'm lucky I never needed one because I'd probably be dead. They don't celebrate holidays, vote, join the military, get involved with politics, invest in retirement funds, or attend college.

"And to explain why, they'll dance around piss-poor, misinterpreted explanations, making their reasons sound rational. They feel it's more important they busy themselves with life-saving door-to-door work, informing householders that the Great Tribulation is upon us, and will soon be followed by Armageddon to rid the world of anyone who doesn't stroke Jehovah's chubby.

"Once Armageddon has run its course, and all worldly people have been burned alive, the Thousand Year Reign begins. Satan is chained up and thrown into an abyss, while Jesus sits as King on a lofty throne to God's right. Faithful sheep spared during Armageddon will be tasked with cleaning up the mounds of burnt, rotted, manure-like flesh of Jehovah's enemies.

"Then, Satan—that rabid little minx—is released from his abyss for one final striptease, leading all near-perfect sheep toward sin and degradation in one last-ditch effort. Those who join Satan's conga line will be destroyed, and the sheep who resist temptation will be rewarded with perfection forever."

"Why didn't you want to say that?"

"When I tell people how I really feel, or how I really see the world, things get weird. It's best for me to say less. Except here. I guess our sessions wouldn't be effective if I didn't tell you how I really feel."

"True. So, what did you say to Phil?"

"I waved goodbye to the memory of a drunken cow, tugging on its udder, stepped out of Satan's conga line and back into reality by simply stating that J-Dubs believe in God, Jesus, and heaven. But not eternal hellfire or the trinity. I told him they didn't celebrate holidays, vote, or accept blood transfusions."

"Was that so hard?" Joel peeked at the clock.

"No. Not until they asked about my parents, and I had to explain why we don't see much of each other. That always hurts, and I suppose is the reason I don't like talking about my upbringing or religion—because the subject of family always comes up. And I miss mine."

Tears welled up almost instantly.

Joel handed me a soft tissue.

"Thanks. The evening ended with me almost choking to death," I said, wiping my eyes and changing the subject.

"Oh?" Joel asked.

"Distracted by my own ridiculous image of Beelzebub's conga-line striptease, I'd over-seasoned my prime rib and when I took a bite, I inhaled nothing but pure black pepper."

"How long had you been away from the Truth at this time?" Joel closed his notebook.

"Five years, and it still had its hooks in me." I crumpled the tissue and put my shoes on after I saw the time on the clock.

"Next week?" he said.

"Next week."

Walking out of Joel's office, I'd never felt so conflicted. On one hand, looking into Joel's mirror and discovering why I was how I was felt so cathartic—as therapy should. And on the other hand, looking at myself and diving deep into my own existentialism was harrowing.

What if I don't like who I see? Suppose my family is justified in discarding me...

Johnnie Walker Wisdom

"HOW ARE YOU this week?" Joel opened his steno pad.

I shrugged. The truth was I didn't even know anymore. Everything we'd talked about thus far had taken me down several rabbit holes, and I couldn't tell if they were alleviating or exacerbating my experience as a human.

"I'm tired."

"Long week?"

"Every week I interpret is a long week. Whenever my hands go up—"

"You can see your parents... But you're not able to see your parents."

I sighed. *Yes.* "I love my job, but I hate my job."

"Missing the Mobil Mart days?"

"Fuck, yes. Things were simpler then."

******

EIGHT MONTHS HAD PASSED. Carter and I were exclusive and had decided to move in together. During the move to our two-bedroom apartment, just around the corner, I called Phil to borrow a tarp, and he was beside himself with joy because I'd reached out. He was genuinely the happiest person I'd met in a long time.

Carter and I worked overnight shifts; me at Mobil Mart, and he at a local heat sink factory. During weekly dinners out with Carter's parents, Phil—after a few glasses of whiskey—told everyone in close proximity that his future daughter-in-law called him to borrow a tarp.

"They needed a tarp and she called me—*me!*" he said, pointing at his chest. Paula and Phil treated me like their own, and I'd almost forgotten what parents could be like.

Frustrated with my increasingly unreliable schedule at Mobil Mart, I gave my notice and started working first shift at Lewis & Saunders (L&S) as an aerospace-metal-tubular-parts-marker. Carter stayed on third shift at his job, and we spent time together between 3:30 and 10:00pm.

Living with Carter I learned that the language he spoke was born of his fingertips, lyrics to his favorite songs, and quotes from his favorite movies.

Exposing his soft, vulnerable underbelly rarely happened unsolicited. I almost needed a crowbar to peel back years of his hardened shell. It was something I suspected at the onset of our relationship, and I accepted that it was just his way.

Each morning, after he left the heat sink factory, he'd stop at L&S to find Deby, my tan Geo Prism. He'd leave love notes, written on the backs of bank deposit slips, on the driver's seat.

They'd relay that he missed me during his overnight shifts, couldn't wait until I got home, and he'd crack my back for me later that night. Pulling me into a tight hug and squeezing his fists into the middle of my back as he went up my spine was a nightly ritual.

Everything changed the day Deby had no note to pass.

I came home and found Carter on the couch, hanging his head. I sat next to him. Sidney broke the silence with a soft chirrup as she entered the room.

"What is it?" I asked.

"Phil's in the hospital, he had some sort of accident, and he's in ICU," he said, looking at the floor.

At Lakes Region General Hospital, we found Paula sitting with Phil in ICU. Two humungous, black- and purple-colored eggs jutted from either side of his forehead.

I touched my forehead remembering when uninvited blows to the head shook me to my core and sent me out into cold winter nights, wandering the small city of Franklin.

Phil's bruised knobs put all of mine to shame.

Sitting at a small conference table in a private room, we learned about Phil's condition. Then, the nurse realized she could no longer dance around the question we all had. She looked the three of us dead in the face, and said, "He has a five percent chance of survival."

The room became uncomfortably still. A faint groan whimpered from the cheap pleather chair I fidgeted in, breaking the unnerving silence.

******

"What in the world happened?"

I shrugged. "No one knows. All we did know at the time, was Phil and Paula were at a dart tournament, drinking with their friends, as usual. When they were ready to leave Paula said she lost Phil in the crowd so, she went outside. She found him lying on the ground, his glasses thrown about twenty feet from his body. When she turned him over, she saw the bumps on his forehead growing."

"And no one knows how that happened?" Joel rubbed his chin.

I shook my head. "There was an investigation. It made local news, but no one knew for sure if it was an accident or...you know... Anyway, Phil was airlifted to another hospital in northern New Hampshire, and that's where he died."

"I'm sorry."

I showed Joel the palm of my hand and nodded, eyes closed. I hate saying or hearing the phrase "I'm sorry" when learning of someone's death. I just do. I ignored his condolences.

"I recall two things vividly. While listening to Paula rehash events leading up to Phil's death, I remembered the elegant plumes of smoke from her Virginia Slims, swirling. I got lost in the way they sprinted a marathon—exiting through the small gap in the passenger door's window, never to be seen again."

"What else do you remember?"

"In the dark, while lying in the bed that night, I touched Carter's face and it was wet."

"This surprised you?"

"The reason he was tearing up didn't surprise me, it was the fact he teared up at all. He was usually so detached."

"Well under the circumstances—"

"Oh, I don't disagree. It was just...different."

"Silly question, but the funeral?"

"There wasn't a funeral. We hosted a celebration of life—basically a party—there was plenty of food and Johnnie Walker Black for everyone. No one stopped pouring until they counted to four. It was far better than any service I'd been to at the Kingdom Hall. No ill-prepared elder gave a talk of remembrance, for a person they may or may not have even known, using the resurrection as an opportunity to convert any non-believers in attendance. Remembering someone for who they were, while they were here, was far better than any hollow hope of seeing them again as a mindless drone in the *New System*."

"How were things afterward?"

******

WE SPENT MOST OF our time with Paula, cleaning out the raised-ranch, and moving her into a small condo along Weirs Beach. While helping her move I doubled over, falling on the sectional, contorting myself into a fetal position. Carter came through the hall to find me balled up on the sofa. He tried helping me up, and I almost fell to the floor. He caught me, picked me up with one swoop, and carried me to the car like a little girl.

I stubbornly endured the pain for a few months.

"It's not just cramps, Bek. If we can't have sex without you crying, there's something wrong. You have insurance, go to the doctor," he said.

I saw a doctor, had an ultrasound, and they detected a potential issue.

"You have a backup of endometrial tissue," the doctor said. "The lining of your uterus goes up into your fallopian tubes rather than down and expelling itself during your menses. It causes pain when the endometrial deposits stick to your uterus and ovaries. It can also adhere to other organs, and that usually ends up critical."

I crumpled my face.

"Basically, what should be leaving your body during your cycle stays, sticking to your fallopian tubes and ovaries. That caused a cyst to burst this time and next time could stick to other organs if left untreated."

My face softened. "What now? Is it curable?"

"Controllable and treatable. But no, not curable. To be certain that it is indeed endometriosis, we need to perform a laparoscopy," he said. "We make two small incisions, put a little camera up there, and see what we can find."

The outpatient procedure was scheduled. Carter and I were at the Franklin hospital to meet the general surgeon by 7:00am the following Friday. I changed into the provocative hospital gown they supplied and sat nervously, watching the anesthesiologist push his cart of sedation toward me.

"Is your equipment sanitized?" I asked inspecting all the tools on his cart.

That's all I need—dirty hospital needles piercing my flesh while Jehovah looks down laughing, admitting in his deep, Santa voice that he planted them there for my comeuppance.

The anesthesiologist laughed. "Of course, it is. I need you to count backward from ten—"

I pushed his hand away. "I won't count until I meet the surgeon." I clenched Frederick, remembering when I used to carry him into Luke's room. I was prepared to drag this out all day.

If I die while still disfellowshipped, before Armageddon, I'm doomed. No resurrection for me. I'm unrighteous and—

Just then, I spotted a tiny Japanese man, eating animal crackers, in faded blue surgeon's gear and booties walking my way.

And there he is—Jehovah—disguised as Japanese Satan in scrubs.

He stepped up to the bed, popping animal crackers into his mouth.

"We do lap-a-ros-copy, yeah?" he asked, gnawing on a little lion cookie.

His accent was so thick I barely understood him.

I looked at him blankly.

He reassured me they were just going to "make small incisions" and that the surgery was "only half hour." Then he skipped away in his booties, swinging his kindergarten snack box.

"Ready now?" the anesthesiologist asked, prepping me with his plastic-wrapped, surgical steel equipment.

I wasn't ready. I knew God was pretty pissed at me, and he was bleeding me out from the inside of my uterus. He'd already mysteriously taken my boyfriend's stepdad, and I was pretty sure my number was up—

I felt a poke and jumped. "Hey!"

"Ready?" the anesthesiologist asked, injecting me with liquid unconsciousness.

"Well, not really buuut..." I drifted off mid-protest.

They wheeled me toward the operating room. I clutched my bear and wiggled my finger at Carter. I saw a blurry version of him wiggle his finger back.

I woke to the shadowy blob of a nurse smiling above me. "You made it, and so did your bear!"

I focused my eyes on her image and as I regained sight, looked down at my right arm. I still had my bear in a death grip. I could make out that Frederick was wearing a surgeon's mask and a hairnet, too. I was wheeled back to the outpatient recovery area.

I looked over at Carter and asked, "How long was I in there for?"

"It really was 'only half hour.'" He smirked.

"My back desperately needs a-crackin'," I mumbled, shifting uncomfortably in the hospital bed.

"I'll give you one later."

After successfully throwing up dry toast and Gatorade, per nurse's orders, they dressed me and sent us home. The worst part wasn't the procedure, the panic of dirty hospital needles, or my thirty-minute brush with death. It was my family's absence; they didn't call or come to check on me once.

******

"Did they know about the surgery?" Joel removed his glasses and wiped them with a cloth.

"Yeah. Carter had told my mom. I wondered what was so different about rescuing me with a broken clavicle one cold winter night, versus being there for me while under the knife... All I could come up with was..." I stopped talking once I realized that as soon as I said the words out loud, they would become facts I wasn't ready to face.

"What? What did you come up with?" Joel put his glasses on, readying his pen.

I sighed. "The older I get, the more I lose them. All of them."

"That's why you think they weren't there after the surgery? Because people age and drift apart?"

"Not entirely, but—"

"Because I can tell you, nothing would ever stop me from being there for my kids. Not old age. Distance. Nothing." He shook his head.

And there they were—the words I didn't want to hear but needed to.

******

IT ONLY TOOK THE weekend and one tiny, little Percocet to recover from the procedure. I wish I could say one cheap-ass pill was all it took to recover from my family not being there, but I'd be lying.

Thankfully, the Mobil Misfits were there all weekend, coming in and out of our two-bedroom apartment, checking on me, feeding me, keeping me company.

When our little Gang of Rebels started growing up, I felt a different kind of pain. Amanda, Kane, and Laz moved to Cambridge, Massachusetts together. Tess and Dustin moved to Queens, New York after announcing their engagement—leaving Angie, Eric, Shari, Kris, Carter, and me behind.

Carter and I filled the void by working the same schedule, now together, at the same company (L&S). Then, we adopted two seven-week-old dachshund littermates. Bartok, the runt of the litter, was long-haired and beautiful. His brother, Moron, was short-haired and quite dapper.

I was not only distracted by puppy love, but I was preoccupied along with Angie as we were being fitted for bridesmaid dresses to be in Tess and Dustin's wedding.

During their wedding reception six months later, the unexpected happened.

Mid electric slide, *boogie woogie woogie*, the music stopped, and I was ushered to the front of the reception hall. Carter stood waiting for me to join him.

"I don't mean to interrupt this celebration, but I'd like to say something," he said into the D.J.'s mic.

I stood in front of Carter, hoping he wasn't about to do what I thought he was about to do.

"I, too, am in love with someone special, and I wanted to know..." Carter pulled a small, black, velvet box out of his pocket, lowering himself to one knee.

My eyes widened and I gently shook my head, mouthing to him from behind my dangling hair, "Not here. What are you doing?"

He looked up, ignoring me, and said, "If she would marry me?"

He flipped the box open and inside was a ring with tiny, little diamonds all along a white gold band. I could feel every eye in the reception hall on me. Gasps and gushes pierced the air, fading into an endless echo. He stood up and placed the ring on my finger. I threw my arms around his neck and cried.

"Is that a yes?" he asked, hugging me.

I nodded, still crying. But I wasn't crying out of joy or excitement.

******

"Why were you crying? Were you averse to marrying him?" Joel scrunched his face.

"No. It wasn't him. I mean, it *was* awkward sharing such a private moment with a hundred strangers, but what shook me was the chaos churning in my chest. In that moment, my mind was in hysterics. There I was, innocently attempting to slide electrically across the dance floor in an ankle-length gown. Then, suddenly, I'm engaged. My mind played a quick game of chess and I saw it all—wedding bands, a puffy white dress, family, kids, and a house with Bartok and Moron."

"That doesn't sound bad."

"No, it doesn't. But I felt bad for Carter. He was happy, he was fucking *emoting.* I was deathly afraid of crushing the growing optimism inside him."

"Why? How?"

"Because Carter's face had our future written all over it. He was ready for marriage, a family, a house, whatever, I don't know. But for me that meant growing up—responsibility. Which meant being responsible for my own impending doom.

"Where Carter saw a future, I saw death and my own grim imaginings of Armageddon; sudden darkness, swirling clouds, rampant lightning bolts, fire, earth-shattering terror spanning all corners of the earth; death, and the rotting flesh of corpses for miles and miles, permeating the air with a stench too repellent for words. And then I saw myself, in a white gown—bloody, filthy, and lifeless—at the top of a human body heap, eyes widened, looking toward the sky."

"Oh. Do you see these things…often?"

I scrunched my face and gestured *so-so* with my hand. "Sometimes. And with that haunting scenario, you tell me—how could I possibly allow myself to be happy? If I'm not fit for God, why do I deserve joy?"

Joel sighed and said, "Because you're human Rebekah, and all humans deserve peace, happiness, and self-actualization. By honoring a promise you *made to yourself,* for the sake of authenticity, you've done nothing wrong. Remember that." He was almost scolding me. "Did you call off the wedding, or any subsequent planning, as a result of this vision?"

"No. I should have. Not because I didn't love Carter but…I just should have. Instead, we spent nine months planning for bridesmaids, groomsmen, a D.J., a wedding cake, seating chart, invitations, RSVPs, flowers, dresses, tuxes, and party favors. It was turning into quite an affair. People I barely knew suddenly appeared on the guest list because if you invite one person, well, you have to invite their cousin."

"Weddings can be a pain. Did your parents get an invitation, even though you knew—"

"Knew they wouldn't come? Of course. Just before the wedding, we braved the dead-end road I grew up on and found ourselves parked in my parent's driveway. I knew they'd say no, but I clung to a tiny bit of hope. I still gave in to the pipedream of a Daddy-daughter dance, while he clumsily sang John Denver's, "Sunshine on My Shoulder" in my ear the way he did when I was little. He always thought he was singing, but the man is literally tone-deaf." I chuckled. "I hand delivered the invitation and practically begged."

"And?"

"My mom said she wished they could, but I knew better than to ask. She requested pictures and flowers from my bouquet. I said I'd bring them by after the wedding, and we left. In the car Carter got pissed. He said if they wouldn't come, he wasn't sharing any part of our day. He said if they wanted anything from the wedding, or reception, they'd have to show up to claim it.

"As we backed out of the driveway, I saw my mom at the kitchen window waving; it broke my heart. No Mother-of-the-Bride-mani-pedi-spa day. No Daddy trying to softly sing John Denver in my ear. I was now left with a slighted fiancé speeding down the quiet road I grew up on."

"Trouble in paradise already…"

I nodded. "I should have run screaming. I should have stopped all wedding planning right there. But it was too late. We were weeks away from the wedding at that point. My gut jabbed hard enough to draw blood. Despite my attempts to fight all systematic indoctrination—where even years of living with Dean, on the opposite end of the spectrum, didn't help—the mind-altering J-Dub dogma still sat incredibly deep. Those villainous fucking mutant claws pierced flesh and just wouldn't let go."

Joel closed his notebook and looked at me. "Do me a favor. Start journaling."

I agreed, wondering what good that would do.

Woman in Chains

THE NEXT WEEK I sat across from Joel with a fresh, almost-untouched journal in my lap. It was medium sized and deep maroon with gold swirlies and paisley shapes. It had a silky ribbon bookmark attached, and its hard cover wrapped itself around the front of the journal, sealing it closed with a long magnet.

"That's a nice journal."

"Thanks. I got it during my weekly jaunt to Borders, downtown," I said, eyeballing it. It *was* pretty spiffy.

"Have you written anything yet?"

"Well, to be honest, it's been years since I journaled; I don't know what to write. But yes. I did." I opened the journal and flipped to the first page.

"Oh?"

"It's a quote I read, somewhere, that I've always loved. 'I sent my Soul through the Invisible, some letter of that After-life to spell: And by and by my Soul returned to me and answered: I Myself am Heaven and Hell.'"

Joel looked at me and dipped his head. "Who said it?"

"Omar Khayyam. An Iranian poet, I guess?"

"Why do you love it?"

"Because that's me...heaven *and* hell. I've sent my soul to some interesting places, and each time have discovered I could be both my own savior *and* my own assassin. The people I was with were only circumstantial."

"If you already know that, why are you in therapy?"

"I guess because I needed more time to figure that out. Also, I still don't know which role to play for myself."

Joel flipped through his notes and asked, "So did you save or assassinate yourself the closer it got to your wedding day?"

I smirked looking down. "I loaded and cocked the gun myself."

******

THE WEDDING PLANNING RESUMED by day, and I fought the clawed demon by night.

Our theme—little kids in baggy clothes acting out adult scenarios—was everywhere. It appeared on the cake topper, the invitations, and the heart-shaped cookie-cutter wedding favors. Along with tiaras, a photographer and flowers and boutonnieres and gift bags for the wedding party and every other little detail you could possibly think of when planning a wedding.

Somewhere in that premarital mess, I found comfort in one tiny detail of the wedding. I swooned over plain, white daisies surrounded by Baby's Breath. They brought me peace. I was fascinated by the infinitesimal lines on each petal and had fallen hard for the yellow, bumpy nodules in their centers. The daisies were just something I felt.

The night before the wedding—after the rehearsal dinner toasts, and final payments had been made—I brought my husband-to-be outside where a ten-man limo was parked, waiting to take the guys wherever they wanted. I supposed the harbored guilt I felt about not wanting to get married seeped through in the form of extravagant gifts.

While Carter and nine guys went galivanting in a limo, I opted to stay behind with my girlfriends. After a couple of drinks out, we spent a chill evening at my soon-to-be mother-in-law's beach condo where Carter and I had been living temporarily.

While spoon-feeding myself Cheerios the morning of the wedding, I felt the honey nut flavor rise. Within seconds I was in the bathroom puking. Anxiety set in, and I found myself fighting the clawed fiend again. Staring into the toilet bowl, forearms resting on the seat as a cushion for my forehead, I closed my eyes and saw the haunting scene play out for the hundredth time.

Dark, swirling clouds hovered low from the sky. People scampered looking for shelter, screaming, "They were right! The Jehovah's Witnesses were right!" And by this time (2001), I expected Peter Jennings to have already delivered the news of impending doom to all those tuned in to ABC...

"Good evening, ladies and gentlemen. The United Nations unanimously declared 'International Peace and Security.' The charge in their preamble closely resembles a warning many may have heard while standing at their own front door with one of Jehovah's Witnesses. For years, it's been their mission to reveal their God, Jehovah, and his plan. The fall of the seventh world power is now upon us. Let's hope their God chooses to remember those of us who haven't heeded the warning..."

******

"Wait, Peter Jennings was going to tell the free world about Armageddon?" Joel said, trying not to laugh.

"In my head, yeah. And after his address, the earth would rumble, and we'd hear the battle cry of God's righteous army. The sky would turn black and fiery balls of fury would be sling-shot from heaven as everything went up in flames."

"These nightmares are quite persistent, aren't they?"

"They were determined to wreck my wedding day. And again, I wondered, 'Why bother building a life if Armageddon is just gonna take it away?'"

"Did anything soothe your panic?"

"Yeah, I remembered that with Jehovah's favor, one could be kept safe from the millions of screaming people, upturned vehicles, crashing buildings, looting, gunfire, and inevitable death."

"By going back?"

"That and making it to a bunker in time."

Joel crumpled his eyebrows and readied his pen.

"While growing up, images of bunkers were planted in our little infant minds. These bunkers were where small, one-hour, Bible study groups were held—the ones my family once hosted from our demon-infested basement."

"Witness Fallout Shelters. Interesting. Do you think you chose little kids in oversized clothes as a wedding theme, because you mourned the innocence of your childhood?" Joel asked off, but not off, topic.

"Hmm. Maybe. Makes sense."

"Anyway, go on."

"Angie, Tess, and Jodi thought it was cute that I was puking. They thought I was just nervous, excited to marry Carter. Little did they know I was fraught with terror."

******

HORRIFIED OR NOT, I became a Mrs. at the age of twenty-four. Our wedding resembled most typical, American weddings; except, as I'd foreseen, there was no Daddy-daughter dance with him softly singing John Denver in my ear. There weren't four over-protective brothers threating their new brother-in-law in jest, like I'd imagined.

It was a very unevenly attended event. Most folks in the buffet line were on Carter's side of the roster. The only people from my side were a handful of friends, Johnny, my nephew, Aunt Kathy, her new husband Keith, his daughter, and Jesse, who was disfellowshipped once again.

Even with them there, I couldn't shake the feeling of my phantom limbs. I saved flowers for my mom like she'd asked, knowing I'd give them to her at some point.

The next day, we met up with my new mom-in-law at her boyfriend's house to gather all the wedding gifts they'd transported for us.

"Did all the guys pay their share for the limo?" Paula kissed me on the cheek as we walked in.

"Um, no. Not yet." I kissed her back.

"Well, I heard the guys went to Massachusetts for the dirtier strip clubs. Lap dance after lap dance. Did you get any Carter?" she said.

"Uh, where are all the gifts?" Carter asked, quickly changing the subject.

I figured ten guys, a limo, and alcohol on the eve of a wedding would equate to some debauchery, but I didn't want to hear the squalid details.

Once we left with gifts in tow, I sat in the passenger's seat, arms crossed, glaring at him from the corner of my eye, and said, "Lap dances?"

"Um, yeah, there were a few," he said, driving down Union Avenue.

"Did you have any?" I kept my eyes forward.

"Does it matter?"

"Yes! It explains why you were all over me in the bridal suite. It wasn't *me* you were hot for—it was all the skanky pussy flaunted in your face from the night before!"

Visions of perverse, sexual escapades filled my mind. I was hot with disgust because I no longer saw Carter. I saw myself competing with Dean's porn collection again.

"It was a gift on *you*!" He pulled over on the side of Union Avenue, got out, and walked down the street, leaving me in the car.

I hopped out, abandoning the car and all the wedding gifts, to run after him.

"What the fuck?" I asked, grabbing his arm.

"Yes, there were strippers and lap dances. But what the fuck do you think happens the night before a wedding? I didn't ask for the limo. Don't punish me."

He stomped down Union Avenue.

Stuck somewhere between pornographic nights spent with Dean and the John Denver ballad spinning on my mind's turntable, was a tangled young woman. My head was clouded by the clean, white innocence of a wedding and the raunchy nightclub girls Carter had most likely bunny-bumped with all night.

Carter, this guy who I thought was so different, was just another voyeuristic freak. And I was now married to him. I couldn't get the lap dances out of my head and felt like a huge hypocrite for even being bothered by them. I'd done more with strangers than those dancing trolls probably had.

Then I did what I do best—I slipped into my chameleon suit. And against my better judgment, I revealed a wild side Carter didn't know I had. I sifted through my rolodex-o-sexual-oddities and dusted off some oldies but goodies.

Rather than the tried-and-true missionary position we'd become accustomed to, I rode him hard, like a wild boar, bucking ferociously until we both lay in a pool of sweat. I went down on him like a starving cum queen and sat on his face, jerking uncontrollably, until he was soaked from the neck up. He wasn't at all displeased. But I wasn't at all satisfied. Amidst my chameleon-like superpowers, something was still missing.

Hopefully we'd find it on our honeymoon.

We were set to stay at an all-inclusive resort in Playa Del Carmen, Mexico. Our room was at the end of a long jungle path lined with gorgeous, lush plants, monkeys in palm trees, and adorable Agoutis.

Daring to leave the resort, we explored the jungle at Excaret, walked the Mayan Ruins, and went snorkeling in the Puerto Morelos Reef.

Well... Carter went snorkeling.

Water and I aren't friends.

I love the ocean and almost everything about it—the breeze, the smell, the negative ion charge, the waves, the saltiness on my skin, and the birds—but I hate the water.

A snorkeling tour in the Puerto Morelos Reef sounded amazing. In theory. I'm not a strong swimmer, nor do I enjoy being in the water for long periods of time. If my feet don't touch something solid, I panic.

I expected my new husband to stay with me and hold my hand, guiding me through the water. Together, we'd see all types of vibrant, tropical fish, and maybe find a bit of romance.

But no. He swam away, joining the excursion group at the reef and left me bobbing in the water—alone and scared.

A nice woman from Ireland stayed with me and held my hand until my panic waned. Then, she joined her own family at the reef.

There I was. All alone in the Gulf of Mexico, heart thumping wildly in my throat. I could hear my own breath like a frantic echo in my ears. I was about thirty feet from the boat. I prayed to the only God I ever knew for strength and courage. I was *that* desperate.

I heard the Mexican guide from our boat shout, "Señora! Señora! Barracuda!"

I anxiously looked around. Snorkel gear wobbling on my head, mouthpiece lodged awkwardly in my mouth, my own breath rebounding in my head; I sounded like Darth Vader underwater.

Without a moment's hesitation, our brave Mexican guide abandoned the boat, swam to me, grabbed my wrist, and forcefully pulled me closer to him just as this long, scaly beast with teeth brushed past me.

He pushed me up into the boat and climbed in after me. I sat shivering as this man gently swaddled me in a beach towel. He took such great care in making sure I was okay. Granted, it was his job, but there was a tenderness in his manner—one I didn't feel coming from Carter.

I looked out at the reef, silently cursing my new husband. He splashed boyishly in the water, gawking at exotic fish, without a care in the world while strange Mexican men rescued me from a barracuda's bloodthirsty pursuit. I could feel my face contorting into a scowl.

"Want a Coke?" the guide asked, handing me a can of Coca-Cola.

I shook my head. I felt nauseous.

"Can you bring me to shore? I see hammocks on the beach," I whimpered.

He smiled, nodded, and brought me to shore. Once I was settled on a hammock, wrapped in a towel like a burrito, he ventured back toward the reef to corral the other nineteen people bobbing happily in the water. I secretly hoped the barracuda would find Carter.

Once we were safely back at the resort, I calmed myself while painting ceramics; it quickly became my favorite pastime during our entire trip.

That night, after dinner, Carter and I wandered the jungle paths, margaritas in hand, planning our next course of action—move out of his mom's condo and try our luck in New York City.

NH hadn't inspired growth. Same jobs, same friends, same scene. I was ready to escape the landscape that had given birth to Armageddon-filled nightmares. Being as young as we were, we could have the world by the ass in the city that doesn't sleep.

******

"Sounds like the marriage was off to a rocky start."

"It was. I thought the honeymoon and plans to leave New Hampshire would push us in the direction of a new start."

"Did it?"

"Briefly. Until 9/11—which happened exactly thirty days after our wedding."

"Oh, I can't imagine that quieted your anxiety one bit."

"Made it worse. My darkest fears were materializing right before my eyes—fire, buildings crumbling to the ground, people running and screaming. My body felt like it was being held hostage. Seeing people jump out of the World Trade Center was just...*unbelievable!* You know? It was surreal. I'd barely wiped the sleepy seeds of Mexico from my eyes before my whole world changed."

Joel nodded. "Everyone's world changed that day."

******

IT WAS AS IF I was watching the Great Tribulation unfold in real time. I wanted to leap out of my skin and find a safe space, but there was nowhere to go. I suspected it wouldn't be long before Peter Jennings delivered the broadcast I'd been waiting for.

Carter and I walked into our shift at L&S in a haze. Our workflow slowed to a snail's pace, and *Enquirer* magazine-type rumors quickly spread. Every news station successfully doled out more fear. It affected our jobs since the contracts we worked on were government, military, and aerospace in nature.

During a candlelight vigil in the parking lot that night, all I did was selfishly wonder if I had enough time to get to a bunker.

When bioterrorist threats came via the Post Office—and letters laced with anthrax were mailed at random—I fell into a deep depression, wrapped in fret.

Buildings had fallen, death spores were being delivered in the mail, no one knew where to turn, and no one had answers. I couldn't eat or sleep. I existed. Our move to New York City was delayed—indefinitely.

Every time I closed my eyes, smoke, fire, crashing airplanes, and people jumping out of windows from a hundred stories up filled my mind. Only, these images were not figments of my imagination, they were things I had *seen* with my own eyes.

Blood, ash, and soot on New York City streets served as the backdrop of Rudy Giuliani's stage while he assured the city they would undoubtedly recover. As biological agents of death intimately kissed envelopes in search of a human to destroy, John Lennon's, "Imagine" played on the radio interminably.

Carter and I stayed in NH, and we had a hard time finding a place with our mini pet shop in tow. It wasn't long before I lost hope in almost everything—humanity, my new marriage, my job, life in general.

I hated my job. It paid the bills, but it didn't feel like me, and our workload was changing drastically. New government contracts replaced aerospace contracts in preparation for war.

I bounced aimlessly from department to department being cross trained as a jack-of-all-trades. I was working in the polishing room, alone, when every one of the poor life choices I'd made up to that moment showed up in the form of ashy smut—mocking me.

I sat in a filthy office chair, spinning in circles, surrounded by Dremel rotary tools, polishing wheels, and enough soot to send my lungs to the ER.

I pulled the teeny, light blue Motorola cell phone from my pocket and made a phone call.

The Kool-Aid Guy

"WHO DID YOU CALL?" Joel asked the next week.

I sighed. "The only person I felt safe calling... Luke."

"Well, you thought he'd save you from Armageddon once. It doesn't surprise me you'd call him. Did he talk to you?"

"He did. I told him I was scared. He told me he would be too if he were me. He said the events of 9/11 were just the nasty side of Christendom (false Christian religions) and everything in Revelation was starting to unfold. It was all God's will. He quoted a scripture, explaining that God had put 9/11 into the hearts of the people responsible for the events, and I should thank Jehovah there was still time."

"Time to get to your bunker?"

"Yep."

******

LATER THAT NIGHT I prayed. Knees on the living room floor, forehead pressed into the couch cushion, hands clasped in earnest supplication.

The rebellious teenage pride once giving me gumption to leave the Truth, swiftly took a backseat. I was now a newly married (and worried) young woman, convinced I would receive an envelope containing anthrax spores with Jehovah's name listed as the return address.

Any sliver of Christian faith still daring to pierce my flesh with its pious nonsense had been previously extracted, left to drown in a pool of my own recalcitrant blood. I couldn't ignore the fact my family had been coached to forget my existence. Their dismissal of my surgery and wedding was still too fresh a wound, yet there I was, praying like a damn fool.

I begged God to prove he was real. Maybe I was out of line, but if he was real, I needed to know. I needed proof. I needed the burning bush. I knew I was testing God and I didn't care.

Fuck it.

I pushed the anthrax-filled envelope across His Holy table. Return to sender. I asked the Almighty for a pet-friendly apartment. And since we had two dogs, two cats, a rat, and a fish tank it'd be a rare find.

C'mon, Jehovah, show me what ya got.

Weeks later when we found a place, I wondered if an interventionist God had surfaced. I convinced myself he had. I believed Jehovah gave me a burning bush, on top of my own hidden hill in Laconia, overlooking the White Mountains.

And on one chilly October evening—while sitting in a cushioned chair next to an unenthusiastic Carter, at the very same Hall in Massachusetts that ousted me nine years prior—I silently made the decision to get reinstated.

Even though many wanted to, no one spoke to me—which was very uncomfortable for Carter. Not only was the meeting in ASL, a language he doesn't use, but after the meeting everyone lined up to shake his hand and welcome him. I just sat quietly with my growing collection of glances, nods of approval, and tearful smiles.

******

"So, you decided to go back... What about your previously conflicted, Witness chameleon suit?"

"I forced myself into it," I said, looking out the window.

Joel scribbled, asking, "And why were people able to talk with Carter? He wasn't a Witness."

"He was never baptized. He didn't know Jehovah, dedicate his life to God's chosen organization, then knowingly walk away with the Truth in his hands. That was me. I did that."

"I see." Joel scribbled vehemently.

"The elders told me because I was married, and not living in sin, my reinstatement would be easy. They said I should go to meetings in Laconia since they were local and a near two-hour drive to the sign language Hall would take me away from my Christian wifely duties—possibly stumbling my *unbelieving mate.*"

"Uh-huh. Did your decision to go back stumble Carter?"

"Oh, yeah. But the way I saw it, I was securing a spot in the bunker for me *and* my unbelieving husband."

Joel was ready. On the edge of his seat.

******

I ATTENDED EVERY SINGLE meeting I could. I petitioned my department manager at work to switch me from nights to days, refusing to miss meetings. I needed to prove I was serious. My schedule changed shortly thereafter and I, again, told myself Jehovah was real since everything was seamlessly falling into place.

Everything except my new marriage, that is.

"So, you're really doing this?" Carter asked.

"Yep. I miss my family and 9/11 stirred me. I know Armageddon's real; it's just around the corner."

"You're sure about that?"

"Look around, Carter! Don't you see what's happening? The Trade Center is gone, people are dead, and it's not over. Jehovah is making these things happen so that we can be in the *New System* soon." I was totally convinced I'd soon be in paradise, hugging my own pet lion.

He shot daggers and said, "Bek, things like war, destruction, and disaster have been happening for centuries."

He walked into the second bedroom of our new, God-gifted apartment. He hid there, in his man cave, often.

I sighed, looking at each of my fur-kids.

Bartok—my beautiful, long-haired wiener—pushed his itty-bitty tennis ball to me with his snout, cooing playfully, grumbling with impatience. I threw it. He returned seconds later, and the same skit played out.

Moron—my dapper, short-haired wiener—lay next to me rolling around with a colorful, stuffed pigeon in his mouth, biting down on the squeaker, taking pleasure in its demise.

Spork, my black Siamese, sat on the kitchen table bathing herself quietly.

And Sidney, the old, fluffy judge of character Dean had given me, wandered around purring, rubbing against me.

In the presence of all my fur-kids, I couldn't help but wonder how each of their distinct personalities could be left to chance.

I continued going to the meetings, studying whatever I could get my hands on. I inundated myself with all the *new light* the *Society* had to offer. I delved deeper down their rabbit hole, grappling to understand things I'd not taken seriously back when I had the chance. I was *putting on a new personality* (theirs) and shedding the old.

My incessant researching caused Carter to retreat into his man cave frequently. The rift between us grew. While I sat on the floor, among a sea of *Watchtower* publications, he mixed records and dawdled on his computer.

I avoided R-rated movies, questionable music, books, and even decreased time spent with our mutual friends and my new in-laws; they were suddenly *bad association*. Carter and I were now worlds away from each other, and I was too far gone to even notice. Then, just five months later, I handed the elders my reinstatement letter.

Using my maiden name was intentional. My family's last name conjured up images of a strong, close-knit, spiritual family among the Deaf community of Witnesses, and I wanted back in.

A week later, Laconia's presiding overseer (head honcho) approached me as I was leaving the Kingdom Hall and said, "We reviewed your letter and are happy to report we plan to announce your reinstatement next Thursday."

I smiled. "Thank you."

"We're always glad when the Prodigal son, or daughter, returns." He smiled back.

I was about to be a Mallory again, securing my spot in the bunker. Carter didn't share my enthusiasm.

"This isn't what I married into, Bek. This isn't what I signed up for. You're so different from the person I married just six months ago."

"Oh, really? You want her back, do you? Unhappy, scared, depressed? Is that who you want?"

The blood curdling events of 9/11 still whorled in my mind, and I refused to be bunker-less when Armageddon came.

"No, but this isn't you. I don't think you *actually* believe any of this; you've been haunted by these beliefs since I've known you."

"I can't look at any of the babies and think they're some *cosmic accident*." I quoted the air around me.

"You look at them and automatically believe in God?" He scoffed, turning his head to the side.

"Well, yeah. Look at Bartok and tell me he was just an accident, the result of a bunch of cells bumping into each other that mutated into a dog. He was *created*!"

Carter rolled his eyes and walked into his man cave, shutting the door behind him. These topics were debated, and repelled, time and time again.

Then they were met with Paula's disapproval.

During our weekly Sunday dinner, while stabbing a fork into my broccoli and cheese pastry puff for the hundredth time, Paula said that joining a questionable religion so soon after our recent nuptials was unimpressive and tricky.

Remembering that mildness was one of the nine *fruitages of God's spirit,* I respectfully told Paula that I was doing this for everyone's benefit.

I was determined to win my new unbelieving mate, and unbelieving in-laws, over with my meek actions and soft tone.

The night of my reinstatement I sat restlessly in the back of the Hall. And just as the announcement was being made, my anxiety subsided. I glanced to my right and saw John Denver's backup singer walk in. My Daddy-daughter dance was about to begin.

Still dressed in his work clothes—dirty t-shirt, old, stained jeans, and baseball cap—he walked to my seat and knelt beside me. He smelled like cleaning supplies. He threw his left arm around the back of my chair. I snuggled into him.

Brothers and sisters in the Laconia congregation, one by one, turned their heads to look back at me, smiling tearfully. And then there was my dad, who'd come to the Hall just in time—filthy from work, no interpreter—just to be with me. I was Daddy's Little Girl again. I could feel his sunshine on my shoulder while Carter's cloud loomed overhead.

The Memorial—the only holiday J-Dubs recognize—was fast approaching. It's not like Easter. No eggs, no candy, no bunny. It's an annual observance of Jesus, his life, death, and the sacrifice he made for mankind. Everyone is dressed to the nines and all around the world at sundown, a plate of unleavened bread and glass of wine is passed up and down each row.

I showed up at the Laconia Kingdom Hall to help clean just before the Memorial. And that's when I saw *her*. She ran up, pulling me into an awkward embrace.

"I'm so happy you're reinstated! Come wipe down chairs with me and let's catch up," she said.

Rene handed me a damp rag and we knelt in front of a row of chairs. It had been nine years. Last time I saw her, I was running off to Dean's and she was buying Sam's Club shirts for Jax.

"Fill me in on the last nine years!" she said.

I had no desire to remember much about the past nine years. I skirted around some half-assed answer, hoping to pacify her.

"You know, just life, working, getting married. The usual." I nervously rubbed a metal chair leg, took the focus off me, and asked, "How about you?"

"Well, I was engaged to Jax briefly and that didn't work out. He wasn't very spiritual—"

"Jax? The Jax you met through me?"

Fuckin' engaged to Jax?!

"Yeah," she said, vigorously wiping the footrest of a chair. "I heard he was disfellowshipped shortly after I broke it off."

Jax. Engaged to Rene. Now disfellowshipped. Huh.

After the Kingdom Hall had been properly cleaned and prepped, it was now the duty of every living, breathing J-Dub to invite anyone they knew to the Memorial. I, of course, invited my husband and mother-in-law.

"Paula, it's just one meeting. One. You don't have to study or get baptized. No matter what you believe, it's just one hour in remembrance of Jesus. That's it," I said.

"Is Carter going?" she asked.

Carter, avoiding eye contact and cutting into his prime rib, nodded.

"Okay. I'm only doing this for you. One time," Paula said, reaching for her glass of beer.

Sitting in the back row of a packed Kingdom Hall, the bread and wine came around. I already knew to simply pass the plate of crackers and glass of cheap wine. Carter and Paula were notably dis-eased as the plate and glass came their way.

"Are we passing? Or eating and drinking?" Paula whispered.

"Passing," I whispered while demonstrating.

Once the evening was over, Paula voiced her distaste for the whole experience in the car.

"Oh! I felt like someone was going to introduce me to Jim Jones," she said as she lit a cigarette and cracked the window.

"The Kool-Aid guy?" I asked, turning left onto Blueberry Lane.

"Yes! Someone I work with was in there. She asked me which one of you was in *the Truth*." She quoted the air with a Virginia Slim dangling from her fingers. "What the hell does that mean?"

"She just wanted to know who the Witness in the family was, that's all."

"Well, it sounds like a cult to me," she said, taking a long drag off her cigarette.

I turned onto Union Avenue and silently readied myself to face Satan's persecution via my new husband and mother-in-law.

Dickless Angels

DURING ALL THE WEEKS of me sifting through jagged pieces of my life, I realized I brought on most of the chaos myself. Unknowingly, of course, but as patterns unfolded and journal entries were made, I saw I'd been a huge influencer on, well, myself.

Joel flipped through his notepad, landing on the topic of Jim Jones. "So, Paula said you were in a cult."

"Yes and, just like when Dean said it, I took offense. Silently but, still, offended."

"How did your marriage fare then?"

"I pretty much started to dismiss Carter's existence. Not right away, our demise crept. Slowly. I tried hard to keep it together but gave up when what I wanted didn't happen."

"What did you want?"

"What every single J-Dub woman with an unbelieving mate wants—for him to study and get baptized. To fall in line, knock on doors, lead lovingly, and cover my chilly shoulders with a goddamn suit coat."

"Well, there's no harm in wanting you and your spouse to be warm and on the same page—"

"True, but it's a page in a book he didn't even want to read. And I didn't respect that."

"What did you do?"

"I fed him to my family. After my reinstatement, my brother Mark and his wife came home for a visit. We planned an entire weekend of informally witnessing to Carter while driving through picturesque New England highways, gawking at the White Mountains, and peeking at the infamous Old Man of the

Mountain—before he fell toward his unfortunate death by way of rock-crumbling nose-dive."

"The Old Man of the Mountain?"

"He's the pride and joy of anyone in the 603, look at any New Hampshire quarter. Anyway, when Mark got me alone, he offered some unsolicited advice, saying, 'Carter's going to see you getting all dressed up for meetings and field service; he may get a little jealous. Sometimes, it's okay to miss a meeting to spend time with him. Be sure to pay him enough attention.' When I mentioned how I wished I hadn't married Carter, and married another J-Dub instead, Mark freaked. He told me not to say such things out loud, not to give Satan any more ammunition."

"Stating your desires would cause Satan to find one of his tools to lure you with?"

I smiled and nodded. "You got it. Because he can't read your thoughts like Jehovah can."

******

THE ELDERS IN LACONIA paired me with a sister, Valeri, who was very *strong* in the Truth. She studied with me and taught me the art of defending scriptures and doctrines, whether I agreed or not.

During one of our many discussions, while playing fetch with Bartok, we analyzed a scripture that didn't make sense to me.

There was a woman married to a man; the man dies. So, the woman married his brother. Then *he* dies. She married the next brother, and he also died. Then *she* died. The question is posed to Jesus, "In the resurrection, which one will be her husband?" Jesus replies, "None of them. In the resurrection, men and women don't marry. They're like the angels in heaven."

Not only did all these poor men die after marrying this suspicious witch, but it meant men and women resurrected after Armageddon wouldn't have genitalia. No penises. No vaginas. No need for sex. I couldn't make sense of it, and I didn't like it.

I brought it up to Carter after Valeri left.

"Lemme get this straight—if you die and I make it through Armageddon, you're resurrected and suddenly a eunuch?"

I nodded. "It's the same if the situation is reversed; I make it through, you die and are resurrected without—"

"A dick? I'm a dickless angel? We pass by each other in this *New System*," insert Carter's air quotes, "as if nothing ever happened? Or better yet, we still have memories of sex and every time we pass each other, I gotta pretend like it never happened?"

I admit the whole idea was preposterous, and even I was having a hard time seeing my husband in the body of a Ken doll. We had so many tiresome, scriptural arguments and the night I came home with my No Blood Card, he was furious.

******

"Now, *this* is what I want to know more about—the No Blood thing with Witnesses." Joel scooted to the edge of his seat, pen and notepad ready.

"It's a hot topic. Every Witness carries a signed, wallet-sized medical directive stating they'll refuse blood transfusions even if death is imminent. This stems from a scripture in Acts telling people to abstain from blood—"

"Well, back in those days it probably pertained more to not drinking it and draining animals properly after they'd been slaughtered."

"Oh, no doubt and I know that...*now*."

"So, it's expected, and okay, to let children just...die?"

"And the elderly or anyone else. There is one exception, though."

"Oh?"

"Depending on a person's conscience they can accept certain fractions of blood, blood platelets, but no whole blood transfusions."

"What's the reasoning behind that?"

I shrugged. "That's when *new light* is credited, and the rules get incredibly intricate. So intricate that most J-Dubs just nod in tacit compliance."

"Who signs the card?"

"Emergency contacts and a power of attorney, which is usually an elder in the congregation."

"Did Carter sign as an emergency contact?"

I sighed, realizing I fueled Carter's fiery hatred for all things Witness related and said, "No. I made a huge stink about how he wouldn't honor my wishes to die a faithful-non-accepting-blood-transfusion Witness, and I wouldn't let him anywhere near the card."

"This hurt him?"

"Pissed him off is more like it. He told me I was right; he wouldn't respect my wishes because he wouldn't want to watch me die. I told him my death would only be temporary, I'd be resurrected."

"And you wouldn't be resurrected if you accepted blood?"

"Not according to J-Dub credo. The argument ended with him saying the idea of me in the *New System* as a vaginaless ghost was not only unappealing, but not far off from who I was becoming."

"Ouch."

"Well, I couldn't see it at the time, but he was right. Our arguments grew tiresome, and we grew apart. Miles apart. Nothing could rekindle what we had prior to getting married.

There was only one person I wanted to talk to, but he was busy."

"Who?"

"Luke, who else? He was roaming the country, working as a freelance interpreter, on the hunt for a new wife—"

"A new wife?"

"He and his first wife got divorced. Even though *Jehovah hates a divorcing* they found some *new light* loophole and *voila!*—divorce. I don't wanna get into that. Their story, not mine."

"Interesting. Go on."

******

LUKE FOUND SOMEONE in Canada of all places. She was sweet, young, and also a CODA, which was pretty important to Luke. When he and I had phone dates, he lit up whenever he talked about Gwen.

I liked her immediately. Luke and Gwen dated long distance, and there were frequent trips between Toronto and the States. I was able to spend a lot more time with them, as their no-heavy-petting chaperone, when I lost my job.

Standing with Carter in the L&S parking lot, holding my severance package, I told him I'd been laid off.

"Are you surprised? You walked around the shop saying that you didn't care if you were laid off because you didn't feel comfortable working on military contracts." He eyeballed the envelope in my hand.

"I don't."

"Well, I suppose Jehovah will take care of you then." He hugged me and walked inside. I couldn't tell if that was sincerity or sarcasm.

I panicked, dialing Luke's number. I told him I was laid off and I didn't know how we were going to pay rent. He told me to get in the car and drive to Boston.

"What for?" I asked.

"Come to Fenway with us. We're going to a Red Sox game."

"I can't go to a game now. I need a job!"

"You won't find one so late in the day on a Friday. Just come. On me."

In a lot of ways Luke rescued me whenever he was able, and whenever the ol' GB sanctioned it. This newfound relationship with Luke, and the trip to Fenway, turned out to be just what I needed. Even though it became another wedge driving Carter and I further apart.

"You're a Red Sox fan now? Jesus Christ, first religion, now baseball. I don't know who you are." Carter slumped on the couch.

I didn't care how Carter felt. My top priority was keeping God happy. I thought if I made him happy first, he'd be sure to take care of everything else—gainful employment, money, and a soon-to-be baptized husband.

I got a job teaching sign language to a little HH girl in fourth grade. *Gainful employment—check. Now to work on Carter by love-bombing.*

Luke and Gwen were soon engaged. Mom, Dad, Jesse, Luke, Gwen, Carter, and I spent many weekends in Toronto visiting and helping Luke move to Canada just before their wedding.

En route to Canada, we stopped at a 24-hour rest area for essentials and an impromptu Star Search performance.

Luke and Dad danced around while lip-synching to Michael Jackson's, "Rock With You" in the parking lot. It was midnight. Their entire shameless performance was caught on video as I sat in the passenger's seat of our car, filming. And when my dad showed everyone his old, white, bare belly—I completely lost it. I laughed, gasping for air.

Carter sat in the driver's seat, lips pursed, staring forward, giving us evil side-eye as we laughed hysterically. At a 24-hour pit stop full of Fozzie Bears, Carter was Sam the Eagle—not amused.

Luke was married once again and after the wedding he and Gwen were off to Italy for two weeks. Carter and I went back to the States and resumed life from separate rooms.

Two weeks later my tiny, blue Motorola trilled. I squished its rubber ACCEPT button.

Luke and Gwen were back in the States and suggested the four of us to take a trip to Disneyworld for more Operation Love-Bomb Carter.

My parents agreed to care for our animals and before I knew it, the four of us were on our way to Florida. I, with a secret plan to feed Carter to my family once more.

To make the trip more affordable we shared a hotel room, brought groceries, a portable electric stove burner to make frugal hotel dinners, and packed lunches to avoid expensive Disney eateries. We went to every park and rode on every ride.

Each night Luke and Gwen did their Bible reading at the hotel. Instead of joining them, I snuggled next to Carter on the bed and read *The Hobbit*. I felt guilty for not doing my Bible reading, but I was desperately searching for some type of balance. Although I cared a lot about what Jehovah, and other Witnesses, thought I didn't want to throw my marriage away. I wanted to read *The Hobbit* without pissing God off.

******

"Were you able to?"

"I don't know. It didn't feel like it. Trying to follow Mark's advice to miss a meeting occasionally felt wrong too, but I did it anyway."

"What did you do?"

"For Paula's birthday, Carter bought us all tickets to see Bill Maher at The Berkeley Center in Boston. The entire night, Bill used 9/11 and molestation charges against the Catholic church as comedic fodder. Pissed off Catholics walked out one by one, and it only egged him on. I surprisingly had a good time but, of course, my conscience poked and prodded all night."

"How'd you deal with that?"

"I decided to *auxiliary pioneer*. Between working and attending meetings, my goal for a whole month was going door-to-door for a total of sixty hours. The same scenarios from my childhood played out—people got angry, slammed their doors, said they weren't interested. But only one thing stuck out to me that entire month."

Joel fidgeted in his seat, waiting.

"While going door-to-door one day, an older sister in my service group waddled her way back to the car after talking with a man on his front step. Once she wiggled her way into the front seat, she started writing brief notes about what happened."

"What happened?"

"She sighed and said that although they had a nice enough conversation, he said he had his own religion. When I asked what religion he was, she said it didn't matter because it was the wrong one."

"Well, you've always known Witnesses claimed to have the one and only Truth, right?"

"Yes. But for some reason when *she* said it, I didn't like it. She said he was in the wrong religion, while parked in *his* driveway, writing notes about *him*. It was disrespectful at the very least. I figured each person would settle the score with Jehovah on their own. But for her to judge him...it just felt *wrong*."

"What did you do then?"

"Pressured myself and struggled internally. I felt like I couldn't win. Either I take Mark's suggested night off with

Carter surrounding myself with political polarization and God shaming, subsequently wanting to send myself to the gallows, or I sit in cars wagging my finger at innocent people. My mind twisted and spun with visions of Bill Maher, No Blood Cards, Armageddon, and the resurrection. Naked, sexless Ken and Barbie dolls lined up to sing the Kingdom Melody, 'We're Jehovah's Witnesses,' leaving me stupefied."

"How were you and Carter at this point?"

"Barely keeping our lips above the waterline. I envied the married sisters, snuggled up to their ministerial servant and elder husbands. Their chilly shoulders were always gently covered with a suit coat whenever the *ay-kah-geesha* kicked on. Most nights I sat, alone and cold, wishing my husband was there. I resented him. I resented God.

"I ceased fire on all things kinky to purify our marriage bed. Any sexual positions or carnal oddities I once okayed, were now prohibited by the ol' GB. Pleasing them, and God, now seemed like a burden and I felt criminal for being a Doubting Thomas."

"Purify your marriage bed?"

"Oh, get your pen ready. You'll love this."

******

IN A POOR ATTEMPT to keep afloat, Carter and I had dinner with Rene and her husband, Colin. He was a bit of a drinker, somewhat inactive at times, and told crude jokes that Carter appreciated.

"The Bible says those things *shouldn't even be mentioned among you,* Colin." Rene scolded.

"Okay, okay. Sorry." Colin smirked, lowered his head, and held up his palm in surrender.

With homemade alcoholic beverages in hand, Rene broke the quiet tension, looked at me, and blurted, "I quit high school because of you."

"Me? Why?" I crumpled my brow.

Rene giggled. "You look like your dad when you make that face." She sipped her drink and said, "When you were talking to Dean and I was dating Jax, I knew you were still upset about it—"

"Rene, stop," Colin said.

"It killed me. I didn't understand why you were so upset. Jax was the one who chose... I think I still have the letter he sent explaining why he chose me."

"Rene." Colin eyeballed her.

"I don't need to see the letter. I'm sorry. I didn't realize I was the reason you didn't graduate," I said.

"It hurt so much to be around you, especially after you were disfellowshipped. I hated not being able to talk to you," she said.

I changed the subject and said, "Let me ask you guys a personal question if you don't mind. Where exactly in the Bible does it prohibit certain sexual acts and talk about keeping the marriage bed pure?"

"Ephesians mentions sexual immorality," Colin said.

"Well, what constitutes sexual immorality? How far can married couples go?" I asked.

It was brazen to bring up such a personal topic, but I really wanted to know. Not only to be closer to Carter again, guilt-free, but...was the GB really sneaking into people's bedrooms?

"Well," Colin sighed, "I won't go into detail about what happens in our marriage bed, and let's say I wouldn't open up to the elders about it either." He sipped his bourbon. The ice clanked. He avoided eye contact.

I knew Carter missed some of the eroticism I'd brought into the bedroom. He was pissed that I'd suddenly stopped and demoted him to missionary man since my reinstatement.

If a couple is found to be rehearsing roles for the next B-rated porno, how do the elders even find out? Does the couple tell on themselves? I was dying to know. I did some of my own research and couldn't find anything specific. Again, the ol' GB writers merely toss around their interpretations, which is speculation at best.

Another notch on my bedpost of doubt.

I struggled with the monotonous sexual relationship Carter and I had. It didn't *defile* our marriage bed, but we were both bored. It was exhausting trying to keep him and the other guy in our bed, Jehovah, happy. And not only was I left out of the suit-coat-covering-chilly-shoulders club, but I was also not invited to the pregnant-wives club. Almost everyone I knew was pregnant.

"Let's have a baby," I said.

"What?" Carter's eyes bugged.

"Why not? I could go off the pill."

"If you go off the pill, we're gonna be doing less than we do *now*." He turned his back to me, opening the fridge.

"Why?" I followed him into the kitchen.

"I am not raising a child with you."

"What?"

"Seriously, Bek?"

"You haven't thought about having kids?"

"I have. I've even picked out names. I just don't think I want to have kids with *you*."

"Why?" I was on the verge of tears.

"It's not obvious? Me—raise a kid in that religion? No way. I don't want my kid going to the Kingdom Hall. I want to celebrate holidays and not feel guilty about it. Our kid would hear one thing from you and something different from me...if they heard anything at all."

"Heard anything at all?" I really hoped he didn't have the balls to suggest what I thought he was suggesting.

"Deafness might run in your family. I'd want my kid to get a cochlear implant. I'm not against them."

******

"Cochlear implant?"

"Yeah, another hot-button issue. Cochlear implants are complex electronic devices, surgically implanted into a Deaf person's head. It's attracted to an oversized, magnetic hearing aid on the outside of the head picking up sound. I say if adults, and kids old enough to decide, want them—cool. But babies, toddlers? Nope—at least not mine. Being raised by 'Big D' Deaf parents, who strongly identify with Deaf culture, it's safe to say our family wasn't a fan of them. Carter knew that."

"Do you think he was trying to provoke you in some way?"

I nodded and said, "I could take responsibility for our suffering marriage. I was prepared to blame God and myself. But the second he lifted that carpet—where all our problems hid—then pointed to my parents' Deafness in cruel jest, he was dead to me. You can fuck with me in a lot of ways. Dean did. But even Dean never said jack shit about my parents, or their Deafness, which might be one reason he's still okay in my book. But when someone stoops that low? Game on."

"Is it safe to say this was the beginning of the end?"

"In more ways than one, yeah. I also wasn't making as much money at the elementary school, and we had to move. *Where* we moved was the problem."

"Which was where?"

"Into the evil-spirited basement of my childhood. We turned it into a livable studio apartment. It was cute—I didn't mind being there at all."

"And he did?"

"Yep, and he was sure to let me know."

"How?"

"He didn't make much of an effort to learn any ASL. My parents bent over backwards for him the way they did for most hearing people—awkwardly using their voices, misunderstanding what they read on people's lips. We'd been married for over a year, and he could barely fingerspell his name. My plan was to save money, re-acclimate myself with Deaf culture, and give birth to my interpreting career. I didn't care about leaving a bitter husband behind in his worldly dust."

"Mm-hmm." Joel looked at the clock.

"Things didn't get any better once Satan and his minions delivered a secret desire I shouldn't have uttered aloud."

"You met another Witness who swept you off your feet?"

"Not exactly."

Shaking the Tree

HERE IT COMES. The reason I looked for a therapist. The reason I'd been making myself comfortable on Joel's couch. The reason I hated myself.

I wanted to run away. I wanted to cry. I wanted to sit in Joel's lap. I wanted shelter and protection. In that moment, for me, he was it. I stared at him, and he looked at me.

"Well?"

I kicked off my shoes. "Everything I'm about to tell you today is the reason I looked for you, the reason why I'm here." I started to cry as soon as my ass hit the sofa.

"It's okay…" He grabbed his box of moisturizing tissues and placed it next to me. "Take your time."

I sniffled, grabbing a few tissues from the box. I swung my feet onto the cushion, heels under my ass, and leaned on the arm of the couch.

I looked down and told the story to my fidgeting hands.

******

CARTER AND I HAD been living in my parent's basement for a few months. I asked the elders in Laconia to transfer my concealed, J-Dub file to the sign language congregation in Massachusetts so I could attend meetings with my parents. Carter didn't seem to mind my absence, and I used the sign language meetings as a foot in the interpreting door. We were worlds apart and neither of us seemed to care.

Jax's sister Gina had moved from New Mexico to Washington, D.C. She visited our humble, basement abode one weekend and encouraged me to send an audition tape to an interpreting agency she worked with.

I wasn't qualified, nowhere near interpreter status, but I recorded myself interpreting a ten-minute speech coming from the TV set. Next, I recorded a Deaf person on the TV screen while I voiced in the background. I sent the tape to Washington, D.C. and forgot about it.

To my surprise, the agency called, said they'd reviewed my tape, and wanted me to come down to work with them for one week. The agency partnered with CloseUp—a nationwide program inspiring middle and high school students to participate in the democratic process. Students, both hearing and Deaf, fly from various states landing in D.C. to learn more about their rights and responsibilities as citizens.

I accepted.

Standing in the security line at the Manchester airport, I clutched recent issues of *The Watchtower* and *Awake!* for dear life. I was still freaked about 9/11 and hadn't flown since our honeymoon to Mexico. I prayed for the entire hour and fifteen-minute flight.

Gina picked me up from the Baltimore airport.

"So, you've done this CloseUp thing before?" I fidgeted in the passenger's seat while she drove to the hotel that was hosting CloseUp for the week.

"A few times. It's incredibly intense. Early days, late nights. Breakfast is at 7:30am, the buses leave at about 8:00 and we're moving all day. Some days we aren't back at the hotel until 10:00pm. So, get ready."

"What's the schedule like?"

She sighed and said, "We'll get a schedule breakdown this afternoon. There's the opening program tonight, where all the Program Instructors—we call them P.I.'s, and they're like teachers—introduce themselves during dinner. After that there's the first workshop.

"Each interpreter is assigned to a P.I. and a workshop of about fifteen to twenty kids, both hearing and Deaf, for the entire week. Two workshop groups share one tour bus, and each bus has its own schedule. We'll tour D.C., the monuments, memorials, museums, and the kids will have an opportunity to prep for scheduled meetings with their state's Senators and Representatives. We have mock debates at the hotel..." she sighed again, "it's a really exhausting but fun week."

I sat in the passenger's seat panicked. I was nowhere near prepared for a week like this. The content alone was intimidating.

I don't know jack shit about politics.

At the hotel we were immediately swarmed with teenagers. After dropping our luggage off in our room, I was ushered to the Program Instructor's suite.

The door opened and utter chaos ensued. The floors, chairs, and beds were heavily adorned with chart paper, sharpies, nametags, folders, handouts, and unfinished schedules.

Busy bodies scampered around the room, feverishly prepping for the intense week ahead. And I just stood there—in the eye of the storm—looking for a quick escape. I scanned the room for anything that looked familiar. Nothing.

My Potbelly's sandwich began to rise. I didn't belong with worldly highbrows more well-read than I was. I could feel my skin breaking out in red blotches.

Just then, a calm and pleasant blond-haired, blue-eyed Toby McGuire lookalike approached me, extended his hand, and offered me a nametag with "Bek" written on it. My big brown eyes met his crystal blues.

He smiled and said, "You must be my interpreter, Bek. I'm Kelly."

"I must be." I took the nametag.

There was something in the way he said my name...

He handed me a schedule, with scribbled notes on what he'd be covering in his first workshop, for later that night. Looking at the paper, words blurred together. I feigned confidence and rubbed my chin, pretending to understand what I saw. I knew damn well I was clueless about current events, the democratic process, and details of government and politics. The only thing I knew for sure was it would all be destroyed soon.

I sat with Kelly at dinner to learn more about his teaching style. I hadn't professionally interpreted anywhere, and I figured the more information I had the better. I grabbed a plate of food from the buffet table, a small carton of milk, and sat next to him.

"How long have you been teaching?" I asked, struggling to open my milk carton.

Kelly grabbed my milk carton and opened it for me. I stared at the open carton realizing how helpless I must've seemed. While Kelly talked about his Modern American History degree, his voice faded, and Rod Serling's took over.

Let's travel to another dimension—an alternate universe that brings us into a young woman's mind spiraling out of control— where religious beliefs, political ineptitude, and a marriage on the brink of death compete for attention. The seemingly benign gesture of opening a milk carton has her wondering if she displays the need for constant care. Is it obvious to others that she perhaps has no knowledge of what she will face...here...in The Twilight Zone?

I looked around the room and realized dinner was over. I followed Kelly to our workshop. I don't know how, but I interpreted in a room full of eighteen high school students for an entire hour and the world didn't crumble.

I envied those kids. They knew more than I did, they were smarter. They'd each written thought-provoking essays, demonstrating their desire to be there. To learn. To be part of something greater than themselves. The only things I did during high school were run away from home, use drugs, and barely survive bone-breaking, knock-down, drag-out fights, while living out degrading sexual fantasies—all just to avoid moving back home to an austere religious environment I didn't agree with and *still* had qualms about.

The days quickly blended together, and I had to make it to Friday. I hadn't even connected with Carter via my new, silver, flip phone. There was no time to piss, let alone make personal phone calls. And what did it matter? He'd taken very little interest in my goals back home. This week was no different.

I fell right in to CloseUp's groove—the lectures, Q&A panels with lobbyists, presentations from journalists and Armed Force members—by Tuesday. My mind swirled with new information, the kind the ol' GB did not provide.

J-Dubs don't vote, join the military, or get involved with the politics of *this wicked system.* And here I was, among hundreds of people, doing just that. Hearing their stories, the passion in their beliefs, then filtering the emotion in their words through my mind and out of my fingertips, made it near impossible not to feel their experiences. Each time it was my turn to interpret, I felt like I was being bulldozed into a corner, forced to confront my own hand-me-down faith and trained neutrality.

With tons of new information filing itself away in my brain's card catalog, the bus ride between stops became my respite from disorienting thoughts—unless there was something worth pointing out along the ride.

Kelly asked me to interpret a tidbit he was about to share.

He stood and turned to face the students. I stood next to him and, while maintaining cat-like balance inside a moving vehicle, interpreted.

"This park is where Chandra Levy's body was found." Kelly pointed to the left side of the tour bus. The students barely lifted their heads.

"I think they're tired," I said, looking at him as we plopped down in our seat.

"Yeah, probably." He looked at my feet. "I like your shoes."

"Thank you." I eyeballed my maroon, Doc Marten Mary Janes.

"You're a good interpreter," he said.

"How do you know?"

"I've worked with a couple. They don't have the same rapport with the students that you do."

"That might be cuz my parents are Deaf. It's an unfair advantage." I smirked.

"You're a CODA!"

He looked at me almost as if I was a mythical creature. I looked at him much the same way, shocked he knew what a CODA was.

Our time on the bus, between scheduled stops, quickly became my favorite part of the week. I felt a deep connection to him and couldn't place why. Nothing was short of amazing to him. He was excited about the world and its endless possibilities. I was in awe of his zest for life. It was refreshing. *He* was refreshing.

An inexplicable longing took hold the few times we were separated during the week. I ached for his presence, and it scared me shitless. I tried to ignore it but couldn't.

Then Gina took notice.

She interfered dutifully, confronting Kelly and I each separately using the phrase "happily married woman." Boy was she wrong. I wasn't nearly as confident in my marriage as she was. But I *was* married, she was right about that. And God knows I'd thrown enough of those proverbial blocks to stumble an entire army.

I used my one evening off, before Capitol Hill Day, to make a much-needed phone call.

"Hi," I said.

"Hey. Wow. I haven't heard from you all week. How's it going?" Carter said.

"Good. Super busy. How are the boys?"

"They're good. They miss you. I had one hell of a time with your dad the other day."

"Why?"

"He needed me to help him with something, and I couldn't for the life of me figure what the hell he was asking me to do. He kept saying *ay-kah-geesha* and pointing to the window—"

"Air conditioner."

"Yes! He wanted me to move the air conditioner. I figured it out after a minute."

"Pick up any ASL?"

"I used the *Joy of Signing* book to sign a few words."

"Crap. I gotta go. The girls are coming into the room and it's about to get loud. See you soon."

"Okay. Love you."

"Love you." Click.

When Wednesday came, the schedule completely flipped. Instead of spending the day with Kelly, and our workshop group, I was scheduled with a different set of students, accompanying them to Capitol Hill.

I knew the P.I.'s needed a day off, but...*shit.* And that's when I knew that I was hands down enamored with Kelly. Our connection was effortless, and I could see it clearly in his absence.

I admittedly didn't miss home or Carter. I had forgotten all about the meetings and had done zero Bible reading all week. I hadn't prayed to my celestial friend in the sky, and my mind was bursting with new information.

I felt like I was seeing the world at large for the first time and I wondered, *If there is still good here—good people like Kelly, making a positive difference in the world—why do we need Armageddon? Why couldn't humanity, together, alter the trajectory of earth and mankind through education and good deeds?*

Reunited in Shaw—a significant D.C. neighborhood during the Civil Rights Movement—Kelly and I stepped right back in line, working together seamlessly, bantering like Abbott & Costello.

Dimpled smiles and side glares confirmed I was not the only one who felt *it*. When we interacted, it felt like we were two separate cell bodies under a microscope, drawn together, perfectly coalescing into one harmonious cluster.

Friday came, giving me the whole day off with nothing planned. I was a bit sad about not spending the day with Kelly but a bit excited to spend the day alone. With enough of the city's surroundings under my belt, I ventured out to wander the streets of Silver Spring, Maryland. Alone. Liberated.

There was no meeting to get ready for. No *Watchtower* study. No Bible reading. And I wasn't arguing with Carter in an effort to break the silent tension between us. The weight of Armageddon wasn't looming. I was somewhere else, learning about many things the ol' GB didn't include in their narrow publications.

This experience allowed me to learn about the person I'd been neglecting nearly my whole life—*me*. Dean's voice echoed in my mind as I wandered through downtown Silver Spring. "Get to know who *you* are."

The last workshop was bittersweet; it was a mellow recap of the week, with a little surprise for me. Kelly had all the students in our workshop sign a huge handmade card, thanking me for my "outstanding services."

"You got a personalized card? I didn't get anything from my P.I.," Gina said.

"I had a mediocre relationship with my P.I. Yours must like you," another interpreter said.

Yes. My P.I. did like me. And it made me quake in my Mary Janes. I was a J-Dub, married to an unbeliever, living in NH. The likelihood of anything growing from this chance encounter was very slim. Besides, what would a scholarly political scientist like him see in a mind controlled, *good for nothing slave* like me?

Who knows? But he saw *something* because Friday night, at the farewell banquet, the attraction was obvious to everyone in the room. And it only intensified when he showed up at a dance club, The Barking Dog, for the interpreter after party.

"P.I. here? Usual not come interpreter after party," signed one of the interpreters, eyeballing Kelly as he came up the stairs.

"I thought any welcome. I told him can come. Wrong?" I signed.

"Not wrong. Odd. He like you," she signed, walking away.

Kelly and I danced into the wee hours of the morning. And when Marvin Gaye's, "Sexual Healing" bounced off the nightclub speakers, begging for a little bump-and-grind, we both knew it wasn't a crush. Our eyes met, we exchanged coy smiles, and that was it. The pull was beyond our control.

While still with the after-party crew, at a local 24-hour diner, Kelly and I sat notably close. Our secret was out. At 4:00am, just before leaving the diner, he tapped my leg with his hand asking if I was ready to head back to the hotel.

His hand, casually on my leg, electrified me. It felt like he'd tapped my leg for the millionth time, as if we were an old couple together for fifty years. And of course, as his wife, I'd know what the tap meant. It was that *natural*.

Back at the hotel parking lot he looked to Gina and said, "It was nice working with you this week."

"You, too," she said.

I told her I'd be up in a minute, hoping she would leave us alone. She pursed her lips, nodded, and walked inside leaving me and Kelly in the parking garage at the hotel's entrance.

"I'm gonna miss you and your cool shoes." He smiled.

I laughed. "My shoes?"

"Well, not just your shoes." He stepped closer. He wrapped his arms around my waist, pulling me into a long, familiar hug. Standing this close to him, our bodies entwined, I swore I'd been here before. The way he smelled, the comfort of his arms, his voice, and his breath all called me home. He let go, looked me in the eye, and innocently kissed my cheek. I kissed the growing stubble on his cheek, thanking him for an amazing week.

As I stepped back, his red rain jacket swished. My leather jacket grated in protest. I turned away and headed toward the parking garage elevator. I pressed the UP button knowing nothing could bring me any higher than he had. The elevator dinged, the doors opened, and I walked in. As the doors closed, my chest ripped itself wide open.

Once alone in the elevator, I hyperventilated. Never in my life had I been caught so unaware. Pairing up with Carter was slow and unsurprising. Meeting Dean and riding his four-year-long roller coaster didn't shock my system as much as Kelly just had. Even *I* wondered if Satan heard me the day I confessed my deepest desire to Mark while gawking at the Old Man of the Mountain.

The elevator doors opened. I forced my breathing back to normal, wiped my face, snuck into our hotel room, and collected my things in the dark. I had no memory of the drive to Gina's apartment. Parked in her driveway, I wondered how we even got there.

I collapsed on her bed. She spooned me, wrapping me into a tight bear hug. I took quick and shallow breaths. The hyperventilating started and before long I was in tears again.

"Did anything happen?" she asked.

"A hug."

I tried desperately to fall asleep, but it was useless. The heavy heart I felt in his absence, turned into a baby Sarlacc sitting in the pit of my stomach—hungry for his aura. This was not the same entity irrationally chewing whatever Dean fed me. This was a persistent gnawing, right in my gut, coming from *me*.

After finally dozing off for what felt like a minute, I woke to Gina's alarm. Once my brain caught up to my body, I started crying again. It was beyond my control. I felt like I was experiencing actual shock—the kind that people feel after a catastrophic event.

"Do you have his contact info?" Gina asked.

I nodded. He'd written his email and phone number on an index card that I'd stuffed into my bag.

"Give it to me. This is Satan's way of testing you. You have to be strong." She wasn't going to let it go, the same way Jocelyn hadn't years ago. I was too weak and sleep deprived to fight. I gave it to her.

Once at the airport and past security, I called Jesse. I told him, through burbled tears, that I'd fallen in love with someone and needed him to come to the house. I needed to tell someone. He agreed only once I'd *clammed dawn*.

Thoughts of 9/11—that had me shaking in fear just one week before—meant nothing to me now. They didn't scare me at all anymore. I leaned back in my coach seat and closed my eyes. My soul was tired, my heart was crushed, and I still didn't understand why. The only thing that soothed me was replaying Kelly's embrace over and over and over. I drifted off blissfully, sleeping for the whole hour and fifteen.

I was startled awake once the plane hit the runway. I looked out the window, past the wing of the plane, and listened to passengers mumbling faintly.

Looking out at the cold NH tarmac, I chose to stay put and watch everyone exit the plane in haste. I was in no rush. I breathed in these last moments alone, moments where Kelly's memory was still intensely alive. I could still smell him.

Forced off the plane, I was the last to depart. I moved slowly along the jetway and headed toward the waiting area. Looking around I spotted Carter, smiling and waving. I couldn't help but feel sorry for him. Excited, he reached out, hugged me, and I sloppily returned the sentiment.

"What's wrong?" he asked.

"I'm just really tired."

I slept on the ride home, comfortably wrapped in the memory of a political scientist.

Once home, I didn't even unpack. I crashed on the bed, cuddling my fur children. Carter lay down next me, much like Gina had, and threw his arms around me. Tears welled up in my eyes.

"Are you sure you're okay?"

I lay there, lifeless in his arms, and prayed to God as hard as I could. I prayed for a strong marriage. I prayed to love Carter and forget about Kelly. I prayed for the gut-wrenching ache to subside. I passed out cold until the barking woke me.

Jesse.

I jumped out of bed and ran upstairs. I grabbed Jesse and rushed him into Dad's office, closing the door behind us.

"Tell me what happened," he said sitting on Dad's futon.

I told him all about D.C., the interpreting, the museums, monuments, the bus rides—only that barely scratched the surface.

What I wanted to explain was that, to me, Kelly was amber. Translucent. Warm. He cleansed me of my phobias. His presence had the power to heal. Being near him, cleared my mind of all fear-induced indoctrination. And for the first time, I could hear my own thoughts.

What I tried to explain was the effortless way we interacted, his familiar smell, the way his body perfectly fit mine, and the age-old familiarity I felt between us. I couldn't explain the ache, the longing. I also couldn't explain how pure magnetism pulled us toward the same hiding place of safety—the one I'd found in my backyard years ago while waiting for the train. Kelly was there. It felt like he'd always been there.

Jesse held me, praying aloud to God Almighty. He asked him to give me strength, begging him to watch over me and send his Holy Spirit as a helper. Amen. *Won't work.*

A few days passed and the nausea worsened. The baby Sarlacc grew into a teething toddler. It now had jagged little teeth for nibbling. I felt like I was dying.

I borrowed Jesse's prayer word for word—asking for forgiveness and strength—powering through days that only bled together. Carter noticed the blood draining from my lifeless body and demanded to know what was going on.

"You won't talk to me, you haven't eaten, you don't wanna talk about D.C... Did something happen there?" he asked.

"No, nothing happened."

I couldn't tell Carter why I wasn't able to eat. He wouldn't believe there was a growing beast, serving as the pit of my stomach, that would only feed on Kelly's amber glow.

Feeling pressured, I went upstairs to Dad's office. I opened my email and at the top of my inbox was an unopened email from Kelly. The bold subject line read, "Your shoes." Excited, I opened the email, hoping my dad wouldn't shift his gaze from the Yankees game to the computer.

The email was short and sweet. He missed my shoes. He missed my laugh. He missed *me*. He understood I was married. He respected that but couldn't get me out of his head. He tried. He couldn't.

I clicked reply knowing I should've sent it to spam, letting it wander cyberspace for all eternity. I said I was married. I said I was a Jehovah's Witness—which was harder than saying I was someone's wife. I said I also had feelings that I couldn't comprehend, but I was married. I said we lived five hundred miles apart. I said nothing could come of this bizarre hypnotic pull. I said I was happy I'd met him. I clicked send.

But I felt hollow.

He emailed back almost immediately. He understood but felt an indescribable pull just the same. He had an aunt who studied with Jehovah's Witnesses. He wasn't familiar with all the tenets but respected my beliefs and wanted to know more.

I emailed again, giving him my cell phone number. *What's the harm in sharing a scripture or two?*

My little silver flip phone rang a few minutes later.

"Hello?" The thought of Kelly on the other end of the line hushed the mini beast in my stomach.

"Hi," Kelly said. His voice sounded like home. I thought my thumping heart would break my rib cage. I just wanted him to talk. I was starved for his knowledge and kind heart. Our conversation went everywhere from family, religion, history, marriage, and onto one topic I recall vividly.

"Gina called me the day you flew home," he said.

"Why?"

"She told me I should lose your contact info. Then she asked me if I liked football. I'm more of a hockey fan, and I'm not interested in football," he said. "I'm more interested in your shoes!"

I had been resurrected.

Hours ago, death felt imminent as this creature awoke in my belly. Dormant blood that drifted lifelessly through my veins just moments ago, now forced its way through. It was as if a water turbine suddenly came to life; it squeaked along slowly, picked up the pace, then began churning rapidly.

Kelly brought me back to life and effortlessly sang the baby Sarlacc to sleep.

A Tryst in Boston

THE VERY NEXT WEEK Joel's basement office felt funereal. I could feel the weight of our recent session lingering. I wondered if any of his other clients could feel it; I sure could. I felt sick to my stomach. Ashamed. Disgusting. I hated myself. And it showed.

"How are you, Rebekah?" He crossed his leg.

I sighed, uncertain if I wanted to answer. "Well, now that you know why I'm really here, and I'm about to rehash all the horrible things I did to Carter, I'm feeling pretty shitty."

"Before you get into all that," he said, showing me the palm of his hand, "I want to say that it's common for people to have affairs."

I was aghast. How could he not judge me as much as I was judging myself? "You're saying it's okay to cheat?"

"No, no. I didn't say that. What I'm saying is, you're not the first person to have done it and you won't be the last. Don't be so hard on yourself."

"Don't be so hard on myself? You wouldn't say that if you knew the details."

"Try me."

"Well, it started out pretty…innocently? It didn't feel like an affair. Kelly was like a gentle pinprick, delivering just one tiny, beautiful poke after another…"

******

THE FIRST LITTLE JAB came the next morning. There was a peculiar notification on my flip phone—one I'd never seen before: TEXT MESSAGE.

I opened my phone and saw a "202" area code. I opened the message.

"Good morning! Hope you have a great day!"

There was an option to reply. After about ten minutes, I had successfully sent my first text via T9. It said, "Thank you. Who is this?" I had a guess but wanted to be sure.

"Kelly." The message read about thirty seconds later.

Thought so.

It didn't take me long to maneuver my way around T9 texting once I knew I could reach Kelly anytime, day or night. Texts got easier, replies were faster, we were unstoppable.

Carter noticed right away.

"What's up, Bek? You're always upstairs with your phone, and if you're down here it's in your hand. What are you even doing with it?"

My flip phone was usually quiet, so to have it constantly in my hand while sitting on the couch, was pretty unusual. And up until Kelly found a way into my pocket, my phone sat on a shelf until "Fur Elise" started playing, which was rare. I didn't get many calls.

I tensed my shoulders, giving Carter the stink-eye. I didn't answer him because I didn't know what to say.

Do I tell him I met someone in D.C., and feel sick to my stomach with crazy excitement?

Remembering that I've never been a good liar, honest to a fault, I kept my mouth shut.

Three weeks had passed since my working vacation in D.C., and Kelly was now fixed on the idea of driving to Boston. He couldn't go another day without my Mary Janes.

I had no idea how to stop what I'd started, and I didn't want to. The pull we both succumbed to was beyond our control. And just maybe some cosmic force aided our weekend plans because, very conveniently, there was a J-Dub sign language convention happening one Sunday and *one Sunday only* at Stanley Theater in Jersey City, New Jersey.

Carter watched me excitedly stuff clothes into a small overnight bag and asked, "You mad that I'm not going to this one with you?"

"Nope."

Thursday night I rode to Boston with Mom and Dad, then handed myself off to Jesse, planning to ride with him to Jersey that Saturday night.

Friday morning, after Jesse left for a short interpreting shift at the hospital, I took the T's Green Line to Riverside.

My stomach flipped, twisted, and spun, bursting with excitement at the thought of smelling Kelly again. I felt safe in his presence.

The train stopped and I saw Kelly through the window. He stood, smiling, with his arms folded, leaned up against a white Chevy Lumina.

I got off the train ready to sprint. My palms sweaty, breath labored, moving past other passengers, roughly brushing by them. The closer I got, the quicker my stride. With shallow breath, I finally lost the crowd. He pushed himself off the car, quickening his pace. Our arms locked tight around each other, bodies melding, inhaling and exhaling.

We didn't need to speak.

In his car, he took my hand and wiggled off my wedding band. I looked over as he placed it on the tip of his pinky. I knew I was playing with fire, and it made me hot.

Kelly's moral compass was just as much in question as mine, and neither of us cared. Being with him—away from the oppressive hand of the Truth, far removed from what felt like a cold, loveless marriage—I could just *be*.

My stomach refused what Friendly's offered during our lunch date. The Sarlacc was content feeding on Kelly's amber waves. More, I wanted more.

We left the all-American burger joint and headed to the Travelodge. Kelly's room was in shambles. Books, papers, charts, sharpies, and pens scattered everywhere… It was the CloseUp P.I.'s suite in Silver Spring all over again.

"Sorry for the mess, being a teacher is a 24-hour job." He laughed nervously then said, "I have a present for you."

He popped a CD in the portable stereo he'd brought and pressed play.

I stood at the door, frozen. He stepped a bit closer, pulling me into the room. He stood, inches from my face, quietly singing along to the song that was playing. He stepped closer again. My heart danced, the room spun, my vision blurred.

"I'm sorry, but I can't wait anymore."

Kelly pulled my face toward his, and the sound of Ewan McGregor's voice floated around the room, serenading our first kiss.

His stubble was soft. His tongue, fiercely tender. His body was home, and I swear for a split second I thought I felt the rumble of a Pullman train under my feet. I took a deep breath. He filled my senses. Jaded, jagged pieces of me started to vanish—guilt, remorse, anxiety, confusion, and fear—all subsided with Kelly's touch. My body swelled with hope and shuddered with anticipation. Those fiery balls slingshot from heaven, red hot with God's apocalyptic anger, faded away— being replaced by an optimistic future.

Suddenly we'd gone from standing at the edge of the bed to lying on it. The weight of his body was my security blanket. His hands grazed my face, moving little pixie hairs behind my ears. He moaned and I swore I'd heard him moan before. I'd smelled him before. I'd felt him a million times before.

The music stopped and we were left to drown in the sounds of our heavy breathing and deafening heartbeats; the rhythm echoed in my ears.

Day turned into night. I was totally spellbound and the little Sarlacc purred, falling fast asleep.

I lay in bed next to Kelly, safe. His arms were wrapped tightly around me, his nose was touching mine, and I suddenly panicked.

I hadn't told Jesse I'd be gone for the night and back in time to leave for Jersey the next day. I grabbed my phone from the nightstand and texted him. Jesse said he was glad I was safe, and he'd see me in the morning. He didn't ask where I was. I knew that he knew.

I set my phone back on the nightstand and rolled over to face Kelly. My phone vibrated again. This time it was Carter and the first time he'd ever texted me.

"I miss you," his text said.

I had completely forgotten I even had a husband. I felt the guilt rise into my throat. I put the phone down and stared at the ceiling.

"Do you need to go?" He looked sad but understanding.

I rolled back over, inhaling. "No. It's just—"

"You're married, I know," he said, eyeballing the white gold, $20 wedding band still wrapped around the tip of his pinky.

"It doesn't bother you? You don't feel guilty?"

"When I look at you, I don't see a married woman. I mean, logically I know it, of course. But when I look at you, I just see *you*. Whatever *this*—" he motioned to himself and to me, drawing an invisible line connecting us, "is...it's strong. I won't fight it. I can't describe how I feel when I'm with you."

I looked at him. I felt it, too. It was extraordinary. No words could adequately describe the passion between us.

"I believe in the inexplicable," he continued. "A friend of mine told me he once knew someone that *this*—" he drew the invisible line that bound us again, "happened to. A man sat next to a woman on a plane, both already married to other people. And on the plane, they happened to strike up a conversation. By the end of the flight, they just *knew*. They each got divorced and they've been together since."

He relayed this love story while moving the mini hairs away from my face, pushing them behind my ear again. I was in shock by how natural everything felt; the pull toward him left me powerless, as if I had no choice.

We slept soundly, glued to each other all night.

******

"Did you sleep together?" Joel asked, wiping his glasses with a cloth.

"You mean did we have sex? No. We were at peace just being together. Kelly never pushed it. Not once. Our encounter was driven by... I don't even know what, but it was literally out of this world."

"What happened the next day?"

I sighed. "It came too fast. We moved like sloths—slow to separate. The Sarlacc—"

"I meant to ask earlier, Sarlacc?"

"Sorry, it was what I nicknamed the sad, hungry pit in my stomach anytime Kelly and I were apart. Have you seen *Return of the Jedi*?"

"Of course. Who hasn't?"

"You'd be surprised. The Sarlacc pit scene was in the beginning of the movie. Lando Calrissian almost fell in—"

"Oh! The thing in the sand that looked like a giant mouth with tremor-looking limbs!"

"Tremors. Well, shit, I haven't thought about that movie in friggin' years," I said, staring off. "Anyway, whenever Kelly and I weren't together, my stomach felt like a starved beast."

"Okay, continue."

"Once the T was up and running, I was back on it headed to Jesse's. I expected a million questions about where I had been and what I'd been doing all night. Not one peep. He was almost ready to go, packing up his toiletry kit, when I walked in."

"I thought Jesse lived in New Hampshire?"

"He did. He bought a condo in Boston years after Jax's visit. Anyway, being at Stanley Theater was a nice distraction from the guilt that surfaced. I wasn't thrilled about being at an all-day assembly, I knew I wouldn't pay one spec of attention."

"How was the health of your faith at this time?"

"Fading. I felt like God ignored my cries for help because I *did* pray. Being surrounded by other Witnesses only triggered my conscience, which beat me into submission."

"Were you sorry for God or Carter?"

"Well, the sad part is, I couldn't tell. And that eventually made me resent God."

"You didn't already resent him?"

"Not entirely. I was still trying to walk the straight and narrow."

"How can you say that given where you were the night before?"

I sighed again, realizing everything was about to sound more ludicrous than it had. I was not only ashamed for carrying out an extramarital affair but for also feeling stuck somewhere between forgivable human fuckups and eternal shame.

"Because I told on myself, hoping that would absolve me of what I'd done the night before," I said, looking out the window.

"Ah. Who did you tell?"

"Not Jesse, he already knew too much."

"Luke?"

I shook my head. "Mark."

"Really? Why Mark?"

"I'm not sure. Maybe it was a feeble attempt at getting closer to him? Sounds fucked up, and it is. But that's what happened.

I told him I developed feelings for another man and did something *wrong*."

"What was his response?"

"It threw me. He pressed his lips the way our mom does and hugged me. He asked if I thought I should talk to an elder. I said the elder I chose to tell was him. He said it was a conflict of interest, and I should find one of my local elders. Then, he grabbed my shoulders, looked me dead in the eyes, and said, 'I just got you back. I'm not losing you again. Fix this.' I lost it, sobbing like a fool.

"I wandered Stanley Theater distracting myself with its high ceilings, gorgeous Italian marble, Corinthian columns, thick, blood-red, velvet drapes, crystal chandeliers, and allegorical paintings while looking for an elder from my congregation. Then the Sarlacc woke, ravenous."

"Why?"

"Because when I thought about what I'd done, I realized my guilt was replacing Kelly's amber—he was fading, and my teething creature didn't like it one bit. We exchanged a few texts and the beast quieted. I was reeling in grief by the time I found an elder from my Hall. I was advised to talk about it with Carter before involving a judicial committee."

"I have to ask—why? You're a grown woman. I mean, I understand the need for some type of discipline and structure. But why now? Why again?"

Joel grabbed his notebook and it's a good thing he did because, well, keep reading.

"I didn't know anything else. I didn't know how to redeem myself from any remorse unless it was sanctioned by local elders. I needed someone else to forgive me; me trying to forgive myself wasn't enough. Even after nine years away from the Truth, it still prodded until I bled whether I was in or out."

"I see." He scribbled in his notepad. "What happened with Carter?"

******

CARTER PICKED ME UP at Jesse's Monday afternoon and I insisted on driving—I didn't think he should be the one behind the wheel when I owned up to my sins.

"I need to tell you something," I said, veering toward the onramp of 93 North. "Something happened. I didn't mean for it to happen, but something happened."

Suddenly Dean's voice, the night we broke up, echoed in my head. I struggled to find the right words to say. Then Carter did it for me.

"You cheated on me." The car fell uncomfortably silent. I felt his glare from the corner of my eye. "How could you? You knew *Phil*."

A tear rolled down his cheek, transformed into a dagger, and drove itself right into my heart.

"I know!" I started to cry. Maybe *I* shouldn't have been driving. "I'm so sorry! It just *happened*."

I stared out at the highway, wondering what I could possibly say. I didn't have the heart to tell him that Kelly made me feel ten times more alive than our own wedding day had. I couldn't look him in the face and tell him our marriage was a mistake, we should have waited.

"How did it? I mean, with *who*? W*hen*?" he asked.

He sat in the passenger seat, and I swore there were two of him—one to take in the news and the other to tell him it was real.

"I'm a shit. There's your how."

On the ride home I told him who and when, assuring him that Kelly and I did not have sex. He settled. And I could see his face planning our next steps, until I mentioned talking with Mark and a local elder.

"You told your *brother*? And a fucking elder? Bek! This is between us! I'm getting pretty goddamn sick of the fucking elders! They sign a No Blood Card instead of me, they know that you fucking cheated on me before I did! This is bullshit!"

He was right, and I was starting to see the ol' GB the way he did. I could have kicked myself for letting 9/11 scare me the way it had, but it was too late. I'd been back in the Truth for about two years by this time and more than enough damage had been done. Once we got home, we crashed and slept in bed as strangers.

After work the next day, I found him sitting at his desk. He turned his chair to face me. I sat across from him, on the edge of the bed, waiting for him to speak.

"I have to know one thing—did you do it on purpose? To get out of our marriage without pissing your God off?" His voice trembled.

It honestly hadn't crossed my mind to *intentionally* cheat. Not once. If that were the case, I *would* have slept with Kelly.

"No, I didn't."

"A huge part of me hates you for doing it." His lip quivered. "At the same time, I don't blame you. Things have been pretty awkward between us for a while. You must feel like you've been married to a ghost. Instead of going to work today, I wandered around, asking myself if I could forgive you." Tears welled in his eyes. "I didn't think I had forgiveness like this in me. I didn't think I was capable. But I can't see my future without you in it. I cried when I thought of never cracking your back again." His voice broke and tears ran down his cheeks.

I really was a shit. I'd destroyed a decent man. He was nowhere near perfect. But still, a decent man.

"I want to try harder. I want us to work. You need to stop talking to him. That's the first thing. And if you do talk to him, I want to know about it."

Honestly, I didn't think I deserved his forgiveness. Or maybe I didn't want it. I agreed to try knowing full well that it wouldn't be easy breaking the news to Kelly—or the Sarlacc.

When Luke got word of my forbidden encounter, he made it his top priority to be in the States, at the Hall, the night of my judicial committee hearing. In an empty Kingdom Hall, Luke and I stood in the coatroom, his forehead pressed to mine. Surrounded by hangers and abandoned suit coats, with no chilly shoulders to claim, he shivered while praying on my behalf.

The elders called me to the basement library. The *second school* dungeon—cold, dark, reeking of judgment. The only comfort I found, sitting at the cherry wood conference table, was being surrounded by books. It didn't matter that they were old *Watchtower* publications.

My warped reflection stared back at me from the shiny glass on top of the table. When I looked up, I saw three men I had known my entire life. All the hugs, BBQs, summer picnics, clambakes, and hikes along the Maine coast flooded my memory at once.

They sat across from me, stone-faced. Hands folded on the table. Suddenly they felt like strangers to me. They urged me to go into detail about Kelly, how we met, and how we found ourselves at a hotel, in the throes of passion.

I thoroughly explained each email, phone call, and text message. I went into detail about Kelly's brilliant idea of driving twelve hours to see me. I shared specifics of what we did and didn't do, with and to each other, while at the hotel.

I couldn't tell if my tears were born of regret or humiliation. Since the elders saw repentance, and some level of remorse, they decided I wouldn't be disfellowshipped but publicly reproved.

******

"I know you explained being..." Joel grabbed a steno pad from his desk containing my earlier years. "Ah, here...*privately* reproved with Trey, but *publicly*?"

"Yeah. When an elder says someone is *reproved* from the platform, the congregation knows it means the reproved did something wrong and would therefore lose their privileges. So, people would know I was being punished for something, but no one would know the details unless I shared them. They'd only know I needed *spiritual adjustment.* I'd be under the microscope until I won my privileges back again."

"What's the point of the announcement if you're not being ousted? Why would anyone need to know anything?"

"I guess so they could decide whether they should continue associating with me. If anyone felt that my spiritually sick germs contaminated their air, they'd avoid me."

"Did anyone do that?"

"A few. Most people pitied me, thinking their spiritual strength would heal me somehow."

"Did it?"

"What do you think?"

"Fair enough. So, what happened after your..." he flipped through pages in his notepads, counting, then said, "jeezaloo, *fourth* hearing?"

"I was shocked the elders didn't disfellowship me—I was sure they would. When I left the basement library, I looked up and saw Luke, still pacing by the coatroom where I'd left him. When he saw me coming, he raised his brow, waiting for the verdict. From about twenty feet away I signed, *warning.* Which is this—" I slapped the top of my fisted, left hand with the four fingertips of my right, twice. "Luke was relieved. He told me to work it out with Jehovah and everything else would fall in line. I had no memory of getting home or telling Carter

255

anything about the hearing. It was all a blur. The only thing coming in clear was Kelly's face."

"I'm assuming the attempts to make things work with Carter were short-lived?" Joel looked at the clock, closing his notebook.

"You assume correctly."

I stood up, grabbing my jean jacket from the arm of the couch.

"See you next week, Rebekah." He swiveled in his chair to face his desk.

"See ya, Joel."

I left, wondering if Joel saw me the way I saw myself—damaged, ruined, unworthy. I wondered if he grew tired of listening to me repeat the same story of self-sabotage over and over. I was getting tired of it myself.

Maybe that was the point of therapy? To tell someone the worst things you believe about yourself, until you finally notice your own masochistic patterns and stop them on your own.

Shameless

WHEN I TOLD KELLY that Carter and I were going to give our marriage some much-needed attention, the Sarlacc gnashed viciously. Its tentacles shot out from the pit of my stomach in violent protest. It howled like a lost child as days went by. I thought I was dying. Until a curious good morning text, hard to ignore, buzzed my phone awake.

"Good morning, chilibean!"

I had to know. "Chilibean?" I text back.

"You're hot like chili and little like a bean."

I had once been Dean's "peanut." Now, I'd become Kelly's "chilibean." Being referred to as tasty, tiny food was oddly irresistible.

Texts and secret phone calls resumed. I convinced myself it was okay because fate had already decided—and who was I to argue?

I didn't argue with fate but with Carter instead.

He shook me awake, early one morning before leaving for work, and asked, "Have you been talking to him?"

I wasn't awake enough to lie and had been straight with him from the beginning. I nodded, rolling over. His open hand met my upper thigh, leaving a bright red, welted handprint.

Fully awake, I screamed, "Ow!"

******

"He hit you?" Joel scowled.

"Yeah. I had it coming. I—"

"No. You didn't. You didn't deserve it with your father, your brother, Dean, or Carter. No, Rebekah. No. It's not okay." It was the first time I'd seen Joel with smoke coming out of his ears.

"You know what that is? The mark of a weak man, waving one huge flapping-shamelessly-in-the-wind *red flag*. Not okay, Rebekah. *Ever*. Remember that."

Well, I know what sets his teeth on edge.

******

CARTER THREW MY PHONE at me and left for work.

I lay there thinking that I'd brought it all on myself. And at the same time, it felt like there was this unstoppable force pointing me in Kelly's direction. It wasn't born of my own selfish desires—of which there were many, I admit—or from the way Kelly's support and adoration made me feel higher than God's celestial throne. It was something else. Almost as if there was some life lesson attached to him.

Unsure which life lesson was due in that moment, I flipped my phone open and called Kelly. While talking with him something came over me. I was suddenly angry with him. I blamed him for pursuing me, for not listening to Gina, and for disguising himself as a beautiful angel of light—like Satan. I decided to push him away. Far away. I told him to leave me alone. Leave *us* alone. He cried. He blubbered into the phone. I hung up. Then he sent text after text, pleading with me.

"Please…" they said. "You make me feel alive… I'm a shell without you, chilibean… Beautiful girl, please…"

With each text I deleted, the Sarlacc shifted. Its anger switched to melancholy.

He called. And called. I let his calls go to voicemail. He left message after message. Begging at first. "Please talk to me." Then he roared, "I'm sorry that you fell in love with me! I'm sorry that I came into your life! I'm sorry that I fill you with hope!"

I knew I owed Carter sincere effort. But when I thought of never seeing Kelly again, my stomach was in knots. I was completely torn—locked in a room I'd put myself in.

Once the weekend came, Carter and I took a scenic drive to an old, rustic, New England restaurant. He sat across from me, holding my hands. I wondered how he could still want me at all.

"I'm sorry for not trying. It isn't fair to you," I said.

"Do you *want* to try?"

"I don't know. I prayed only I feel like God's ignoring me. He isn't giving me the strength I keep asking for, and I can't help but wonder..."

Carter leaned forward, looking into my eyes.

"If the Truth is really the truth." I fought the tears I felt welling. He rubbed my hands, pursed his lips, and gave me an I-told-you-so look.

I started to miss meetings and *fall away* from the Truth. As I did, I could hear the Gin Blossoms song "Until I Fall Away" playing nonstop, along with congregant whispers...

"Oh, she was publicly reproved. She's inactive, weak in the Truth." And in the sign language Hall, it's more like: "Sister Bek regular meeting no more. Weak."

******

"How did that feel?" Joel had *clammed dawn* considerably from his recent scolding.

"How did what feel?"

"All of it. Trying with Carter and *falling away* as you put it?"

"Weird. I didn't just miss Kelly, but I was unhealthy, I guess? I wasn't eating. Not really sleeping. Work was annoying."

"Did reconciling with Carter and missing meetings feel like things were somewhat back to normal for you two?"

"Not really. I was kind of hoping it would feel that way, but it felt more like we were two strangers shoved together after some catastrophe, trying to make sense of it all. The sad part is we'd only been married for two and a half years. We shouldn't have been so *estranged*."

"Marriages don't typically fall apart when things are going well. You two were estranged long before Kelly came around. How did you feel missing meetings?"

"Guilty. We lived with my parents. So, they'd come downstairs to see if I was going to a meeting, and if I was, did I need a ride? Every time I said no, I just... I could see the hurt in their faces. My mother, god, she killed me. She was a bit overweight at the time, and it took a lot of strength for her to even come down the stairs. Watching her turn around and slowly go back up, gripping the handrail, disappointed, broke me. I felt like such a shit."

"They were the real reason you went back, 9/11 was scary for a lot of people, but even that fear would eventually dissipate. You wanted your family back more than anything." Joel didn't even look up as he was writing chicken scratches in his notepad.

I hated him for being so goddamn right.

******

CARTER AND I TIPTOED around our dying marriage. While we tried in vain, our lost love was writhing on the floor. We managed to step over it and only heard it crying in the dead of night.

Days without Kelly felt like years. I could feel him all around me. After weeks, he sent texts simply reading "..." and I knew, beyond all doubt, that he was home to a Sarlacc, too.

I sent "..." texts back.

Then, Kelly dared me with light, texting conversation. "How are you?" he'd ask. "Are you doing okay?"

And without fail, we were right back to the painful longing neither of us could ignore.

And neither could Carter; he knew me too well. Turns out I didn't know him as well as I thought because he suggested something shocking.

260

"Go ahead and meet up with him again," Carter said. "If you two *do* anything expect to do it with me when you get home."

My eyes bugged. He was giving me permission to cheat, as long as I was willing to repeat the whole adulterous scenario with him.

******

"Why on God's green earth would he even suggest that?" Joel was disgusted.

"I really don't know. I've thought it over quite a bit. All I can come up with is, he's sadistic?"

Joel removed his glasses and leaned back in his leather swivel chair. He laced his fingers together and rested them at the base of his head, looking up at the ceiling. He was just as stumped as I was.

"What a clever chess move…" he said to the ceiling. "I think, this would either force you to keep Kelly at arm's length—repulsed at the thought of re-enacting events with Carter—or Carter simply resorted to perverse and cruel revenge. You, sleeping with him after sleeping with Kelly, would put him back in the driver's seat, or at least he'd *feel* more in control."

******

WHAT CARTER AND I had lost was gone long before Kelly showed up and pointed at the squirming creature we'd been sidestepping since our wedding day.

I needed *something*. I found part of what I was looking for in a brand new 2004, deep indigo, Mazda3 Hatchback. I fell in love with Lysah, the hatchback, instantly. She was my ticket to sovereignty. Cruising down 93 South in my brand-new ride, sunroof open, I could smell the freedom. *Zoom Zoom.*

I thought about what Carter said and decided I didn't care. If he was giving me permission to see Kelly that's what I was going to do. I knew I was being reckless. I knew I was being shitty. But I never lied about it. Not once. I figured if he knew, came up with asinine rules, and stuck around expecting a play-by-play that was on him. I couldn't take responsibility for my sins *and* his.

Kelly drove to New England once again. Only this time, his big white Lumina shamelessly brought him straight to NH. Heart racing madly, I pulled into the hotel parking lot where we planned to meet. Kelly was leaned up against his car, arms folded, wearing a shit-eating grin. He lowered his sunglasses to get a better look at the new ride I parked next to his. I smiled, ear-to-ear from the driver's seat, as he circled the car emancipating a wolf-whistle. He stopped at the passenger side door and opened it.

"Damn, chilibean! Nice ride! Did you name her?" Plopping down in the passenger's seat, he started scrutinizing her many gadgets. He opened the glove box and reviewed the manual. He had a thing for manuals.

"Lisa, spelled L-Y-S-A-H, cuz she's fast and easy," I said, running my hands over the steering wheel.

We left Lysah next to the safety of his big, white boat and ventured inside with plans to stay for the night.

One night turned into three.

All weekend long, we were in a lovesick haze. Driving Lysah around the 603 during a clear, warm, perfect, spring weekend taking in its beauty was just the break I needed.

We drove her to the top of Mt. Washington, we stopped to swoon at moose grazing along back roads, we ordered in, we ate out, and snuggled at the hotel while watching movies. We relaxed naked in the tub, still virgins to each other's intimate touch. He cared for me the way no one ever had.

With him, I didn't need to be anything other than who I was at my core. I didn't know who she was, but he was introducing me to her in small but very significant ways.

He didn't measure my level of spirituality. Lurid sex play wasn't required. And he didn't act as though a piece of paper instantly deemed me his property.

He saw the erratic whirlwind gusting inside me and set out to be the eye of my storm; I longed to rest beside his calm. Everything about him was hauntingly familiar. He loved every part of me that I hated.

We wandered into the Children's Museum off Main Street in Concord, talking at length about the kids we'd have, names we liked, where we wanted to live, who we wanted to be, the ways we viewed the world, and how that would shape every decision from there on out.

We planned our life together that day.

Just outside the Museum's entrance, sitting on a bench shoulder to shoulder, he threw his arm around me, nuzzling my ear with his nose. I inhaled, committing the moment to memory, and he whispered, "Marry me."

The current flowing between us was powerful—like electricity. You don't see it, but you know its harnessed power can generate the light of a billion bulbs with the flip of one switch. Kelly was my switch.

Sitting comfortably inside Lysah, after one of our long drives, we breathed in her new car smell while listening to one of our songs. I leaned my head against the headrest, sharing my fantasies of a Hollywood movie kiss—the song would reach its instrumental climax, he'd pull me into a deep kiss, and the world would spin around us.

I asked what he saw.

"A door opening; I open a door and see you inside with our kids."

And here it comes, the part we'd both been romancing in great detail. The music softened, then rose to a crescendo. He leaned in close, then playfully pulled away from my kiss. I pouted.

"It's not time yet," he teased, forcing me to wait for the height of the song.

His face was millimeters from mine, his hand was on the back of my head, stroking my hair. By this point, I was nearly begging. He looked into my eyes. The peak of our song crashed through Lysah's speakers, and he pulled me closer with urgency. His kiss was deep and fierce. I melted into him, slowly fading, forgetting every little part of who I thought I was.

Glassy-eyed, I looked at him and said, "Maybe someday I can give you your fantasy."

We were interrupted by my buzzing cell phone.

"I realize I allowed this," Carter's text read, "but you don't have to put me through hell. I deserve better. Everyone thinks so."

It had been three days of bliss for me and pure hell for Carter. He was right—he did deserve better than the two-timing trollop I felt like.

******

"Two-timing trollop or not, he told you to go!" Joel shook his head.

"I know he did—"

"Rebekah, listen. I'm not excusing the choices either of you made. You were having an affair, yes, but you didn't hide it, you came clean to him and your elders. What he was doing—instead of saying, 'I deserve better, we're over, I'm leaving,'—was manipulating you *vengefully*. I want you to see that. Now, what did you do?"

"I tried to make Carter leave," I said, shamefully to my nervous hands.

"How?"

I sighed, knowing I was about to start picking at one mother-fuck of a scab.

SITTING IN MY FREEDOM RIDE I felt imprisoned.

Kelly looked at me; the worry lines on his face were waking up.

I pressed my lips. I knew that he understood how conflicted I was.

He looked out the window, silent.

I studied Kelly's face and hiding between each crease, and every grain of stubble, were endless possibilities. And coming through his blue eyes, hope.

I looked through the trees, toward the highway going north, and only saw frustration, captivity, resentment, and defeat. I sighed, knowing I was the one responsible for all the turmoil.

Thinking about the roles we play in each other's lives, how sometimes, some people show up right on schedule—I made a split-second decision.

I closed my flip phone, turned off Lysah's engine, looked at Kelly, and said, "C'mon."

I got out, slammed the driver's side door, and grabbed his hand, leading him to the hotel's back entrance. I flung the door open and yanked him into the stairwell. The door slammed shut, echoing. I stomped up four steps until I felt him pull back.

I turned to scowl at his resistance. We stood a few feet apart. I fixed my gaze on him from two steps above.

It was dissonantly quiet.

Then he said, "Like this?"

"Yes."

I grabbed his hand again and marched.

A million thoughts ran through my mind charging up those steps. Carter deserved better and so did I. I wanted to make things easier on everyone and I knew what would do the trick. I didn't want to do it in angst, but I knew it was bound to happen sooner or later; I was just speeding up the inevitable.

I could make it easier for Carter to walk away and leave. If he asked me again, I could say, "Yes, I did it on purpose." There were enough people in the Truth doing it on purpose, getting out of unhappy marriages. If that's what the ol' GB wanted, then that's what they'd get.

I also couldn't wait another minute; not after that kiss in the car; not after our entire weekend of bliss. And not after Kelly whispered, "Marry me."

I wanted him, and goddamn it I was going to have him.

I opened the door to our room and hurried us both inside, letting it close behind us. I pushed Kelly up against the wall and threw my body onto his. My breath was quick and shallow. I knew his hesitation from the stairwell would be short lived.

He moved in closer. I backed away, teasing him. I laced my fingers behind his neck and pulled him in. Every kiss I'd ever had, up until that moment, culminated into this one perfect embrace. He moaned, pressing into me, unable to stop what I'd started.

We quickly undressed each other—fingers fumbling, breath heavy—and fell onto the unmade bed. The weight of his body comforted me. His skin was soft, he smelled like home. We'd been naked in the tub just two days before, but this magically felt like the first time we'd really seen each other.

He eased his way inside. The passion between us flooded my senses and I cried. I don't mean, one single tear streamed down my cheek. I mean, every emotion I'd ever felt in my whole life burst forth, and I cried as he pulsated back and forth. Our bodies melted into one. We came simultaneously, awestruck. We remained still on the bed—breathless and tangled. We didn't dare move; moving meant the weekend was over; moving meant he'd be leaving soon.

He held me closer. I was still crying. He was shuddering. I secretly hoped the cure to our magnetic pull was sex. Maybe the draw to each other would subside now that'd we'd given in to carnal temptation. Maybe it would satisfy the Sarlacc, ending our time together.

But I was wrong.

Parting ways that Monday was excruciating. Kelly and his Lumina went back to D.C. while Lysah and I sat quietly, reliving moments from the weekend to keep my creature well fed.

Leaving Concord, I thought about what I'd say to Carter. Trying to make it work now would only be nocuous. He was hurting. I was hurting. We were hurting each other. Me, by continuing the affair, and he, by resorting to manipulative schemes.

I texted Carter, telling him to meet me at my aunt Kathy's house. Shortly after she and my uncle moved to NH, they had my baby cousin, Gianna, and I'd been staying there, on-and-off, helping out.

Meeting on neutral ground seemed safe. Carter came inside and found me sitting on the couch. Unfortunately, we were alone. He stood on the other side of the room glaring at me.

"Did you sleep with him?"

I wasted no time. "Yes."

He pulled off his wedding ring, threw it at me, and stormed out.

I chased him into the driveway, throwing myself onto his truck. "No! Don't leave yet! Let's talk!" I screamed pounding on the driver's side window.

******

"Why did you chase after him? Wasn't that what you wanted?" Joel asked.

"I knew you'd ask that. What's funny is at the time, it was instinctual. Even though I'd just delivered a hard blow, I *did* want to talk; to mollify what I could. I hated all the hurt we'd caused each other. And I knew deep down, talking might have stopped him from—"

"Manipulating the situation even more?"

"Bingo. He was hurt, and I didn't blame him. But what he did next was shitty, and I'm finally starting to see that."

"A breakthrough! Hallelujah, Rebekah!" Joel threw his fisted hands in the air, shaking them in victory.

"I guess so, thanks to what you said about manipulation. I don't know why I didn't see that before—"

"You may not have been ready to. What happened? Did he stay and talk?"

"No. He peeled out. But before he did, he asked me if I'd want to talk it over with my family. See, they knew nothing about where I'd been all weekend, and he was about to tell them."

Joel shook his head and pursed his Larry David lips.

"I could hear the J-Dub whispers, echoing in my head after he left. The whispers became heckles. The heckles became judgment. When I thought about people heckling in small groups, talking about *my* personal business, images of the *second school* came to mind. Which meant another judicial committee hearing. I couldn't go through another one. I panicked. Carter had me in a pickle and he knew it."

"Of course, he did."

"Well, my family was now undoubtedly aware of my secret weekend rendezvous, and the following weekend was like an intervention, my very own *After School Special*. My brothers and their wives drove to the house, inserting themselves into my marital tragedy. And every J-Dub who knew, had made it their primary concern. People from both congregations called offering unsolicited advice and begged me to 'think about what I was doing.'"

"Did anyone give you a red 'A' to embroider on your dresses?" Joel joked.

"They really should have because the focus was showcasing my wrongs so that I'd be forced to make them right, the way *they* all thought it should be done. No one seemed to care about what I was going through. Maybe the damage I'd done didn't deserve compassion. But I couldn't help noticing that the focus was put on how I'd hurt Jehovah and jeopardized my place in the *New System* line, stumbling my Witness family and in-laws along the way. Even concern for Carter fell near the bottom of the list. Dead last was my general well-being and curing me of my love for another man. 'Just pray, Bek' was all I heard. I wanted to say, 'Oh, okay, cuz *that's* working!' I'd prayed so much and, nothing."

"Was there anyone you could talk to?"

"Well, my mom was as supportive as she could be. If I *did* confide in her, even for the tiniest thing, she felt pressured to tell someone because that's what Luke told her she should do. I know she wanted to be there for me, she waddled up and down the stairs to our studio apartment often enough. But she most likely didn't want me to tell her too much because she'd have to give my secrets up to someone."

"What did your brothers do?"

I sighed recalling the last time I saw Mark.

"Mark and I walked to the coffee shop we grew up going to with Mom and Dad—Jim's Drive-In. At a tiny truck stop off the highway, surrounded by truckers stuffing their faces in between pit stops, Mark dug right into my marriage. He said I was married to a good man who *let me* go to meetings without a fight. He couldn't believe I had the nerve to fall for a worldly man, commit adultery, or that I still wanted to leave Carter even though he'd forgiven me. I knew sharing my heartbreak wouldn't matter, and neither would describing the ravenous Sarlacc in the pit of my stomach. I kept the gaping holes in my faith to myself as we left Jim's Drive-In and walked home in silence. Approaching the driveway, I bolted ahead for shelter.

But Luke was waiting for me by the split entryway. I pushed past him, and he followed me down the stairs, cornering me."

"It really *was* like an intervention!"

"I wasn't kidding. He asked if I really thought I could treat people however I wanted, without a care in the world. He got right in my face and said, 'Do you think I'm gonna let you do such a thing to *my* God?' He said since I was committing adultery, stealing and murder were in my near future. He told me I needed to forget Kelly and work it out with Carter. Then he glared at me and went upstairs. A few minutes later, Carter came down and lay beside me on the couch."

"Oh, now he wants a snuggle?"

I held my breath, shrugged, then exhaled. "I guess after my affair, and him telling everyone about it, we were tired. The sad part was, while lying there with Carter, I could almost remember a time when we were okay."

"Did he ever bring up wanting to re-enact your lovemaking with Kelly?"

"Come to think of it, no. Maybe he thought he'd done enough damage? Maybe he never really planned to? I don't know. I envied Carter because he only needed to heal his own broken heart. I was tasked with making things right with Jehovah; making things right with Carter; making amends at the Kingdom Hall; earning my privileges back; *and* severing the tie with Kelly. I had a lot more on my plate than Carter and I just wanted to sleep. It was too much and what *I* needed wasn't a priority. Once again, I felt like I was expected to be everything to everyone. I can only wear one chameleon suit at a time and with Kelly, I didn't need one. So, we stayed in touch; he was the only calm I found in the shit storm I'd created."

Joel looked at the clock and closed his notepad. "Do one thing before next week. Think of more ways Carter also contributed to the demise of your marriage, more ways in which he was responsible. It takes two, Rebekah. When you've done that, see if anything resembles other relationships you've had. Journal it all. Okay?"

I inhaled thinking about how much journaling that sounded like. I mentally scheduled a time, figuring I'd have to sandwich journaling in between all my government, alphabet-soup interpreting assignments. *Good thing I ride the Metro.*

I exhaled, blowing air from my cheeks. "Okay. I'll do my best."

End Scene

SITTING ON JOEL'S COUCH, I clutched my maroon and gold swirled journal. I was ashamed to say I hadn't come up with much.

"So? How did it go?" Joel asked seated on the edge of his leather chair.

I buried the fingertips of my right hand into the outgrown, wavy, mess of curly hair and scratched the side of my head. "It went? I don't know."

"What did you come up with?"

"Not much. I mean, the more I think about the end of my marriage, and can for one second stop blaming myself, I see a couple things? But not enough to fill the journal."

"You didn't need to fill it. What did you see?" Joel grabbed his notepad and pen, ready.

I opened the journal, flipped past my favorite quote, and skimmed the little bit I'd scribbled on the way to my three-times-a-week interpreting assignment.

"Well, the more I thought about all the crap that happened, I realized maybe one reason he told me to go ahead and see Kelly was so he could spend the weekend telling whoever would listen where I was and how excruciating it was for him. He could be the victim for *my* assassin. He got what he wanted when everyone he talked to told him he deserved better. And talking to my family, well, he knew about certain Witness rules; he knew adultery was the only way out of a marriage unless there's forgiveness," I said.

"Forgiveness how?"

"According to ol' GB scriptural misinterpretation, if the adulterer and victim consummate the marriage again (after a transgression) the slate is wiped clean. No divorce granted; it's technically forgiveness. If the adulterer and victim *don't* have sex, that means the victim couldn't get past it, couldn't forgive. Therefore, divorce is permitted."

"Had you and Carter consummated the marriage again—"

"Oh, my god! No! When we were trying to make it work, and I stopped talking to Kelly for that short time, I half-assed my way through sex with Carter. But Kelly and I hadn't slept together at that point. After Kelly and I actually *had* sex, I certainly didn't want to cheat on my boyfriend with my husband, so, no. Wow. Why am I *just* seeing that?"

Joel smiled. "Journaling."

"Given what Carter knew about J-Dubs, because he did tune in to conversations from time to time, he knew exactly which buttons to push. And he pushed them to torture me with my own faith—a faith he resented."

"Yes, Rebekah! Did this mirror anyone else in your life?"

I thought for a minute. "Luke. Carter must've gotten that idea from him. Luke is a major button-pusher and only pushes when he's hurting. He's always been master at finding the weakest spot below the belt, then hitting hard." I nodded to myself. "Yep. Luke probably coached Carter."

Damn! How had I not seen this?

"What about Mark?"

"No. Mark never did anything like that, but he did keep to himself. A lot. So did Carter. My dad is a mix of Mark *and* Luke; he doesn't push buttons but tries to manipulate using guilt. My mom has always been the eye of their storm—patiently waiting for the waters to settle."

"What about Dean?"

"Dean? Huh, I hadn't factored him into the equation. I guess Dean and Luke were somewhat alike; both were hot-headed, manipulative, saw me as something to protect, and exploit, maybe? Although I don't think either of them truly *knew* that's what they were doing. Sometimes I felt like Dean's pet. Luke's, too. Obviously for different reasons. Dean for amusement. And Luke, admiration."

"Admiration?"

"When I was reinstated, Luke took me all over the place, introduced me to everyone, proudly. Out of everyone in the family, I always thought he and I were most alike. He was proud to have a carbon copy of himself around until *I* found *his* buttons. I found Carter's eventually, too."

"Oh?"

"It was around the time Dad's big brother, my uncle Teddy, was dying..."

******

UNCLE TEDDY WAS DYING from Cancer. Hospice made regular stops to his tiny apartment in Danbury, Connecticut as he flirted with death. I made plans to drive down one Friday afternoon and stay at a nearby hotel.

Carter offered to come with me.

I didn't want him there. We'd been living with my parents for over a year, and he hadn't learned any sign language. I still saw him as the walking dead when he said he'd give any kid we had a cochlear implant.

My uncle Teddy was also Deaf, and I didn't want Carter anywhere near him. They had also never met and to meet him as he was dying was just in bad taste.

And let's not forget, Carter had told my family things—resulting in an ill-timed scriptural intervention, worsening our matrimonial chaos.

"No. Someone needs to stay with the pups," I said.

I hugged and kissed all my furry friends, hopped in Lysah, and took off for Connecticut.

And as I drove, Kelly flew to Providence, Rhode Island.

I just wanted to be there, sit with Uncle Teddy, hold his huge boxing hand, tell him I loved him. But when a priest showed up to sing "Amazing Grace," and deliver last rites, I was asked to interpret.

My cousins, CODAs by definition, couldn't sign their way out of a paper bag, and no one thought to hire an interpreter. It wasn't like interpreting for a Kennedy on Capitol Hill, where I had support if I floundered. This was my uncle's deathbed.

I signed "Amazing Grace" while everyone around him sang. Teddy tossed and turned as the morphine wore off. He looked me right in the eyes and signed, "Angel you?"

No, Uncle Teddy—I'm far from an angel.

In the hotel bathtub, wrapped safely in Kelly's arms, he scooped warm water into the palm of his hand, pouring it over exposed skin to warm me. More and more, he showed me what true intimacy looked like. It wasn't about animalistic fucking or being someone's property on paper. It was loving someone when they couldn't find a way to love themselves.

Uncle Teddy died shortly after my visit. His giant, signing mitts had boxed their last fight.

Back home, Carter took me by surprise when he suggested we take a road trip. He saw what he'd done by entangling my family into our wedded mess and suggested we give it one more shot.

I conceded, feeling guilty for having had a clandestine tryst in Connecticut. And I didn't want to end things without saying I absolutely tried as hard as I could. Even if I was exhausted. Even if I couldn't tell why I was willing to try. Was it for family? Carter? God? Vanity? I felt pressure coming in from all sides.

Carter let me choose the destination. To satisfy the longstanding crush I had on a dead celebrity, we went to Fairmount, Indiana. I'd had a thing for forlorn actor, James Dean, since my freshman year of high school. Somewhere in

Indiana, I hoped to find missing pieces of myself buried beneath the ruins of an American icon. I instinctively knew nothing between us could be revived.

I'd done some reading on the long drive and learned an interesting fact: genetic bacteria can be more suitable with one person compared to another. If the existing chemistry between two people is interrupted with someone else's *more compatible* chemistry, it's near impossible for the original couple to reconnect biologically. The fact that our mediocre scientific attraction was disrupted by a friendlier source, bio-chemically speaking, meant it was unlikely anything could be resurrected. Or maybe I just didn't want to resuscitate it.

But what the hell? We took the trip anyway, and it was a miserable disaster.

We visited the James Dean Museum, where I purchased an original copy of John Steinbeck's, *East of Eden*, introducing me to one of my favorite authors. We saw James' gravesite, drove by the house he grew up in, and parked outside his old high school. It was empty, abandoned, and vandalized.

Colorful graffiti covered the faded, once vibrant, red brick. Doors were boarded up, and the windows on almost every floor were busted. Much like our marriage—crumbling and near unsalvageable.

Sitting in the car, staring at Fairmount High, I teared up. There were the stomping grounds of a once young, hopeful James Dean—on the school's drama club stage—giving birth to his very short acting career. And all of it was laid to rest in a decaying, vacant building. A painting of his face dressed the city's water tower. I could feel his ghost lingering painfully from street to street.

And that was the moment I accepted my marriage was over. End scene.

We decided to cut our trip short and head home. Stopping at a Denny's on I-80, to let the torrential downpour pass,

Carter and I had the conversation that finally laid our short marriage to rest.

He told me he didn't think I was very smart—I had the potential to be, but I wasn't. He chuckled to himself while shaking several sugar packets, emptying them one by one, into his heavily creamed coffee. He stirred his coffee, then lifted his mug to the same lips I'd once planned to kiss for the rest of my life; I shuddered at the thought.

"You had no knowledge of me driving to Connecticut, and finding your car, the weekend your uncle was dying." His face wore contempt like he was getting paid. "I drove to all the hotels nearest your uncle's until I found your car."

"Why?" I asked; my eyebrows furrowed, limbering up for their passionate tarantella debut. I could hear the accordions in my head start to compress and expand. I was ready.

"If I found your car, I knew I'd find Kelly's; D.C. plates in Connecticut would be easy to spot, especially parked next to your purple car." He was so impressed with himself, and I was very disturbed by his investigative efforts. "That's not what I found, though," he said, sipping his coffee. "Finding your car alone, I was relieved and thought you just went to see your uncle, then study for your interpreting test, like you said. Halfway back to New Hampshire, it dawned on me that you probably picked him up from an airport."

"You're fuckin' creepy."

I mopped up dribbles of egg yolk with my toast and decided, in a Denny's dining room, that we were most definitely done. I didn't blame Carter for his paranoia, or his misguided grief. But his private investigation caused me to feel just like I had growing up. Small. Helpless. Stuck.

We started separating our things once we got home. Carter made plans to stay with his mom. And I, with all the animals, stayed with my parents. Carter took all the good vinyl, along with the original Star Wars comics, movie posters, and action figures. That pained me more than his leaving.

With Carter's exodus, the inevitable force between Kelly and I only grew stronger. I was terrified by the passion between us. The trail of destruction our bond had created not only left me in anguish, but I was also convinced I'd never find anyone else I wanted as much—what I felt for Kelly was unearthly.

It would've been easy to find a hollow-headed Yes Man in the Truth; finding anyone to develop lukewarm feelings for, would be a cinch. I'd already done that. The Sarlacc stirred when I realized I might never feel *this* again. Whatever *this*— invisible line connecting me to Kelly—was.

Kelly and I were the only ones able to unfold the mysterious pull between us, looking at it from every single angle of our respective world prisms. And even then, we were only halfway to understanding. What we shared was unstoppable. Beyond our control. Meant to be. Anyone hurt in the process was doing so for fate's ego.

And Sign Language Associates (SLA) must've also seen something they liked because they called, asking if I wanted to fly down to D.C. for working vacations. Which was just the push I needed to start interpreting for real.

No more one-on-one classroom situations, acting as the glorified babysitter hired to communicate with the school's token "hearing impaired" kid. Deaf people, Deaf *professionals*, were willing to take a chance on an ignorant CODA with no degree.

Challenge accepted.

******

"Why do you call yourself ignorant?" Joel wrinkled his brow.

"Because at the time, when it came to interpreting, I was pretty green. I don't have a degree, just Deaf parents. That doesn't necessarily make an interpreter."

"Did you ever take any college classes?"

"When Carter and I were dating he asked me what I wanted for Christmas. I told him I wanted feetsie pajamas and a college education. That year he gave me a giant fleece onesie, and a gift certificate for one class at a community college. One class easily turned into two semesters. I loved it—Philosophy, Creative Writing, and Psychology were my favorites. Then we got married, 9/11...you know the rest," I said, waving my hand.

"How did you feel around Deaf highbrows?"

"Scared. Nervous. But I always teamed with seasoned interpreters. I wasn't left to my own devices that often."

"Were you and Kelly together during these working vacations?"

"Oh, yeah and I loved every minute of it. Between my work assignments, I'd get out along various Metro stops, visiting the Lincoln Memorial, DuPont Circle, Union Station, Chinatown, and Tenleytown—where Kelly's apartment was. Every stop became my home away from home."

"Did anyone find out you stayed with Kelly while you were there for work?"

"Everyone assumed I stayed with Gina since she also worked with SLA. When the elders asked her, she corrected them, and their witch-hunt would continue. Since no one actually *saw* me with Kelly, nothing could be confirmed, and I successfully avoided judicial hearings."

"For how long?"

"About a year? Maybe a little less. Working with SLA, learning about a world the GB keeps their rank-and-file apart from, and being with Kelly, opened my eyes to how life could be. And it was then when I *really* started to resent the Truth and all its chicanery. I saw nothing but lies—and a worldwide organization underhandedly keeping people inside—with threats disguised as council, fear dressed as love. It didn't make sense that the Almighty shook his celestial fist at my infidelity but not at the countless injustices plaguing the planet. I mean, how does that add up?"

"Why didn't you just write another letter, excusing yourself from the faith?"

"My family, parents especially. The Governing Body held them hostage." I started to think about my life while gazing at a lint ball attached to the sleeve of my shirt. I picked it, rolling it between my fingers, and said, "Being raised a Witness felt like drifting along thoughtlessly on the GB's conveyor belt of mind control—repeatedly being stamped with guilt, fear, shame, depression, doom, and exile. Once enough self-doubt, groupthink, and indecisiveness are instilled, the GB then points to a shiny, red button at the end of their assembly line—tormenting anyone not in compliance. Threatening the button with their forefinger, triggers the inner-ticking-time-bomb-of-terror which is stamped sometime between infancy and childhood. I can see the upper echelon grin, flash a photo of my family, and whisper, 'Do you really want to do this again?'"

"That's quite a mental image." Joel raised his eyebrows. "I can't imagine what that's like."

"I have an over-active imagination. Thinking about losing my family again, hurt. What felt worse was the thought of being a hypocrite. I have to live with me for the rest of my life. I gotta be okay with who that is."

"You didn't want to be a *double lifer*."

"No, I didn't. I know every family is different. Every person, whether in or out, does what they have to do. I won't judge anyone else for that, but I knew I'd judge myself. One thing I like about myself is my integrity. I'm a terrible liar and I'm glad. I don't know if I should credit being raised a J-Dub or if that's just *who I am*, but I knew what I had to do. *Double lifing* didn't feel right. I ejected myself from the conveyor belt of systematic indoctrination, flying right into another judicial committee hearing."

"Rebekah, you're a glutton for punishment!" Joel said.

If anyone else had said that I may have taken offense but given everything we'd talked about so far, I smirked and said, "I myself am heaven and hell. Besides, by this time I was numb to it. It was almost—"

"Part of who you were, part of who they trained you to be. So how did your…" Joel flipped through his notes counting, "…*fifth* judicial hearing come to be?"

"Before I tell you, I want you to understand that besides Kelly, I had no one; I'd shut everyone out. I feel stupid even remembering this and how pathetic I allowed myself to be." Tears welled up, and I avoided eye contact but could feel the weight of his stare.

"I'm not going to judge you or the fact that you were heavily influenced by mind-altering propaganda. It's *me*."

From the corner of my eye, I saw him smile and hand me a box of Kleenex.

"What? No aloe?" I teased.

"Tomorrow's grocery day… Whenever you're ready."

******

CRITICAL THINKING IS NOT a Governing Body approved stamp-of-indoctrination. And I sure wasn't using any when I chose to confide in Valeri, the J-Dub who had studied with me after my reinstatement.

I didn't want to confide in my mother and put her in a tough spot—she had enough to deal with surrounded by the men in our family, constantly questioning her. I wanted someone uninvolved.

I drove to Valeri's.

Lysah's sunroof was open, and the distinct hallmarks of early NH summers revealed themselves one by one. The smell of humidity, earthy dust from old dirt roads being kicked up, the lavender, the dandelions spread out like a blanket along the roadside, and the sound of a Black-capped Chickadee singing its infamous two-note song brought back memories of driving in the Caprice Classic with Mom.

Pulling into Valeri's driveway, Lysah's tires rumbled over gravel with disapproval. Parked, I hung my head, forehead touching the steering wheel. Lysah begged for us to leave but it was too late. Valeri had run to the driver's side door and opened it. She, along with many other J-Dubs, already knew about my unchaste predicament.

While sitting on a blanket in her backyard, I skimmed over the past year—Kelly's visits, failed attempts to save my marriage, and even my secret doubts about the Truth. She responded exactly how I thought she might.

Tears welled in her eyes, and she said, "How can you not love Jehovah? If you get to know him, *really* get to know him, you'll see he is just *so good*."

I looked at her, thinking it would've been nice believing in something the way she did. Some sort of higher power. God. A force that would take care of everything. But I knew in that moment—while listening to her go on about how good God was—that I never really did. I was never moved to tears. Fear, yes. In love with Jehovah, no. And sitting on that blanket with her I realized, their Truth merely had the *appearance* of genuineness. It was nothing but smoke and mirrors, weak verisimilitude at best.

She urged me to take responsibility for my choices and confess to the elders. If I didn't confess within her designated time frame of a week, she would be forced to tell them on my behalf. I said okay and left.

Relieved once I reunited with Lysah, I opened her sunroof, welcoming the sweet fragrances of summer drifting around me. On that drive, I decided to end my time in NH and take SLA up on their offer to hire me full-time.

I was packing for my move to Silver Spring, when Valeri called to ask if I had spoken with the elders. No. No, I hadn't. She reminded me if I didn't, she would. She was eager to wipe the blood of my sins off her own hands. Fine, I told her. I'll call.

Dialing the presiding overseer's number, I thought about how J-Dub women, *sisters in faith*, encouraged each other to repeatedly place themselves beneath men—in the *second school* of shame—reliving their transgressions over and over in the presence of "older and wiser" men.

Did any of them get off on this?

I told the elder my affair had not ended, and I was moving to the D.C. area within a month. He said we needed to schedule a hearing.

Before long, I was back in the hot seat again. Three elders sat across from me in silence. One sat with tears in his eyes. Another hung his head. The almighty presiding overseer met my eye.

With his hands folded, and voice low, he said, "I don't want to disfellowship you a second time. This is killing your parents. I hate doing this. If you said you were moving to Las Vegas, we'd probably just reprove you again. The fact you're moving to D.C.—*to where he is*—really only leaves us with one choice. Are you sure about this?"

I stared at the other two elders. They both said nothing, and it was deafening. I started to cry. "I love Kelly, I can't help it. We've planned our whole lives—"

"Oh, Bek. We all fantasize. It's human to idealize a future, but does it compare to the one Jehovah is offering?" the overseer asked.

I shrugged and looked away. I no longer believed in the one Jehovah was offering. Kelly's offer was tangible, full of scary wonder.

"What happened between the two of you? I mean, are they disfellowshipping offenses? Loose conduct? Adultery? Are we talking A to Z?"

I didn't want to tell them anything. The overpowering emotion Kelly and I felt being together—both of us bursting into tears when we made love—was none of their business. They'd laugh hearing me say Kelly and I were like two stars floating in space, forced together as part of some cosmic plan. Separate, we were weak embers faintly glowing. Together, we ignited an uncontrollable flame, overwhelming us both. They didn't need to know we'd named our unborn children, or that our bodies melted into each other's effortlessly.

I just nodded. I didn't know what A to Z meant to him and I didn't want to.

"Are you repentant?" he asked.

No. I wasn't sorry about any part of the last year and a half. Kelly was my switch. All systems go. I shook my head in tears, knowing that they were about to push the GB's shiny, red button. I saw an old family photo flash in my mind—one of those campy, Old West photos where someone dresses you up in saloon clothes and gives you a fake gun along with a bottle of whiskey.

"We won't announce your disfellowshipping right away. We'll give you a ten-day grace period, time with your family and time to connect with local elders in D.C., so you can be reinstated when you're ready."

******

"A grace period?"

I wiped the tears and shook the old Disney photo from my memory. "Yeah. I don't know how often they do that, or what scripture they misinterpreted to allow it, but they did it for me."

"How much time passed between Valeri, your hearing, and the move?"

I sighed, looked down, and shrugged. The truth was it all happened so fast I couldn't really remember. "I think like two or three weeks. I'd found an apartment on one of my working vacations, and the landlord was nice enough to allow all the animals and hold it for me."

"Wow. Not many landlords are willing to do that."

A few more tears escaped. "I just know my family could have loved me through my own bullshit if the *Society*, the GB, had let them. I mean, imagine *liking* your family, ya know? Then some fucking publishing company, with foolish biblical principles, tells them from the top down to just cut you off. I hated delivering them up as a sacrificial lamb. I think even Carter felt sorry for me, and maybe he even felt bad for the tumult he caused, because he loaded up his truck with my things and moved me down to Maryland."

Joel's pen stopped and his eyes bugged out. "Come again?"

"Carter didn't think I'd go through with the move; maybe he wanted to witness me getting scared, changing my mind. And if I did, maybe he wanted to be the one picking up the pieces, keeping one over on me for as long as I'd let him. Or maybe he just wanted to be with our boys, Bartok and Moron, before I took them out of arm's reach." I shrugged. *Who knows* why *he moved me down?*

"That's kind of noble of him."

"Sort of. He did ask if we could 'say goodbye' and from that, I figured he was seeking some type of recompense. I obliged and that was that. Aside from Carter buying me groceries and staying with me until I secured a rental car—"

"A rental? What happened to Lysah?"

"Taking Carter to breakfast before his drive back to New Hampshire, Karma found us in a busy intersection; she took my electric purple hatchback as payment when a moving truck hit us head on."

"Oh, no! Were you hurt?

"Surprisingly, no."

"And, of course, you thought you had it coming."

"Didn't I? On the one hand, there's my boyfriend—a mere half hour away from me, chomping at the bit. And then there's my husband—moving me closer to the man I'd left him for. Carter stayed the night to be sure I was okay, and it was totally undeserved. I guess I was okay with spending more time saying goodbye to Carter, but watching him drive off the next day, waving farewell, meant hello to my grace period. So, I called Luke instead of Kelly."

******

"HELLO?" LUKE SAID.

"Hi, it's me." I said, wandering around the corner of my small, brick apartment building.

"Hey, where are you?"

"Maryland."

"Working again?"

"Yes. But there's more." I hesitated to continue. "I just moved down here. I start full time at SLA this week." The line fell silent. I looked at my phone to see if we were still connected.

"Where are you living?" he asked.

"In a basement apartment with the dogs; it's a one bedroom. I'm alone."

He seemed relieved I was living alone until I told him my disfellowshipping would be announced in nine days. Despite our many tiffs over the years, he was my brother—therefore one half of me—and I was being forcefully ejected from his life.

I could hear him fighting tears. "This doesn't have to be for long. You got reinstated in a few months' time just a couple of years ago. You can do it that quickly again," he idealized. "Steer clear of Kelly and *come back* soon, make sure it doesn't end up being another nine years." His voice cracked.

There was just too much hypocrisy, mixed messages, and conditional love weighed down with guilt and fear—so much pain wrapped around the promise of *everlasting life in paradise on earth*—I just couldn't tell him I wasn't planning on going back.

Calling Mark felt like being called to the principal's office at school; he was curt, condescending, and cold. He disapproved of my recent move and even had the nerve to suggest when things didn't work out with Kelly, I may "turn lesbian."

"How do you figure?" I fumed.

"You won't want to be alone—getting discouraged with men and the cycle you keep repeating—you may try being with a woman."

I was speechless. The Bible was shoved so far up his ass he was spewing total ignorance.

My dad drove down a few days later, making sure he stayed within Jehovah's timetable. He stayed one night, savoring his last moments with me.

It felt like I was watching my own funeral play out—everyone surfaced to say goodbye.

At breakfast the next day he, of course, voiced he and Mom wanted me to *come back* soon.

That night, carless and broken-hearted, I got ready for bed. I ignored Kelly's efforts to reach out; I just needed some time. And in the bathroom mirror, I saw *her* again.

A very gaunt, sad, young woman stared back. Her once long, dark mane was now cut into a disheveled, overgrown pixie.

She recalled lopping it off, despite her husband's pleas not to. There were dark circles under her eyes, and she'd lost a considerable amount of weight. Her cheeks were sunken, worry lines were drawn above her dark eyebrows, and her full lips were now shaped into a perma-pout.

The pups tap-danced all around her while she stood at the mirror. Bartok jumped up with an itty-bitty ball in his mouth ready to run down the hall and fetch it. And Moron sniffed around the bathroom floor familiarizing himself with his new bathtub—he loved hot showers.

Her fingertips grazed her thinning face, and a single tear trickled down her cheek.

What the fuck are you gonna do now? I asked her.

Sleep, she said.

The next day I was scheduled to meet with one of the managers at SLA to fill out new-hire paperwork. Luckily, my Silver Spring basement apartment was a short walk away from a Metro stop.

I sat nerve-wracked in the manager's office, wondering if Lysah's repairs would affect my assignments. I only had the rental for a couple of days and had already returned it. Well, SLA not only offered to keep me on Metro-only assignments until Lysah and I were reunited—they filled my schedule with them.

While reviewing paperwork, we came across the income section of my salary form. Having no degree, I was sure I'd be scrounging for pennies in the dirty city as a part-time job. But my rate *increased* after the manager checked off the "Deaf Parents/CODA" column.

I rubbed my eyes and looked at the form again to be sure. Being a CODA equated to years of experience in the field. She said that even though I didn't have a formal education, I instinctively had a knack for seeing the subtle nuances of ASL. And since it was technically my first language, they quickly noticed my ability to pick up on minute details during my recorded evaluation.

I wasn't academically taught Deaf culture. I didn't know what "non-manual markers", or "classifiers" were by name. But you better believe I knew the complexities of eye gaze, lip curls, and the power of the eyebrows since Mom and Dad's faces danced wildly every time I got into trouble.

Things at SLA were looking up. But phone calls from Luke, and VRS calls from Mom and Dad, came to a screeching halt once my disfellowshipping announcement was made.

******

"VRS?"

"Video Relay Service is a step up from the antiquated TTY device that used to squeal obscene beeps into my ears as a child. Deaf and HH folks converse with non-ASL users in real-time, using a videophone and an ASL interpreter with a headset as the go-between. Since I didn't have a video phone of my own, it was how Mom and Dad talked with me until the announcement. All the calls stopped after that. Even being somewhat prepared, it was excruciating."

"How did you feel, being shunned a second time?"

"It was like being in the middle of a violent game of tug-of-war. At the time, things with Kelly were wonderful, everything I imagined. But I still couldn't shake the ghosts of infidelity or the fact that I'd lost my family to an imperfectly governed organization *again*. I was excited at the thought of living freely, spending every moment possible with my twin flame. But the *Society* left me with a shattered and altered sense of reality."

"Mm-hmm. Go on."

"Because of everything that happened with Carter and my family, and because of being raised with such iron-fisted religious programming, I struggled to operate within the norms of commonplace human decency; unsure if I trusted the right people or doubted the wrong ones. I either weighed myself down with irrational, prudish statutes or veered way off course, finding myself in questionable situations."

"Oh?"

"Then, and even sometimes now, I lashed out at Kelly, judging him for pursuing me—a married woman. I blamed *him*. And other times, I allowed myself to get lost in carnal excitement. One time, at a DuPont Circle movie theater while watching *Inside Deep Throat: The Documentary*, we gave way to temptation—hoping fellow movie goers didn't catch our impromptu passion."

"And now?"

"I've gotten better about not blaming Kel, but the constant back and forth is insufferable. It feels like irreparable damage has been done. That brings us to another reason I'm here. I'm *still* struggling. I don't trust myself, and I don't trust people, or even Kelly after all we've been through. Sometimes, *just sometimes,* I wonder if it really is the Truth. *Sometimes.* Barely ever…but still. Ninety-nine percent of me doesn't believe the hype, but that one percent…"

Joel looked at me, and I could tell he was thinking, mulling something over. His face was still weighing pros and cons. I looked at him and wrinkled my face. He stood up, walked over to his bookshelf, grabbed a black book, and handed it to me.

"I've been wanting to show you that for a while, but I thought it best to wait. Now's as good a time as any," he said.

He sat back down in his leather swivel chair and crossed his leg. With his elbow on the arm of his chair, chin resting on his thumb, and first two fingers pressed into his cheek, he waited for my reaction.

In my hands I held, *Blood on the Altar: Confessions of a Jehovah's Witness Minister* by David A. Reed. Except for the title—and *Watchtower* symbol drawn in red on the front—the book was black. I shuddered. That Watchtower symbol always creeped me out. I opened the book and read the flap. Just as I thought—apostate literature, written by a former Witness. I can't say I wasn't curious, of course I was. Morbidly curious.

"Well?" Joel said.

Sitting there, holding this apostate book, I wondered, *Am I mentally diseased for leaving? For holding this book?* Then I said, "Well, I'm a little freaked."

"Why?" It's almost as if he knew I would be and had known all along, letting me carry on all this time.

"Well, it's written by a former Witness which makes it apostate literature, and all apostates are *mentally diseased*."

"Are they?"

I thought back to one summer convention and said, "They don't seem to be. I really don't know. I remember at one convention my dad and I were walking across the street, toward the Civic Center in Providence. My little hand drowned in his hairy mitt as he pulled me along, saying, 'Want good seat, we go early.' And along the way, some people standing on the corner were handing out small brochures. They approached us and Dad yanked on my arm, rushing past them, avoiding eye contact. I turned to see who they were, and my dad said, 'They apostate, be careful.' I looked back again, shamefully interested, hoping I wouldn't turn into a pillar of salt."

"Well, no pressure. Borrow it or don't borrow it but, uh, I thought it was an interesting read."

******

LATER THAT NIGHT, *Blood on the Altar* laid on the coffee table, taunting me. My nightly routine of vegan take-out from Whole Foods, puppy-poop-walks, and watching *Sex and the City* could only divert me for so long.

I picked up the book and muted the TV. The author's preface opened with the topic of child sacrifice mentioned in the book of Jeremiah, and two notorious cult leaders who led people to their death by the hundreds. He suggested that Jehovah's Witnesses fit the mold, inconspicuously. Reading the history of Jehovah's Witnesses, from the vantage point of anyone *not* in the Truth, was harrowing and a bit refreshing.

I cringed with the turn of every page, reading story after story of each man, woman, and innocent child dying from the GB's No Blood rule. Those numbers were in the thousands, and difficult to capture since they happen one by one around the globe. They don't make headlines like "Over 900 Dead in Jamestown from Mass Cyanide Poisoning" does.

I couldn't put it down. I learned more about how Pastor Russell, a racist pedophile, formed his own following—the Russellites—and how the next chief in command changed the growing group's name to Jehovah's Witnesses.

I read about the Governing Body and just how they came to govern the way they do—by making it up as they went along. And *new light* was just what I'd always thought—something needing to be changed due to changing times.

Then, the author went deep into his own personal experiences as an elder and the incredible guilt he felt for keeping blood transfusions away from his flock. I finished the book before my next visit with Joel.

And I had one burning question on my mind.

******

I handed the book back to Joel, devoured.

He looked disappointed that I'd returned it so quickly. "Did you read it?"

"Yes! Finished. Devoured." I sat down on the couch and kicked my shoes off.

"Really?"

"Really. And I have a question. If you knew about the J-Dubs stance on blood, their beliefs, and their history—among other things—why did you want me to go into such detail? Why did you take notes? If you read that book, you already know a lot."

Joel leaned forward in his chair, elbows resting on his knees, hands clasped, and said, "Because I wanted to hear *your* thoughts. I know what the author of this book said. I wanted to hear your take. If I sat over here, and told you that I already knew a lot about the Witnesses, would you have opened up as much? Discovered all these things about yourself?"

"Probably not."

"And you really needed to, Rebekah; you needed to hear your own thoughts, your own voice. So...what did you think?" he asked, leaning back in his chair, notepad-free, crossing his leg.

"I...it..." I sighed, closed my eyes, and tried to grab hold of just one of the many thoughts rushing through my mind. "I used to be so afraid of those eschewed mental cases when I saw them standing outside Civic Centers and Assembly Halls." I snickered at my vivid imagination before continuing. "I used to think that once they were overcome by demonic forces, they'd start speaking in tongues, fall to the ground, and gyrate as their apostate literature burst into flames."

We both laughed.

"So, here we are," Joel said.

I nodded. "Yup and I still feel fucked."

"Why?"

"Well, what do I do with all this now?"

"All what?"

"All this new information. I mean, almost everything exposed in that book are things I've believed my whole life, things my family *still* believes. Even when my intuition told me not to, I forced myself to believe it. I let the Truth get under my skin and out of my hands. How do I..." I sighed. I didn't even know what I was trying to say.

"Let's switch gears for a minute. I want to hear more about work. Tell me about interpreting." Joel grabbed another notepad.

I sighed, a bit dissatisfied, but answered. "What do you want to know? I can't go into detail—confidentiality and all."

"Oh, I understand ethics of the job. Just tell me about SLA. How's it been so far?"

"So far? SLA's been my fucking lifeboat. Moving here to work for them is one of the best decisions I ever made. Ha! Finally, a good decision."

"What about SLA makes them your lifeboat?"

"They accept me. Trust me."

"How?"

"I play on the company softball team, we go out for happy hours, I don't feel judged for moving down here to be with Kelly. They must trust me because I work a few high-profile gigs regularly, and sometimes other cool events. So, I guess the work I do must not suck."

"What events?"

I thought before answering. "I guess since they were public, I can tell you. Gigs like the Takoma Park Folk Festival, the International Children's Festival, those were pro bono. The most fun was probably the Steve Miller Band concert, those guys are cool backstage." I laughed, remembering how much fun I had. "The most challenging was probably the Democratic National Convention. Oh! And John Waters was cool, even though I didn't know any signs specific to gay or drag communities. Then, Obama's Disability Inaugural Ball. Obama was—"

"Did you hear yourself just now?" Joel looked up from his notes.

"Yeah? Why?"

"You're proud. Happy. And you should be. You deserve to be." He looked at the clock and closed his notebook. "Before next week—and journal this if you'd like—think about the changes happening in your life and how *you* are responsible for them. Okay?"

With playful sarcasm, I said, "Okay, *Uncle* Joel."

I grabbed my jacket and stood, thinking about the many changes I'd experienced in the past year. Walking toward Lysah, parked on the street in front of Joel's, I felt perplexed.

Trying to understand how *I* was responsible for all these changes would be challenging. I'd gotten so used to shifting either blame or reason to the *Society's* indoctrination, and for the most part I wasn't wrong.

While driving home to Silver Spring, I recalled Mark once telling me that throughout my whole life I'd always gotten what I wanted. I thought he was calling me spoiled in so many words. But now, after Joel's homework assignment, maybe Mark meant just what Joel wanted me to unveil—I was responsible for everything that had happened in my life, thus "always getting what I wanted."

I parked Lysah at the Wayne Avenue garage and walked to the center of "Silver Sprung"—a clever nickname due to a major makeover Silver Spring's downtown had received a few years prior. I headed into my church, Borders, in search of more apostate reading material.

I needed more.

Amber

"HOW WAS YOUR WEEK?" Joel asked, leaning back in his chair.

"Good! I went to Borders after our session last week and found this!" I handed him a book and sat down on the couch. "It's a rare find, and I can't believe I found it there. And it's *legit* written by Raymond Franz, former GB member."

"Did you finish this *already*?" Joel flipped through the 447-page expose of the *Watchtower Bible and Tract Society.*

"No, not yet. I'm barely a quarter of the way through. He includes articles, letters, and like, *actual* documented proof that the Society is a total fraud—a faulty organization."

"Wow." He handed the book back. "How does this help you identify responsibility for *your* life?"

"I thought about that, and I remembered something my brother Mark told me. He said, I always 'get what I want.' Until last week I thought he meant I was spoiled. What he meant was every choice I made was my responsibility, resulting in whatever I wanted at the time. After that slap to the forehead, it was much easier for me to think about my choices and everything I've done; leave home at sixteen, head to Dean's, mess around with his friends... I didn't have to do any of that. I could have said 'Fuck you, Dean' and left—"

"Yes...but remember, you were technically a child. Being raised the way you were—thinking you couldn't tell anyone no—I'm not surprised that you stayed for as long as you did or that you loved Dean. You couldn't always control what happened, or the consequences handed to you, as a child. Which is why I've not really had you delve too much into your

Dean years; you were impressionable—not *totally* making conscious choices. And you were abused, plain and simple."

"I guess, but *I'm* the one who made those choices, so I *was* responsible. It was my choice to marry Carter, go back to the Truth, then cheat, and leave again. Those *were* my choices. Adult choices." I hung my head.

"Well, yes, they were. And certain things *did* influence your choices—some were right, and some weren't. But do you see the pattern?" Joel showed me all his (*my*) steno pads; there were now three of them.

"Maybe you should invest in legal pads for clients like me," I joked.

"I went through these," he said, holding the notebooks up, "and over and over, the same thing happens—you go against the grain somehow, are severely punished in some way, look to someone else for redemption, and then the cycle repeats. Don't hang your head and don't punish yourself. Cycles are hard to stop, especially when you're the one stuck inside it. The *Watchtower Society* has a lot to answer for. Now that you're free to make your own choices, *better* choices, don't you feel—"

"Empowered?" I cut him off.

He nodded.

He's onto something because I did feel lighter. *I hope he can help me with this choice then...* "There's something I want your opinion on. Sort of. I mean, I know you're not technically supposed to advise clients but this falls under the umbrella of making choices."

"Okay, shoot." He crossed his leg.

"Well, Kelly called me a few days ago and told me something that sort of shook my world. I'm not sure what to do—regardless of any newfangled, empowering choices—I feel pretty lost right now."

"What did he say?"

I started to tear up. "He applied to a teaching program a little while after I moved down, providing them a list of underprivileged cities and school districts he was willing to work in. He was accepted. And even though he put D.C. on the list..." I sighed, "he's going to Memphis."

"Oh, boy." Joel reached for a fresh notebook.

"I paced the apartment as he told me his work assignment would last two years." I started shaking my ankle at warp speed. "I yelled. Cried. Told him it wasn't fair that I risked everything—uprooted my life to move here, lost my family in the process—just so he could leave less than a year later." My voice cracked. "He said there was nothing to figure out, we could do long distance again, and as far as he was concerned that's what we were doing. Case closed."

I looked out the window hoping to see my friend, the bird.

"What happened then?"

"I hung up on him and had a panic attack. I haven't had one of those in—"

"Years. Last one was when your mother was reinstated, right?"

A stream of tears fell down my cheek. "Yeah..."

I saw a photo of my mom in the kitchen, wearing one of Dad's sweaters, with a dishtowel draped over her shoulder. She was half-smiling, signing the word *pig*. I closed my eyes, shook my head, and continued.

"After I hung up, I couldn't breathe. I felt sick. Fear pulsed through my veins, my heart beat erratically. Nothing looked familiar. I felt like I was floating above the room. I could see myself below—freaking out, unable to help myself, wanting to scream—only nothing came out. Then I felt Bartok, licking my hand. I opened my eyes and saw that I was on the floor. Bartok, and his itty-bitty ball, brought me back to reality. He cooed, waiting for me to throw it."

"Smart dog."

"They both are, but Bart *knows* me."

"Have you considered going to Memphis?"

"Kel asked that, too. For fun, I researched Memphis' Deaf and interpreting communities just to see what was there and came up with nothing. SLA isn't just a place for me to work, with great benefits all around, I feel like I've found a family there. Plus, how could I find another therapist as good?"

He laughed. "I assure you there are many good therapists and psychologists out there. But this isn't really about work or therapy, is it? Why don't you want to go? Initial response. Three, two—"

"Because I'm fucking pissed! I mean, two years?! I moved here, risked a-fucking-lot and he's just gonna go? I get it—" I lifted my palms in surrender, "my *choice* to be pissed, but he's choosing to go and fucking leave me here. Alone with our ghosts, wandering the city. Every fucking Metro stop, every restaurant, every memorial, and monument... He'll haunt me, freezing our memories in time. Fuck!" My face contorted. Tears and snot leaked from my face, and I started burbling. "I feel like I've been shot... And I'm... Just... Bleeding out."

Joel sat silently, holding a box of aloe-treated tissues. For the rest of our session, once I gave myself permission, I talked about Kelly and the fact that we were indeed *still together*. I painted a masterpiece in his honor.

Kelly was my nerdy history and WWII buff; a Red-Wing-loving-pasties-eating-Mackinac-Island-vacationing Tigers fan who would point to a place on his palm, illustrating where in the great Wolverine state he was from. Most of his sentences ended with "eh," he loved the cold fronts coming in from Canada, and he loved old folk songs that told strange stories.

He had this odd habit of keeping every receipt. He kept a small shoebox of receipts on top of his dresser. When the shoebox was full, he'd empty it into a bigger box he kept on a shelf in his closet. Once the shoebox was full again, into the bigger box his receipts went, and the cycle continued. I never asked why. It was one of the many quirks I found strangely endearing about him.

Kel had this lip thing I adored. Anytime he talked about something passionately, his lip quivered. The first time I noticed was while visiting the Holocaust Museum. Walking through the museum was sobering—dead silent—even with crowds of people. At exhibits, he'd lean in and whisper nuggets of history in my ear. My eyes fixed on memorizing every detail of his face, and that's when I saw the lip thing. It trembled in such a way that if he could've taken out Hitler himself, he would have. It quivered in seriousness, passion, sadness, and defeat.

There was absolutely no one else on this tiny blue dot I felt at home with. When we made love, tidal waves of ecstasy culminated with carnal frenzy—and uncontrollable tears—*every time.* We shared real intimacy, safety, trust, and for the first time in my life, *un*conditional love. No one in my life loved me the way he did.

He encouraged me to just be myself. He seemed constantly amazed with almost everything I did. He commended my courage, passion, and beauty. He adored the wonder and curiosity I had for things that didn't come in a pre-packaged box labeled "Necessary Belief System for Armageddon's Survival."

He watched me interpret every public event he could attend, and, while hand flapping, I'd gush with pure schoolgirl giddiness. Someone in my life had faith in me when I had none in myself. He believed I was more than a *good for nothing slave, a weaker vessel.* He saw the person I wanted to be, long before I knew she even existed. I felt beautiful around him. Flawless.

That's love.

I looked up at the clock and saw it was at the top of the hour. I sniffled, wiping my nose. "Sorry, I kind of went off the rails there."

"Don't apologize." He sighed, smiled, then said, "Good work today, Rebekah. There's hope. And trust me, you *will* figure this out. That gut you started listening to at the train tracks—listen again."

******

I'D FORGOTTEN ALL ABOUT the tracks. Everything that happened with Carter, my family, and Kelly made me almost forget about my longstanding love and pinky-swear promise to the B&M Railroad. Standing at the tracks had once brought me so much peace and many squished Lincoln heads.

I thought a quick little road trip home, in search of some clarity, was in order. I called my NIH intern friend, Sammy, to see if he was up for the drive.

"Hey, luv! What's up?" he asked.

His British accent was engaging; one of my favorite things about him.

"The boys and I are driving home early on Saturday. Back on Sunday. Wanna come?" I asked.

"Of course! Let me call you right back. I'm just leaving the office." He hung up.

Sammy and I hit the road early Saturday morning, as planned.

Sammy was beautiful. His dark hair, black-as-night eyes, button nose, and slender frame were endearing. His effortless wit and charm frequently forced my crooked teeth to grind behind pursed lips, concealing my envy.

Cruising along the highway—passing state lines with Sammy, Lysah, and the boys—lent me pure freedom. The distance between me and the ghosts Kelly would soon be leaving behind was a must. I didn't *want* the distance, but it felt necessary. And just maybe the tracks would provide some answers.

"I know your relationship with your parents is…estranged. Have you got a secret path to your backyard, or something?" he asked.

"There's another way to the tracks."

There had always been another way.

"Oh. Isn't I-95 quicker?"

"Highway 81 to 84 avoids tolls, is quieter, and prettier. It's the way my dad suggested. It's the way I always go."

Ten hours later we arrived in NH. Tired and hungry, I took him to my favorite restaurant downtown—Tilton House of Pizza.

"This place has been here since I was little. Good, huh?"

Sammy moaned with pleasure.

We crashed at my friend Jessie's and made plans to scope out my backyard, from my beloved tracks, the next morning.

Before our trespassing adventure the next day, I suggested coffee at Jim's Drive-In—the old truck stop by my parent's house. Jim had passed, but the Drive-In was still going strong.

"Shit," I said, looking down at a full cup of coffee.

"What?"

"My parents just walked in. They saw me. Fuck."

Sammy turned and waved hello.

"What are you doing?" I said in a hushed whisper.

They walked over to our tiny table and sat.

"Who?" My dad signed, pointing at Sammy.

"Friend. D.C.," I signed. I was stunned that they sat.

My mother looked tired, beautiful but tired. She smiled, and in her adorable voice said, "Hi Mecky. What you doing here?"

"Here one night. Visit."

"Oh, oh. Okay." She smiled again.

"Hey, you go meeting?" My dad voiced.

I looked down at my coffee, and without looking him in the eye signed, "Not yet. Will."

I hadn't been to any meetings since my move down and hadn't planned to, but I had to give the man something.

Dad softened after my half-assed promise to sit through fictitious drivel.

It had been about thirty minutes before Dad stood up, and said, "We go now, have go shopping." He looked at Sammy and said, "Remember sign C-O-F-F-E-E," while showing him his favorite sign for coffee.

With my parents out running errands, it made being in my backyard much easier. Only I couldn't bring myself to do it. Going there when they weren't home, even just to *peek* at the tracks, felt *wrong*.

Instead, I parked Lysah at the little corner store by the train tracks. Sammy and I leashed up the boys and walked to the tracks. All anyone ever had to do to get to the tracks was find a spot somewhere in town and hop on the foot trail; it brings you wherever you want to go.

We started walking the tracks and with every step on each railroad tie, we got closer to my backyard. After a minute I stopped and looked down the rails, fading into the horizon. I stood, petrified. The boys tugged on their leash to keep going.

Sammy stopped next to me, turned, and then said, "What's the matt-ah, luv?"

I didn't answer because I didn't know what my matter was. Something in me fidgeted, unable to step any closer. I stared into the distance. The amber silhouette I once saw dancing along the tracks, the bronze outline of Kelly, was no longer there. I couldn't feel him. I inhaled and my body shuddered.

Bartok turned his little wiener head to look at me. He stopped tugging and walked toward me. Moron followed suit. I spun around and walked back to the car. Sammy flicked a cigarette as his shadow fell behind us.

The car was silent for hours.

"So, what happened back there?" Sammy asked, lighting a Camel and cracking the window.

"Can I have one?" I asked, holding up the first two fingers of my right hand, left hand on the wheel.

He lit another cigarette and handed it to me as I cracked my window. "I don't know. Something felt off."

"Listen, I don't know if it's the weird, religious family shite bothering you or if it's the whole Kelly thing, but either way... No one's judging you, luv. So, stop judging yourself."

"Did I tell you he was leaving D.C. and moving down to Memphis?" I took a drag, remembering how much I love a nasty butt sometimes.

I felt his head slowly turn to face me. "No!"

"Yeah, he thinks we can do long distance again. I don't know maybe we can. But since he told me, I've lost him somehow. I lost *it*."

I sucked on that Camel like it was my last and stared out at the highway. Rolling hills of Pennsylvania cried out to me as Kelly's face faded between the valleys.

Being back in the dirty city, after my last-minute trip home, forced me into a decision. Only I wasn't ready to make it just yet. Instead, I took Kelly up on his offer to help him move the life he planned to share with me down to Memphis. I used five days of vacation time from work, then called Joel to cancel that week's session.

"Cancel? But you're making such great progress," he said.

"No, no I don't mean cancel as in 'never again.' Cancel as in 'postpone.' As in 'I'll be back next week.'"

Cancel Joel? Not a chance.

"Oh! I'll see you then. Can't wait to hear about your trip. Take care, Rebekah."

Sammy stayed at the apartment with the boys and Spork, while I helped Kelly leave me.

Penance. That's what this is. Fucking penance.

With Kelly's Budget truck all loaded up, we pulled away from his little, basement apartment in Northwest D.C. This would be the last time I'd have any reason to come to this gorgeous side of town.

Kel, always trying to find the silver lining said, "You know, chilibean, the teaching program is only for two years. When I'm done, I'll have a good chunk of my student loans paid. Then we can go anywhere. We can make it two years, beautiful girl. Just..." he sighed, "let your hair grow."

"My hair? What? You don't like it?" I asked grabbing chunks of the overgrown pixie that was now almost to that awkward, shoulder-length-mullet phase. *Maybe a new 'do is due.*

Kel laughed. "No. You letting it grow represents time. When it's longer, we can be together for good. Wherever. Just, focus on your hair."

It was the most romantic and most painful symbol of our relationship to date.

Once through the traffic of the D.C. beltway, the rolling green hills and giant bales of hay in the Shenandoah Valley stole my breath. Damn were they gorgeous. Kelly clicked on the radio.

"I love this song! Ever hear it?" he asked, turning up the volume.

I shook my head.

"It's 'The Wreck of the Edmund Fitzgerald' by Gordon Lightfoot. It's about a ship that sank in Lake Superior in the 70s!"

He sang along. I had to hand it to him for making the best of a shitty situation. He was good like that.

I looked out the window as the song played for six and a half more minutes, and I concluded that our relationship's demise was fixed within the same stars once fusing us together; much like the sinking of the SS Edmund Fitzgerald. An uninvited conversation between Luke and I ran through my mind…

"You can move down there, but it won't last," Luke said, laying a ceramic tile down in Mom and Dad's kitchen. "It never lasts between two people who commit adultery."

"He's not married," I said, leaning against the kitchen counter. "So? He's not committing adultery."

"You know what I mean." He stood up, walked toward me, reached around my waist, snatched his wallet and Boliva watch that had been laying there, then said, "I better hide these, you might steal my money or my watch. You're cheating on your husband; lying, stealing, and murder aren't too far behind."

Sitting in the passenger's seat with my head against the window, watching the hills of the Shenandoah Valley pass by in streaks of vibrant green, I let Kelly go and didn't even know it.

Memphis was like no place I'd ever been before. Folks just roamed the streets with no place to be, wandering along double yellow lines, aimless.

Businesses established in the 50s, complete with old neon signage and decrepit facilities, filled the city. I loved it. I clicked the radio on and tuned in to the city's anthem, "Walkin' in Memphis," for the sixth time that day.

The Budget truck made a wide turn into Kelly's quaint, new neighborhood. Well-groomed lawns met long porches with rocking chairs and porch swings at the front of every house. A white house with a similar landscape became Kelly's new home. On this insanely hot and humid June day, we hauled his old life into his new apartment.

He took me to Graceland, which was easily my favorite part of the trip. The Jungle room was the best—with its green shag carpeting, a wall of horizontal brick, a giant, stuffed teddy bear cuddled up to an acoustic guitar in the corner, a polished, solid-oak coffee table, and wild plants in almost every nook—I wanted to make myself at home there and never leave.

Aside from our tour of Graceland, I spent a lot of time on Kel's porch, rocking in a chair with a drink in my hand. Kelly stayed in reviewing his curriculum repeatedly, committing it to memory.

My last night there, Kelly brought me to the center of Memphis. Among the horse-drawn carriages, moving right along with traffic in front of the blue-lit-M-shaped bridge, 311 sang, "Amber." The audience sang along, and I had to laugh at Karma once again for putting me in my place. I really wished she had a face so I could bitch slap the sardonic grin she was wearing.

We walked up and down Beale Street. I waited all night to feel ten feet off the ground but felt more like I was buried beneath it.

Later that night, Kel sat on the edge of his bed watching me stuff clothes sloppily into a suitcase. He said breaking it off wasn't an option. We did long distance before and could do it again. We *were* doing it again, end of discussion. What we had was too special to throw away.

I wanted so much to believe him.

My newly softened and amenable heart, curious about life and love, backslid to a rigid and hardened tool; its only job was to circulate blood I no longer cared to pump.

We made crazy love that night. Of course, I cried. Of course, *he* cried. That's just how it was for us—like a cheesy Lifetime movie love scene. We tried to fuck like hungry animals, and every time we did passion trumped lust; we drowned in tears instead of sweat.

At the airport, slow to separate once again, we hugged for an exceptionally long time. I gave Kelly a weak smile and he said, "I'll be up for Christmas."

My voice cracked the words, "Okay, see you then" and I headed for the escalator. As my body escalated, my heart dropped. I looked back at Kelly, standing below with a huge smile, waving the *I love you* sign.

I cried while putting my belongings into a grey bin. TSA employees steered me toward the millimeter wave scanner. There I stood, imprisoned. With my arms up high overhead, I surrendered everything.

******

"How was the trip?" Joel asked the following week.

I inhaled, puffed my cheeks, and blew the air through my lips.

"That good, huh? How did you leave things? What *choices* did you make?"

"Oh, fuck choices," I said. I was too torn to make any.

"Okay, let's talk about it."

"Before I talk about Kel's departure, I gotta tell you about something weird that happened when Sammy and I went to New Hamp—"

"Sammy?"

"Yeah, Samuel. Sorry, sometimes I call him Sam—"

"You've never called him anything, I don't think you've mentioned him." Joel squinted his eyes and looked at the ceiling, trying to remember.

"Oh! He's an NIH intern; I met him at an assignment I had there."

I told Joel all about my gorgeous, gay, brilliant, little, British scientist friend. Though we hadn't known each other long, Sammy somehow knew what I was going to say long before I said it and usually knew my next move before the thought was born.

"He sounds like a good friend to have. Do you have any other friends?"

"Um, yeah. Kara, a staff interpreter at SLA. She's from Colorado. And I swear, this woman's got Telluride Bluegrass pumping through her veins. She's an amazing auntie to my boys, they just love her. I trust people my dogs approve of, and Kara's badass."

"How does it feel to have friends, *worldly* friends?"

Truth be told, I hadn't given it much thought. Sammy and Kara were just *there* one day, and we'd been inseparable since.

"I don't really know. I guess…" I thought for a minute. "Well, if I had to look at each group, juxtaposed, my worldly friends seem to have more integrity. When they do good, it's because that's *who they are*. When J-Dubs do good, at least the ones I knew, it was for personal gain; they were always looking toward the *New System* and how many tally marks were on their field service reports. Their good deeds were good, I think their hearts were in the right place, but they just didn't seem as genuine. I don't know. My worldly friends seem *real*."

"And Kelly, how did that go?"

I rehashed the gut-wrenching trip in detail, right down to our last intimacy.

"What do you think you'll *choose* to do?"

"Ugh, I knew you'd ask that. Right now, I don't know." Any emotions I felt, just a few weeks before, were left behind—one sizable chunk was left at the tracks in NH, and the other with Kelly in Memphis.

"What weird thing happened in New Hampshire?"

"Oh, well, in a nutshell I lost Kelly."

"You *lost* him?"

"I brought Sammy to the rails with me. And I swear I thought the tracks were a safe place to keep Kelly…" my voice cracked. "But he's gone. The train conductor took him instead of me."

Joel handed me a of box tissues. "Sounds like you've already made a choice then?"

309

I sobbed. "My gut made it without asking me. I'm not ready to let him go!"

"Then, take your time. I understand the guilt you may still feel being with him, but if what you say about your connection is true, maybe give long distance a try? No one, not even your gut, is saying you can't."

I didn't mention running into my parents for coffee, or the half-assed promise I made to my dad about going to a meeting. The only thing on my mind was Kelly, his absence, and our imminent demise.

******

THE TRUTH WAS, I was hell-bent on my own undoing as well. I started to drink heavily. At home. Alone. With each sip of every homemade Cosmopolitan, I let myself go. My bout with endometriosis came back with red hot anger and snuggled right up to the Sarlacc—who was also back with a vengeance.

Kelly kept true to form—calling and texting every day. I still felt him, longed for him.

My inability to care for myself didn't go unnoticed. Sammy stayed with me a couple of nights a week shortly after our NH trip. He always seemed to know when I needed him.

He'd surface with take-out, suggesting we stay in and cuddle with the boys watching *I Love Lucy* and *Family Guy* reruns. Other nights, we ventured out to gay bars in DuPont Circle. We drank heavily and watched gay porn from the bar's TV screens, gawking in hysterics.

Then, Sammy set up my first social media profile, opening the door to online dating. I didn't want to date anyone else, but I didn't stop him.

Maybe I'll make some new friends.

God knows I was lonely enough since calls and texts slowed due to Kel's packed schedule. I asked if maybe we should start seeing other people. Kel said no. And when I said he might meet a cute, scholarly, southern bell, he'd say, "Not a chance." He wanted to stick to his plan and fly home for Christmas. Period.

I had plenty to keep me busy before then.

My interpreting career had certainly taken off and I'd done something to impress the CEO because she gave me a raise and a promotion. I went from being a Staff Interpreter to Staff Interpreter *and* Professional Development Congress Chair—in charge of contacting presenters, scheduling dates, times, and locations for continuing education workshops.

Shortly after my surprise bump in pay, SLA's annual end-of-the-year staff meeting commenced where I won the Team Player of the Year award. Apparently, I was "a joy to work with for fellow interpreters, Deaf clients, and account reps in the office."

Aside from awards, free food, and the opportunity to see my interpreting family, year-end bonuses were direct deposited into our accounts. It turned out to be a well-timed distraction.

Once off the Metro in Silver Spring, Sammy met me at my favorite pub, McGinty's, for drinks.

"What'll ya do when Kel gets here?" he asked.

"I don't know." I sipped my Cosmopolitan.

"Luv, watching you go through this is like watching a woman go from soft to stoic. It's almost like he's gone off to war."

That's what it felt like. Kel was in Memphis—his fatigues were suits and ties, his battlefield was an underprivileged high school—and I was nursing a never-ending hangover until his triumphant return.

******

"How's it going this week?" Joel asked.

"Not bad. I got a raise and promotion." I said, sitting down.

"That's great! Congratulations!"

"Thank you. I got an award at the staff meeting, too."

"Rebekah! This is great—why aren't you more excited?"

"It's stupid."

"Tell me."

"I don't feel like I deserve it. I feel nauseous every time the CEO calls me into her office, closes the door, and hands me a sealed envelope."

"Why?"

"Bad memories, maybe? I know it was just her office, but it felt so authoritarian. I know that wasn't her intention but—"

"You mean it felt like you'd done something wrong? Did it feel like a judicial committee was waiting for you?"

"I guess, even though I've had a couple breakthroughs, years of systematic religious abuse and emotional terrorism don't just go away." I snapped my fingers.

Joel sighed and said, "No, I'm sorry that one is going to take some time. But you're aware of it and that's a step in the right direction. Did you finish your recent book purchase? It looked like an intense read."

"*Crisis of Conscience*? I did. It was very helpful. Like, logically my brain understands what I experienced growing up; it comprehends the source of my pain. I just can't seem to wiggle free yet. The fucking shackles are still there. Loosened, but still there. I'm so tired of the mind fuck."

"Keep reading. Something will start to pick the lock."

******

THE LOCK WAS FINALLY picked by another therapist. No, I didn't replace Joel. I found a book written by a mental health counselor that shook my world.

Combatting Cult Mind Control by Steve Hassan was my third read on the way down the ex J-Dub rabbit hole. Steve wasn't a recovering Witness, but the details of his experience with The Moonies sounded all too familiar. It spawned his research on cults, thus making it his life's work to unveil them and aid anyone trying to recover from their own cult experiences.

While reading, I couldn't believe that right there in black and white, it had been confirmed: I was raised in a mind controlling cult. I felt relieved to learn that "no one *chooses* to join a cult knowingly they just postpone the decision to leave." Cults prey on the broken while instilling dread, sprinkled with false hope. The GB had been using God, and his paradise, as a springboard for over a century.

I can't be angry with my parents. They did their best. I don't for one second think they sat at the kitchen table over coffee deciding to raise me and my brothers in absolute terror, training us to be devoted to a group of fear-mongering old, unsophisticated writers. They really thought, and still think, that they're doing what *God* wants by way of his earthly mouthpiece, the GB. I just can't be angry with them. And I'm not.

It was easier being angry at myself while using Kelly as a punching bag. Which I did when Christmas brought him home, knocking on my door.

"Hi!"

Kelly rushed in bringing a storm of excitement with him. He pulled me into a tight hug, then dropped his overnight bag on the floor to get down and see the boys.

"Oh, I missed you guys!" he said, ruffling their fur, then he stood to squeeze me again. "I missed you, too."

His distinguishable scent was back. I inhaled deeply as his red rain jacket swished the same way it had the first time he ever hugged me. He put his things in the bedroom, leaned on the doorframe separating the bedroom from the kitchen, and watched me finish dinner.

"Seeing anyone?" I eyeballed him.

"No," he half laughed. "I told you, I don't want to. I still haven't even had the desire to watch any porn since I met you. I just want you." *Why is he making this so hard?*

He pushed me up against the wall in my tiny kitchen and planted a deep kiss. Just like that, I found myself in the throes of earth shattering, irresistible passion again. When we kissed, time stopped. I vanished, my vision blurred, my breath got shallow, and I became putty in his arms. I stopped him and pulled away.

"You used to love that, Bek." He sighed. "Look, I know it's hard but—"

"We can do it. I know." I looked away.

It was too easy for me to sabotage things when they got hard. I was a pro at slamming doors.

"Are we done? I mean, is this it?" His lip quivered.

I ignored his question and handed him a bowl of vegetarian chili. We ate in the living room and filled each other in on the last few months.

He was unimpressed with Memphis. The teaching was going well and by the end of two years he'd have his teaching certificate. But it was safe to say he hated it there. As for me, my new position at SLA was turning into the only thing I was proud of; SLA was home for this abandoned orphan.

After dinner Kelly went into the bedroom.

"No," I said.

"Whaddya mean, no? Where am I supposed to sleep?" His voice cracked.

His lip quivered as I pointed to the couch. He sighed, grabbed his bag, and slumped toward the couch. I went into my bedroom with the boys. I heard him sigh repeatedly. He zipped and unzipped his bag a few times, sighed again, then sobbed.

I turned out the light, spooned my bear, and watched the unique and irreplaceable flame that glinted between us fade into darkness. I quietly cried myself to sleep.

In the middle of the night, I snuck into the living room. He was asleep in the fetal position. I stared at him and thought, *There's the man I left my husband and family for; the man who left me here alone.* My anger and my longing were at war. Torn between holding on and letting go, I let go and snuck back into my room.

******

"I made a choice," I said to Joel as I kicked my shoes off and plopped down on the couch.

"Oh? Go on." He got into position—elbow on the arm of the chair, thumb under his chin, two fingers pressed to his cheek.

"I broke it off with Kel. I had to. I knew if I tried long distance, I'd just sabotage anything he left me with here and I have to feel him everywhere as it is and our ghosts linger like James Dean's in Fairmount—lonely, homeless and I need to move forward. If I don't, I'm afraid of what I'll become." I inhaled after the short speech shot past my lips.

"That was a mouthful. How do you feel?" He wrinkled his brows.

I thought for a minute. "Numb."

Joel turned the corners of his lips down and bobbed his head. "Is it over?"

I nodded, refusing to look at him.

"What else is going on?"

"I'm super busy. I finally got my security clearance after three fucking polygraphs."

"Congratulations. Why three?"

"I don't know. I certainly haven't done anything worth setting off their radar. I guess I just house enough shame for everyone in the room." I looked out the window. "I'm gonna miss him. Who'll worry now?"

"Worry about what?"

"The endometriosis. Kel was always so worried about the amount of blood I shed each month. He always said I was too tiny to be bleeding that much. He begged me to go to the doctor's every month. Sorry. TMI."

"No, it's fine. I have a wife. I get it. How has that issue been for you lately?"

"Terrible. Treatable my ass… You're not gonna like this but to quiet the melancholy Sarlacc, I need him to be anesthetized. Unfortunately, his drunken stupor teases the endometrial bitch, and she has fuckin' fiestas while the Sarlacc's passed out. It's one or the other, and right now my choice is to hush the sad beast and let the other wreak havoc on my uterus. I drink to numb what I can."

"Be careful. Too much could do irreparable damage." He sounded like a parent. It was nice.

"And I know it's *my* choice. As far as I'm concerned, the damage doesn't matter. It doesn't matter whether my body's capable of keeping soft, bloody tissue healthy. Kelly's gone. The thought of having children died the day he left."

"You don't want children?"

"Bringing a child into this world, for the sole purpose of seeing myself run around, seems like a shallow ego boost at best. I think taking care of me, and my own shit, is more than enough. Consider it my gift to the world—Rebekah refuses to spawn."

Joel laughed.

"I'm serious! Think about it. I have absolutely no business molding a young, unadulterated mind. Knowing me—and all the fucking twisted thoughts that keep me up at night—I'd unintentionally subject an innocent child to the brainwashing abuse I went through. I have enough sense to know the mind control, *that I'm in fucking therapy for,* would somehow find a crack in my armor and pierce the flesh of my offspring. No kids. I don't trust myself."

"That's fair." Joel saw no sense arguing with a donkey.

Life in the Grey

THURSDAY NIGHT ROLLED AROUND bringing Jesse into town. He was out once again and—knowing how prone to self-destruction I'd been as of late—had come to spend a long weekend with me.

As always, traffic was insane when getting him from the airport. To make my weekly date with Joel, Jesse came in tow.

"He has a waiting room, right?" Jesse asked.

"Yeah, in the basement next to his office."

"Then I'll just relax. I need my beauty rest if we're going out tonight." He winked.

Once at Joel's home office, Jesse grabbed a magazine from the coffee table and made himself comfortable on an old, flowered loveseat.

"Have a restful hour," I said to Jesse, turning the corner into Joel's office.

Joel turned around from his desk. "A restful hour? With you?" he joked.

I smirked. "I was talking to Jesse. He's gonna sit in the waiting room if that's okay."

"Jesse, your brother?"

I nodded.

Joel got up from his chair and walked to the waiting room. I kicked off my shoes as usual and waited on the couch. I heard Joel introduce himself to Jesse, then *invite him in.*

My brother, Jesse (a tall Black man who looks like a freakin' linebacker), and Joel (the Larry David lookalike), walked in together.

I scooted on the couch to make room for Jesse, totally fazed.

"I don't normally invite family in, but it's just so nice that you're here. I've been working with your sister for quite some time now. She's a good kid."

"She is. A bit mixed up sometimes, but she's a good girl." Jesse winked and smiled at me in the endearing way he always had.

"So, you were also raised a Witness?" Joel asked Jesse.

"Yes…" Jesse's voice faded.

I ignored their conversation almost completely. I was taken aback that he was invited in and using up part of my hour. Not angry. Just flummoxed. Their brief conversation ended, and Jesse returned to the waiting room.

"I don't normally do that, but I really wanted to say hello. I hope that's okay."

"Yeah." I inhaled, raised my brows, smiled, and exhaled.

"Nice fellow. So, he's disfellowshipped right now, I take it?"

"Yeah. He's been in and out a couple times, like me."

"Do you think he'll go back?"

"I don't know. He's always said that the relationship he has with his creator is no one else's concern. I can respect that. So, I don't ask. Just between us, I'd love it if he didn't. I like having him around."

"Does he visit often?"

"Lately, yeah. This is the second time he's come down to visit."

"What do you guys do?"

"See the city. Have dinner. Go to bars. Watch movies. Get into trouble."

"Oh?"

******

THAT NIGHT, JESSE AND I had dinner in the city then I dragged him to The Barking Dog; home to my first CloseUp interpreter after-party and from time to time, Kelly's ghost.

Since the club was loud, and Jesse and I were both ASL heritage users, we signed while everyone else shouted to each other. Sign language is not only a better way to communicate in loud spaces, but it can also be alluring to folks; especially those just *dying* to know what's being said. And knowing that, sometimes I'd use my first language to woo a cute boy.

Jesse and I had full conversations in ASL while laughing at other club-goers, watching intently as they attempted picking up their one-night stands by shouting. All of them, fools.

Except for one brave soul I happened to make eye contact with.

"I took a class once. I can remember one sign," a tall, young man shouted to me.

I turned and saw a gorgeous, dark-haired, dark-eyed Latino with a characteristic nose, smiling at me. He interned in the Senate House for a Senator whose name I didn't care enough to recall.

I looked him over, leaned my head to the side, and asked, "What sign?"

He attempted the sign for "awkward" and I laughed, while correcting his handshapes and palm orientation. We carried on, away from the noisy dance floor, in a quieter part of the bar. We talked about duck-billed platypuses and their awkwardness, wondering if they were extinct. I hoped not, they're my favorite animals.

I don't know what it was about this guy, Ben, but I fell for the way his presence hushed Kelly's ghost for even just a minute. He almost had me entertaining thoughts that maybe someday, I could be happy with someone else.

Ben asked for my number to set a sushi date for the following Friday in Shaw—another spot where Kelly's ghost mournfully lingered.

"Who?" Jesse signed, mid cabbage patch.

"B-E-N. Cute. Work Capitol Hill," I signed.

"Brave," Jesse signed.

I guess he was brave; not too many people attempted to use ASL to get a date.

Months before he left, Kelly had given me a stuffed platypus knowing how much I loved them. On my first date with Ben, I brought it along. I thought it would be a great icebreaker, serving as awkward conversation fodder, which it did.

The platypus tagged along all evening—in the car, in the sushi restaurant, and while wandering around the historic Shaw neighborhood.

Later that night while *American Psycho* played on a TV in the background, the platypus became a pillow for my head while Ben fucked me doggy style on his couch.

He was so well-endowed I had to bite my stuffed animal gracelessly in protest, gripping the arm of the couch with my hands. He mistook my grunts of pain as moans of pleasure and plowed harder. He came and collapsed on top of me. I could barely move.

Ben jumped up, heading to the bathroom to dispose of the condom I could only assume was labeled, *Magnum.* I slowly moved my arms and hugged the platypus—its webbed foot still lodged in my mouth.

Ben chuckled when he saw me on the couch, still immobile. I slowly rolled over, sat up, and noticed my black, knee-high, heeled boots were still attached to my feet. He sat next to me, leaned closer, and gently moved hair away from my face the way Kel used to. I looked at him, panicked, and shot up from the couch, ignoring the painful pulse coming from my crotch.

"I gotta go," I said.

I gathered my clothes and quickly dressed in the bathroom.

"Lemme walk you to your car." He dressed in a hurry to follow me outside.

I hopped in Lysah, relieved to be somewhere familiar. I turned the key. He tapped on the driver's side window, and I rolled it down.

"Thank you." He smiled in a way that was so hard to ignore.

"You're welcome?"

"You, uh, left your boots on. That was hot." He looked down, smiling.

I waited for him to kick the ground and say, "Aw, shucks" like a Little Rascal—he was that adorable. I smiled and drove home.

I left Shaw with no intention of contacting Ben the Brave.

******

"How was the rest of your brother's visit?" Joel asked.

Our sessions had gone from weekly to bi-weekly—Joel said I was ready. Whatever that meant.

"Good. We had dinner, went clubbing, I met a cute boy." I said, tucking my feet under my ass on the couch.

"Oh?"

"Mm-hmm. We went out for sushi in Shaw."

"And?"

"Um, I'm pretty sure I won't see him again."

"Why is that?"

"Well, I was just trying to choke Kelly out, rid him of haunting me. And I used a nice enough guy to do it. I'm a shit."

"Did it work?"

I sighed and said, "No. Kel's ghost is still haunting me, and Ben was really nice, ya know? I felt bad using him. And for some reason, I crave rejection from him. I mean, it feels like Kel rejected me when he left, and I'm sure Ben would get around to it eventually. It doesn't really matter who rejects whom, I just need it. *Soon*."

"You've been rejected time and time again from your own family, the Witnesses, you've gotten used to it. Do you think you'll see Ben again?"

I shrugged.

******

TO MY SURPRISE, BEN came to my neighborhood for tacos and live music a week later. I drove him home. He asked if I wanted to come in. *Yes, I do.*

He sat on the couch, and, within seconds, I devised a plan to see how far I could get his monstrous baby arm down my throat without puking. I could not allow my on-the-mend vagina, or uterus, to endure that anguish again.

I wanted him to writhe in pleasure so I could feel better about the looming rejection. I wasn't doing it because he was an asshole but because he wasn't. I couldn't let myself fall for Ben; leaving him sexually satisfied seemed like a nice parting gift.

I knelt in front of him. He was huge in my hands. I wrapped my lips around him and started to chug, gazing up every so often to catch glimpses of his expressions. I accepted those as payment and continued. I used my left hand to cup his balls and I tickled his asshole with my middle finger, just for a second.

He moaned, breathing heavily. Then, he tried to stop me. "Slow down, there's time…"

There won't be another time. This is it. Now or never, pal.

I ignored him, wrapping my right hand around the bottom half of his huge tool, and jerked enthusiastically. My mouth bobbed up and down furiously around the head of his cock. I used everything I could in that moment to drive him mad; my right hand jacked feverishly, my mouth and tongue were starved, and my left hand was somewhere between his balls and asshole.

His breath got quicker, turned shallow, then he exploded into my mouth. At the first taste of cum, I quickly removed my mouth and dodged the rest, leaning to the side. I knew he'd blow a load I couldn't carry. My right hand finished the job, and he melted into the couch with satisfaction.

"Oh… My… God," he said between breaths.

I stayed on the floor and rested my arms on his knees. I relaxed my head on his upper thigh, near his still-swollen penis and I looked up at him, thinking, *That was easy.*

Then, I realized Dean's indoctrination also sat deep and I was immediately disgusted with myself; unsure why I felt the need to please, then reject.

Ben moved his hand closer to my face, playing with my hair again. "I like spending time with you." He wound strands of my hair around his finger then let them go, watching them bounce back up.

"Well of course you do," I said.

"Not just because of *that*," he exhaled. "Bek, I'm not looking for anything serious, but I do wanna see you again, and just, ya know, see what happens."

I remained silent while he talked about his family. Said I'd probably like them. For one tiny second, I could see it all: I'd meet his sisters, they'd be like the sisters I never had. He'd bring me to family gatherings. I'd meet the parents. Between my assignments in the city, we'd meet up for lunch breaks near the Senate House and wander the city with expensive lattes in our hands. He might even move the hair away from my face and let it dance between his fingertips until it was grey.

I shook the fantasy and seized my opportunity in the rejection zone. I jumped up to use the bathroom. Once I was ready to leave, he hugged me, moved the hair from my face, tucking it behind my ear, then kissed me like he *really* meant it.

I never saw Ben again.

It wasn't him; it was me.

****

"Okay, I tried the dating thing, and I can't do it." I told Joel the next visit.

"Okay. Why?" He crossed his leg and rested his chin on the heel of his hand.

"Because no matter how great the guy may seem, it just can't work."

"Oh?"

"The feelings I might be able to develop for anyone else would be lukewarm. Or worse—I'd fall hard, and he wouldn't. Kelly left behind some huge shoes to fill. Those suckers don't stand a chance."

"You just need some time. I don't foresee you being alone for the rest of your life. Not at all. Quite the opposite. So, take your time."

"Sammy set up a social media profile for me. I don't want to date anyone, though."

"Let's see it. C'mere." Joel swiveled his chair, turning his back to me, and logged into his computer.

I stood up and stepped toward his desk. "You wanna see my Myspace?"

"Sure. Why not?" he asked.

He pushed his keyboard toward me, and I logged into my account.

Joel scrolled, reading a few things, then said, "Hmm."

"What?"

"Your writing is good."

"Thank you."

"You should do more of that."

I sat back on the couch. "Do you ask to see all your clients' social media profiles?"

Joel turned to face me. "Eh, sometimes. Rebekah, I'm trying to show you how to live somewhat sensibly in a world without the Truth. I want you to see that people—non-Witnesses specifically—*can* be well-intentioned without using fear, guilt, shame, or conditional love to manipulate you. That's not to say some won't, but not everyone *will*.

"It's really no wonder you spent four years with Dean. He was on the other side of the spectrum, so *his* intrigue—sky high." Joel raised his hand to the ceiling. "Even though he *did* seem to love you, it was a warped type of...possessive love. His approach mirrored the *Society's*. Maybe not intentionally, but the approaches were similar enough to keep you bowing to another golden calf."

"How do you explain Carter? I mean, I kinda fucked him over."

"No doubt, but he made choices, too. With Carter, I want you to see that you don't need to crucify yourself when you make a mistake. You did then what you knew how to do at the time. And you're doing better now because you're here."

"Thank you," I said.

"Sure. As for your Witness friends, it's just what you said a few weeks ago—they're constantly looking forward to Armageddon. A new earth. Their good deeds are good but not always genuine, not coming from a truly altruistic place. Perhaps for some, but even then, who are they really doing it for? It's understandable you'd have difficulty trusting people. You were born into an automatic network. And it's ripped out from underneath you all at once because *they're* sending you away for your mistakes, not helping you through it. Of course, you'd continue the trend with yourself."

I took it all in. It made perfect sense. Everything I'd been reading and every relationship I'd had until this point, came to a perfect head. Except... "My family. That one..." I teared up.

"That one is going to be a challenge," he said.

"Leaving the Truth a second time almost feels worse—I'm not the same person I was at sixteen. This time I didn't leave home after thrashing an old coffee table. I was married, technically an adult. I got to know my family and I saw them differently. I *like* them and that makes it harder."

"It's not fair, I know. The *Society* is indeed holding them hostage. Unfortunately, the ransom is you forgetting who you are, forsaking the deal you made with your younger self."

I closed my eyes and felt tears stream down my cheeks. I saw little four-year-old me, crouched near the rusty, wired fence between our backyard and the train tracks with a fistful of pennies.

"I need to go back again."

"Back…where?" I could hear the worry in his voice.

"To the tracks. Alone. I need to find *me*."

"Weren't you just there with Sammy?"

"Yes, and I was there looking for Kelly. I wasn't looking for me. I need to try and find little me. Maybe she can help me remember…"

"If you find her, hug her, and tell her she's perfect just the way she is. And take a few of these…"

Joel opened the top drawer of his desk and fished out some spare change. He handed me a couple of old pennies and smiled.

******

I DROVE HOME THE following weekend. Alone. I avoided places I could potentially run into anyone I knew. This wasn't a social visit—I was on a mission. I'd seen a strange girl-turned-woman in the mirror that I answered to for some reason or other, but I hadn't faced little me in quite some time. I needed *her* to guide me. I could feel she was smarter than me somehow. She knew things. She trusted herself.

I parked Lysah at the same corner store and started walking the tracks. Nervous about whether I'd see myself, I walked along the rails noticing how corroded they were.

Close enough to my childhood home, I stood near the old, rusty, wired fence. It sunk deeper into the ground—I almost couldn't find it. It was still bent in the same place we used to push it down, jumping it, then letting the wire spring back up into place.

This place was overgrown with despair, covered in shame. The ferns were crying. A tree had literally uprooted itself out of the ground right next to the tracks. My beloved in-ground log sofa—where I used to sit comfortably, singing to myself with a handful of pennies—was so far into the ground, it was buried, almost invisible.

The path from the tracks to my backyard was barely there. I could feel it crying out, begging to be trampled on by curious sneakers, if only I could see it. I put my hand in my pocket, jiggling the pennies Joel gave me, looking for the path. I didn't see it, but finally...I saw *her. Me.*

She stood in the backyard with a fistful of dandelions for Mom. Her tiny little body was dressed in hand-me-downs. She wore a tacky, 70s, tan, yellow, and brown striped shirt, mismatched with light blue, flared-denim pants. Her long, dark hair was bound in two ponytails by those tight, god-awful, bobble hair-ties. Her bangs were too long, but I could still see her huge, dark, brown eyes and already thickening eyebrows.

She walked toward me.

Her blue Trax sneakers, sporting three white stripes, braved the path without missing a beat. She's already walked it a hundred times. She stood at the in-ground log sofa with one little hand full of pennies and the other still clutching dandelions.

"Hi!" she said, pushing the fence down with her flower clutching hand, hopping it all by herself.

She crouched down and started laying her pennies on the rail, one by one.

I bent down to meet her eye. "Hi."

"Are you waiting for the train, too?" she asked, laying her pennies in a perfect line while counting them.

I reached into my pocket and pulled out my pennies, setting them down next to hers. "I am. I also came to see you."

She looked at me then asked, "How come?"

She was still counting in ASL, using the small fingers of her right hand as her left hand clung to yellow weeds.

Damn she's adorable.

I wiped a runaway tear from my cheek. "I um, wanted to, um—"

"C'mon!" She motioned for me to follow her. "Hop the fence! You can't be that close when the train comes! It goes wicked fast!"

She tugged at the wired fence, pushing it down so I could step over it. Her little hands were filthy, and I smiled—happy that she hadn't started working for McDonald's Happy Meals yet.

I stepped over the fence and turned to face the tracks with her. She looked at me and smiled. Kneeling on the log sofa, we both waited with anticipation.

Right then, I realized there would be plenty of time for me to tell her why I came, what I'd been through, what I'd learned, choices I'd made along the way.

But this wasn't the time for that.

I just wanted to *be with* her—this gorgeous, perfect child. Standing next to her was the best choice I'd ever made. It made me forget why I came.

I put my arm around her little shoulder. In the distance I could hear the bells, warning us the train was coming. As it got closer, the wind picked up.

I looked down and her left arm had found its way around my waist, clutching my side with excitement, still gripping dandelions.

"Here it comes!" she squealed.

Her little hand dug into the flesh of my waist. I pulled her closer to my side, looked up to the sky, and closed my eyes just as the train horn wailed.

In that second, I forgot almost everything I'd seen and done between heaven and hell.

"You're gonna miss it!" she screamed, competing with the oncoming train.

The ground rumbled and as the train whooshed by, I looked down to see her little ponytails flapping wildly. Her right arm had made its way around the front of my waist. She was hugging me…

She was hugging *me*.

I hugged her as tight as I could, and as the line of Pullmans rushed by tears streamed down my cheeks. When things quieted, I felt a slight, gentle vibration. It was coming from her. She was humming, without a care in the world.

She was perfect.

And she already knew it.

Acknowledgments

THIS BOOK WOULD NOT have been possible without some key people. There are many to thank and honestly, this section kinda blows. Does anyone even read this?

Thanks Mom and Dad for bringing me into this crazy, fucked up world, gifting me with your rich culture and unique life experiences worth writing about. I wouldn't trade my time with you for anything, regardless of our differences. I thank my brothers for toughening me up and inserting a badass warrior in me; the torture made me stronger.

Thank you Jax for *seeing me* and being my safe place. Thank you, Dean, for introducing me the world's macabre, nefarious underbelly and showing me who I am. Carter, thank you for tolerating some real bullshit and showing me who I'm not. We live, we learn.

Kelly, jeez, how can "thank you" even begin to show my gratitude? Thank you for showing me what unconditional love really looks like and for being someone I can call upon as a friend.

Thank you, Jodi Rhodes for beta reading, your feedback, and twenty years of friendship. I love you.

This book really would *not* have happened if the following people weren't part of bringing it to life. My writing coach, Lauren Sapala, thank you for taking a chance on unknown author, for pushing me in the most loving way possible. Kayli Baker, thank you for your mad copy editing/beta skills, and for being so kind and patient.

Jo Harrison, what can I say? You're a fucking formatting queen; your hard work, skill, and patience is unparalleled. Ryan Ashcroft, thank you for *all* your hard, amazing work on the book covers. Jacob Nordby, thank you for leading me to Lauren, and for the endorsement. It's an honor, sir.

Holly Rioux, thanks for checking my Deaf culture facts; mad love, lady. Heather Herring-Boli for all your hard work on the website and logos, I am so thankful for you. Melissa and JA Plosker, you're both amazing. Thank you, Jeremy Jack (black heart, gold heart forever), Patricia Kirsch, Katherine Turner, Jas, and the INF Club—mad love.

I gotta thank Uncle Joel, wherever he is, for being the best listener, my first therapist, for loaning me all the apostate material, and pushing me down the most interesting rabbit hole. If he hadn't, I wouldn't have read Kyria Abrahams, David A. Reed, Ray Franz (RIP), or Steve Hassan's books, which helped me through some pretty dark times.

My husband for supporting this long ass journey. I luve you; our story awaits. PSI Seminars, Team 558, C128—specifically Junkyard—and Jennifer McBride. Thanks to everyone that has been part this crazy ride—Erica, Ang, Kris, Shari, Eric, Laz (RIP), Amanda, Kane, Tess, Dustin, Kara, SLA…I wouldn't be me without you. Brian, had I not run into you years ago and started remembering shit, well, I may not have written a damn thing.

And to you, the reader. Thank you from the bottom of my heart for giving enough of a shit about my story, buying a copy, and reading it. You have no idea how much that means.

Note From the Author

Thank you so much for reading *Train Gone*. While writing, a major shift in healing took place. Although this has been one of the hardest things I've ever done, writing has been a massive therapy session for me; exhausting, wonderful, scary, cathartic, and everything in between.

While writing and mending, I discovered my younger self again. Writing this not only helped me see patterns but shoved that little four-year-old toward me, regardless of whether I was ready to see her. Connecting with who I was before wreaking havoc on my own life—while using sharp pieces of both heaven and hell to do it—healed me more than I could say, more than I could ever write. Even though my mini-me made a mere cameo appearance, her character was much louder than any of the others. And she was present for every one of my therapy sessions.

If you, Dear Reader, know anyone who could benefit from this memoir/creative nonfiction, or anyone who would be comforted knowing they're not going through their own personal hell alone, anyone who needs to reconnect with their younger selves to heal, please pass this book along and be sure to tell them—it's not over; I'm rooting for them.

I hope you'll consider posting a review on Amazon and/or any other internet medium. To keep up with blogs and future book releases, please add yourself to the mailing list on my website. I'd love to stay in touch.

Website: www.rebekahmallory.com